D0141949

Self-determination and the Social Education of Native Americans

SELF-DETERMINATION
and the SOCIAL EDUCATION
of NATIVE AMERICANS

Guy B. Senese

PRAEGER

New York
Westport, Connecticut
London

Copyright Acknowledgments

The author and publisher gratefully acknowledge permission to use extracts from the following:

Guy Senese, "Promise and Practice: Important Developments in Wartime and Post-War Indian Education Policy: 1940-1975," *Journal of Thought*, Fall 1984.

Guy Senese, "Self-determination and American Indian Education: An Illusion of Control," *Educational Theory* 36, no. 2 (Spring 1986), pp. 153-64.

Library of Congress Cataloging-in-Publication Data

Senese, Guy B.
   Self-determinaton and the social education of native Americans /
Guy B. Senese.
      p.   cm.
   Includes bibliographical references and index.
   ISBN 0-275-93776-3 (alk. paper)
   1. Indians of North America—Education. 2. Indians of North
America—Government relations.   I. Title.
E97.S46   1991
370'.8997—dc20   90-20011

British Library Cataloguing in Publication Data is available.

Copyright © 1991 by Guy B. Senese

All rights reserved. No portion of this book may be
reproduced, by any process or technique, without the
express written consent of the publisher.

Library of Congress Catalog Card Number: 90-20011
ISBN: 0-275-93776-3

First published in 1991

Praeger Publishers, One Madison Avenue, New York, NY 10010
An imprint of Greenwood Publishing Group, Inc.

Printed in the United States of America

The paper used in this book complies with the
Permanent Paper Standard issued by the National
Information Standards Organization (Z39.48-1984).

10 9 8 7 6 5 4 3 2 1

LIBRARY
ALMA COLLEGE
ALMA, MICHIGAN

For Mia and Zoë

Contents

Preface

This book is the result of fourteen years of interest in, observation, and study of, the issue of Native American self-determination and community-controlled schooling. No language more greatly captures the democratic pluralist vision of educational potential than the language of self-determination. This concept has been used to martial support for a variety of participatory democratic, self-empowerment efforts which are the heart of progressive social policy. Ironically, the power of this language to win minds for policy initiatives has resulted in a wide gulf between the rhetoric and reality of self-determination. My involvement in the issues surrounding self-determination began during the two years 1977-78, when I worked as a youth counselor in a juvenile facility serving a large number of Tlingit-Haida school-aged children in southeast Alaska. It was there, at the Juneau Receiving Home, that I became aware of the strong contradictions that affected the lives of these children. Their material poverty was radically opposed to their community and extended-family connections, a connection which most of our Euro-American children did not have. This poverty was in contradiction to the great natural riches their surroundings implied and also to the growing administrative, political, and educational influence of the Sealaska Native Corporation, which owed its own wealth to the greatest single exchange of land for money since the Louisiana Purchase—The Alaska Native Claims settlement.

Throughout my experience I was greatly affected by the unique position of Native Americans in the twentieth century and the complex dimensions of culture, politics, and education in their lives. I developed a particular interest in the resilience and restorative dimensions of the Native American community. I was not too surprised, upon further study, to discover my concerns preceded by those of a long line of interested observers of Native American community democracy. I discovered others who have pointed to the fundamental health of American Indian community structure; who also developed an enthusiasm, an urge to cheer on efforts toward the reclamation of community and tribal sovereignty. This enthusiasm was tarnished by an increasing skepticism regarding the genesis, actual purposes and effects of the various social progressive movements for Indian reform, each of which, in slightly different ways, contained a call for increased self-determination.

I was nonetheless excited when, in 1981, I had the opportunity to interview for a position in the high school social studies program at the Rough Rock Demonstration School, the flagship of neo-progressive bilingual, bicultural education on the Navajo reservation near Chinle, Arizona. The opportunity was, for me, a chance to be a part of an educational experiment whose principles coincided with my own - schooling with community democracy at its core. As my wife and I, with our six-month-old daughter, traveled down Interstate 44, I remember feeling confident that I had learned a few things in Juneau, and now better understood the issues facing Native American students. I believed that teaching in a school dedicated to community self-determination would be much more rewarding than had been dealing with the struggles of the Receiving Home residents, trying to succeed in public schools that made little effort to adjust to their unique experiences, and whose inflexibility, ethnocentrism, and occasional hostility made meaningful achievement highly problematic.

The next two years were the most thought provoking, interesting and frustrating of my life. Like most Anglo teachers on the reservation, I settled in unsteadily (it was called culture shock) and despite what I thought was my best effort, based on good preparation and what I believed was background in the issues that mattered, learned a great deal more than I taught. I hope I contributed something to what I believe is, despite its problems, one of the great educational communities. Rough Rock is an institution of great vision and promise, but frequently unfulfilled ambition. Soon after I settled into my teaching, questions began to arise: Why was it so difficult to compete with the area Bureau of Indian Affairs (BIA) schools and the public schools for funding? Why was there so much trouble negotiating a yearly contract, which left its teachers frequently without a position—until August, or never? Why has it been so difficult for the community to successfully argue that its unique educational standards and goals count as fundamentals in an appropriate education? Why was so much pressure being applied for the school to conform to federal and public school standards? These questions, as well as staff divisions regarding the purpose of the "demonstration," led to a school where dedication often met its match in frustration, a school climate fraught with crisis planning and overreaction. My allegiance to its fundamental principles led me to the study of which this book is a culmination.

My study led me to an exploration of the concept that formed the basis for the existence of Rough Rock, but has in fact been the ground for most, if not all, postwar government-Indian tribal debate and policy. As such, this study raises a number of questions which, while they include analysis of the community school movement, transcend it, developing a general analysis of a concept influencing all tribal social educational policy during this time.

With roots in twentieth-century liberal progressivism, self-determination carries certain meanings and intentions which begin to explain some of the aforementioned questions. It is my belief that an objective view of the development of this concept argues for cautious vigilance on the part of those who value the extension of tribal sovereignty and community democracy in America. For myself, who once saw self-determination as a natural antidote to social, economic, or schooling programs leading to eventual termination, a look at the development of this policy language has been sobering.

Self-determination, as an operative policy concept, is fundamentally contested terrain, with built-in contradictions. It is, furthermore, a contest in which the future of tribal sovereignty and social autonomy is at stake. In it, the language of democratic pluralism has obscured the juggernaut of progressive managerial planning under which educational policy is subsumed.

Certainly the policy contest was fought by those who defined self-determination as a community democratic effort to strengthen economy and increase meaningful sovereignty. But little attention is paid to the power of those policy contestants who saw something quite different in the future of Native America; who saw in self-determination, a final solution to the "Indian Problem," once and for all, reconciling the inevitable logic of the expansion of the progressive-liberal state with the ideological requirements of ethnic pluralism and the constitutional limitations of the federal-Indian trust relationship. This book is a beginning effort to describe that star-crossed reconciliation.

To a very great extent the academy of American educational policy scholars has been silent regarding the relationship between contemporary Native American education and U.S. education policy in general. There is a voluminous literature analyzing the complexities of Indian students' achievement, curriculum, attendance, learning styles, etc. Yet social and philosophical analyses of educational policy development have been extremely scarce. The standard reference in the field is Margaret Szasz's *Education and the American Indian: The Road to Self-*

determination, which is a thorough and responsible chronicle of twentieth-century Native American schooling since 1928. However, very little sustained critical work has been done beyond this to amplify the impact of current government Indian education policy.

This book is an effort to extend the interpretive effort in this direction. It is an attempt to critically analyze the most crucial conceptual development in American Indian social and educational policy, the idea of self-determination. It is not intended to be a comprehensive treatment of postwar Indian social or education policy. Nor is it a chronicle to describe the sequence of events leading to or encompassing self-determination as a policy era. For that the reader may consult Olson and Wilson, Deloria and Lytle, or Francis Prucha's fine overview of government-Indian relations.[1] This book is a critical analysis of important components of a policy which has become the linchpin of the present generation of Indian social and education programming. It attempts to magnify the constellation of progressive liberal policy which has been trapped in the orbit of the language of "self-determination."

Olson and Wilson's account of twentieth-century Indian policy is a good example of a general standard in the field of government Indian policy interpretation during this period. They write of the great local control efforts made during the 1960s and 1970s, culminating in the Indian Self-determination and Education Assistance Act of 1975. They are wise to note, that "given the course of Native American tribalism, however, the entire thrust of self-determination has not pleased all."[2] They go on to discuss the dissatisfaction with which "militants" view the concept—as another illegitimate offspring of BIA sponsored elections. They note the fear which many tribes expressed, that self-determination is a code word for termination, in another form, of the federal government's trust responsibility. Yet, despite these crucial warnings, which deserve exploration, they conclude that, "if current self-determination is not a panacea to all native Americans, it is nevertheless a major change in Native American history, *considering the probability that for the first time officials of the federal government are dealing correctly with Native American concerns and demands*"[3] (italics added). This statement, coming at the conclusion of their book, unites Olson and Wilson with virtually all the other comprehensive analyses of this period, which, in full view of a problematic period, react strangely as one, in the belief that self-determination is the tool with which Native Americans have finally broken the cycle of disempowerment. The numerous warnings of caution regarding this conclusion are treated by most writers as a hypothetical undertone, sounded mostly by the disaffected critical fringe.

Rupert Costo repeatedly cautioned scholars to temper enthusiasm for the liberal managerial structures related to the tribalization moves of the New Deal, which are the social-philosophic forbears of self-determination. He argued that the Indian Reorganization Act (IRA) "was the last great effort to assimilate the American Indian. It was also a program to colonize the Indian tribes. . . .The IRA had within its working and in its instruments, such as the tribal constitutions, the destruction of the treaties and of Indian self-government."[4] If Vine Deloria is right, that one cannot make much sense of self-determination reforms without understanding that they are an extension of Collierism and the Indian New Deal, then these comments may be applied here, too.

Emma Gross, in her 1989 study, suggests the potential need for a closer critique of the ideological uses of self-determination.[5] Her interviews of policymakers determined a number of varying interpretations of self-determination, from full nationhood sovereignty for tribes to development of economic self-sufficiency toward eventual termination of federal tribal status. Gross recognizes that eventual termination can indeed hang in the balance of interpretation around this crucial concept.

The administrations of John F. Kennedy and Lyndon B. Johnson are remembered as the beginning of a watershed period in the development of an ideology of economic self-help, in community development and as an apparent move away from the policies of rapid termination of the federal-Indian trust relationship which characterized the preceding postwar period.

Scholars of Indian policy have most often cast a positive light on this period as a time of crucial gains in the effort to consolidate and increase Indian tribal and community sovereignty. However, few have critically analyzed the historical development of the contemporary self-determination policies.

Francis Prucha's thorough and authoritative study *The Great Father: The United States Government and the American Indians* is another standard of reference for the history of government Indian policy. I will attempt in this book to elaborate on Prucha's claim that if one wishes to understand the meaning of self-determination in American Indian policy, one must begin with three seminal forces: first, the findings of the Fund for the Republic Commission on the Rights and Responsibilities of the American Indian; second, The American Indian Chicago Conference; third, the Task Force on Indian Affairs under the direction of Stewart Udall in the Kennedy administration. Prucha emphasizes the importance of these policy bodies. Indeed, they reinforce each other by mutual and compounding influence, culminating in the Udall task force report, which Prucha identifies as "most significant because it became the basis for official policy."[6] "Official policy" after this period is, in important ways, the developing policy of self-determination. I agree with his contention that the Udall task force is the most important driving force behind this policy. This book is an effort to develop the "educational" significance of these and other efforts. As such, it is not only a discussion of schooling, rather a discussion of the varied ways social and educational policy intertwine. It reflects my belief that Native American social policy is broadly "educational" in intent, and in ways that extend beyond schooling.

I have intentionally sacrificed breadth in the quest for an analysis that magnifies the social meaning inherent in the genesis of policy. Magnification makes this book less a chronicle of the period than a critique of the prevailing meaning of self-determination. Too much official language has been taken at face value by scholars of policy who have placed their emphasis chiefly on the scope of events during this period. Szasz, Olson and Wilson, and Prucha, as much by omission as commission, have wrongly accepted at their face value the ideological commitments of the individuals involved in many of these seminal policy bodies. By setting an admirable standard for breadth of analysis, they have won a reputation for accuracy of interpretation. The consequences of this are great. Self-help, self-determination policies have subsequently taken on an unwarranted association with the moral commitments of the civil rights, community control, and Red Power movements. Contemporaneity has become tantamount to historical moral equivalence. A closer look, a magnification, reveals how different these themes were in reality and commitment. For example, Szasz chronicles the development of education since the progressive-era Meriam Report. Her study reads as a thorough, yet relatively unproblematic chronicle of progressive education policy, characterized by the social scientific approach to educational and social administration, begun by Lewis Meriam in *The Problem of Indian Administration*. The feeling here is that, except for the interlude of renewed rapid termination feelings in the years immediately after World War II, progressive administration and social planning have proceeded haltingly apace toward a brighter day for Indian people—darkness to self-determination, from the dawn of progressive planning.

Indeed, centralization and bureaucracy in Indian schooling and economic policy administration have been attacked more by the democratic-liberal than by the neo-conservative critic during this century. Szasz notes the inexorable positive development toward an empowered Indian social and educational pluralism, without much critical interpretation. Yet, as with Prucha, she seeks not to analyze the importance of what David Adams has termed the "deep meaning" of Indian education.[7] By omission, she condones a tacit interpretation of New Frontier and Great Society self-help initiatives, culminating in self-determination policies, an omission that fundamentally underrepresents the themes of administrative oligarchic control, human and capital resource exploitation and implicit termination, lying not far beneath the surface of these progressive-liberal programs. It is truly instructive for students of twentieth-century American democracy that there remains no irony in the fact that, given the persistent progressive liberal involvement in policies furthering resource exploitation and internal colonialism, the codification of self-determination legislation took place during the administration of Richard Nixon.

This book is written in three parts. Since it is fundamentally a critique, these parts are thematic and not primarily chronological. It contains no effort to misrepresent the development of events, but rather seeks to nest events in analysis and interpretation of central ideological commitments. All of the parts revolve around the effort to question the basic assumptions of Native American social education. I use the term "social education" to emphasize my contention that the history of government Indian policy is an effort that fails to separate social and economic-development activities from education, and education from social and economic development. Prucha notes correctly that "educational development was always linked with economic development and in fact economic self-sufficiency always depended on educational improvements."[8] Certainly, the earliest federal social policies, for example, the Allotment Act of the late nineteenth century, were as much devices to educate Indian people for competent participation in the tradition of the Euro-American yeoman farmer, and eventual assimilation, as these were simple efforts to dispose of Indian lands. Likewise, nineteenth-century boarding schools were centers of vocational education and not infrequent sweated labor, working to develop educational competence in concert with what Charles Eliot would call the assumed "evident and probable destiny" of the students enrolled in the modern school.

This pattern was greatly extended in the twentieth century, particularly in the reforms after the Meriam Report, which supported a renewed commitment to the symbiosis of work, community, and schooling, so prevalent in progressivism, and which has been the recurrent theme throughout this period of reform. Indian people have not escaped the relentless development of educational bureaucracy as an arm of human capital development in this century. "Social education" reminds us that we may look again at federal Indian education policy and see development, and at federal Indian economic development and see education.

Part I of the book is a look at the ground upon which the seeds of self-determination were sown. In these chapters I will map out what appear to be the ideological concomitants of a post-termination policy. I argue that self-determination grew as a response to the moral requirements of reservation "development" in a political climate of resurgent Americanism after the war.

The uses of self-determination language, then, grew from the practical and moral failure of the termination of federal supervision, where a combination of Indian resistance and a resurgent spirit of liberal social planning after the Eisenhower administration, opened the door for a new antitermination, pro-self-determination policy. This part serves to argue the educational nature of the new policy. Economic self-help, in some ways, like the allotments of the nineteenth century, would act to train tribes for the competency required for full participation in American life. Self-help took root with deference to the full requirements of capitalist expansion and participation in mind. Much of the outline of policy took shape in the caucuses of several highly influential administrative, philanthropic and unelected oligarchies, commissions and task forces. Their actions, while representative of the style of progressive planning in the twentieth century, do not necessarily reflect the most authentic spirit of the concept of self-determination, nor the fundamental interests of the people whose lives were affected.

Part II of this book shifts the focus of self-determination more directly to schooling. In this part is a discussion of the development of the community control concept from programs in the Office of Economic Opportunity through the Self-determination and Educational Assistance Act of 1975 (PL 93-638). It shows how educational self-determination, like economic self-help, mimicked in many ways the methods sought by economic planners to secure labor cooperation in nascent commercial colonies like Puerto Rico. For example, it argues how the motivational utility of "maximum feasible participation" is best understood not as a commitment to community control as much as a method to secure the cooperation of a minority previously hostile to the prerogatives of development. It also argues that the supposed limitations of feasibility have worked like a virus to infect the efforts of communities to operate their community projects, whether they were assembly plants or schools, in accord with the real needs of community people.

Part III is an analysis of the dialogue of Native Americans in many ways united, in others divided, by the meaning of self-determination.[9] I discuss how this fragmentation is the result of the logic of capital development serving to divide Native people, as it has the rest of our society, along class and ideological lines. In this section I also discuss the way the concepts of trust and sovereignty have created fertile ground for expropriation of the meaning of self-determination. These concepts are the fulcrum over which the meanings of self-determination balance, a fulcrum of meaning which complicates Native American educational policy critique in ways which do not apply to other American minorities.

This is an investigation of government involvement in the social education of a diverse people. I am well aware of the limitations present in any attempt to generalize the Native American experience. What I have tried to do here is to reflect problems and issues which had an impact on a large number of Native Americans who struggled to redefine their relationship with the U.S. government during a crucial time in the postwar period. The development of Indian competency in this period was an effort to educate on a variety of levels: in school, but certainly not exclusively there; in industry; in the community; indeed, anywhere there was an opportunity to involve Indian people in their own institutional training—their own training, self-determined. Self-determination has been hailed as a bright new direction in Indian policy, a reform which finally would confer upon Indian people the right to legitimately control their destiny. Perhaps historical coverage, thoroughly accomplished by the authors mentioned here, has prepared the ground for critique. Yet the relative scarcity of critique may explain why there has been so much attention paid to the narrowly rhetorical rather than to the full meaning of self-determination. This policy most often has been attributed to the efforts of reformers to redress the wrongs of the termination period which preceded it and to solve, finally, the problem of Indian poverty and dependence. Indeed, this policy growth, which began in earnest during the early 1960s, was finally codified by PL 93-638 in 1975. It was certainly accompanied by, and to some extent, resulted from, the criticism of Indian and white antiterminationists.

However, the earliest architects of the self-determination efforts were not attacking the termination policy per se. Rather, they recognized the political and moral failure of rapid legislated termination and sought to develop a program which could create the human and material conditions of a justifiable termination.

The data that support this analysis are comprised partly of the correspondence of the Association of American Indian Affairs and the Ford Foundation Fund for the Republic Commission on the Rights, Liberties and Responsibilities of the American Indian, along with the papers of Indian commissioners Glenn Emmons, Philleo Nash, and William Brophy. These, along with a variety of supporting documentation, have provided a crucial lens through which to view the germination and growth of Indian policy during this period. Any understanding of the present meaning and possible consequences of self-determination is illuminated by, and is indeed dependent upon, critical analysis of the social and intellectual milieu within which policy was incubated.

NOTES

1. See James S. Olson and Raymond Wilson, Native Americans *in the Twentieth Century* (Provo: Brigham Young University Press, 1984); also Francis Paul Prucha, *The Great Father: The United States Government and the American Indians,* Pt. II (Lincoln: University of Nebraska Press, 1984); Margaret Szasz, *The Education of American Indians: The Road to Self-determination* (Albuquerque: University of New Mexico Press, 1977); and Vine Deloria, Jr., and Clifford Lytle, *The Nations Within* (New York: Pantheon Books, 1984).

2. Olson and Wilson, *Native Americans,* p. 206.

3. Ibid,

4. Kenneth R. Philp, ed., *Indian Self-rule: First-hand Accounts of Indian-White Relations from Roosevelt to Reagan* (Salt Lake City: Howe Brothers, 1986), p. 48.

5. Emma R. Gross, *Contemporary Federal Policy Toward American Indianns* (Westport, Conn.: Greenwood Press, 1989).

6. Prucha, The *Great Father* p. 1089.

7. David Wallace Adams, "Fundamental Considerations: The Deep Meaning of Native American Schooling, 1880-1900," *Harvard Educational Review,* February 1988.

8. Prucha, The *Great Father* p. 1100.

9. Since both forms are employed in customary tribal and community usage, throughout the book I use the term "Native American" interchangeably with "American Indian."

Acknowledgments

To my wife, Jamie, goes my deepest gratitude. Her intelligence, guidance, and wit were crucial in the course of the years during which this study was developed. I could not have accomplished it without her.

I would particularly like to thank Mark Sorensen, and Terry Denny, for the friendship and intellectual support without which this study could not have been possible. My colleagues, friends, and students at Rough Rock Demonstration School were also a source of great insight. To Olson and Gucina Redhorse, Tom Simpson, Luanne Summers-Yazzie, Eleanor Velarde and many others, I extend my thanks.

It is a pleasure for me to acknowledge the individuals who supported my scholarship during this study. I thank Professors C. Benjamin Cox, James Anderson, Clarence Karier, Ralph Page, Rudolph Troike, Steve Tozer, Judith Mogilka and Paul Violas for their help during early stages in the development of this work. Professors Jack Forbes and Roxanne Dunbar-Ortiz, and Wilma Miranda also provided valuable critique, as did Sharon Senese, who helped me both get "started" in the area of Native American Studies, and finished. To Nina Neimark and Jane Willis goes my gratitude for an expert job of formatting and final editing. A special thanks to Steve Talbot for giving generously of his time and critical acumen, and to Jeffrey Mirel for being a generous colleague and friend. Finally, I would like to thank my parents, Victor and Ida Senese for their support and encouragement over the years. Whatever merit these pages possess, for the intellectual challenge of the past fifteen years, I owe these individuals much.

To the following individuals I would like to extend my gratitude for permission to interview them regarding this study: Susan Allman, March

1983; Jimmy C. Begay, May 1983; Ben Bennett, April 1982; Wayne Holm, May 1983; Lee Kiyanni, March 1983; Carl Levi, March 1983; Sidney Mintz, by phone, May 1990; and Robert Roessel, February 1982.

Introduction

Self-determination has been described as "the right of all peoples to determine their political future and freely pursue their economic, social, and cultural development— [and that it should]...operate both externally and internally to ensure democratic government and the absence of internal or external domination."[1]

Unconditional self-government always has been a concept problematic for Indian people due to the complicated interdependent relationship they have forged with the federal government. Yet, the ideal of self-determination may indeed be instantiated within a quasi-dependent political relationship as well as from within a relatively independent one. In his discussion of Indian self-determination, Steve Talbot cites the National Lawyer's Guild's definition of self-determination, as

> that right to choose whatever form of political organization and relationship with other states it desires. It does not necessarily mean independence, although it may very well and often does. It may result in a people choosing to be associated with or dependent on another state. They may choose confederation with other less-than-totally independent peoples."[2]

Talbot argues that the heart of the 1972 Trail of Broken Treaties and Pan-American Quest for Justice was the demand that the U.S. government restore to Native American nationalities their Indian sovereignty. "Sovereignty," activist Hank Adams has said, "is the collective authority of a people to govern themselves."[3]

For many, strengthened American Indian tribal sovereignty is at the heart of the ideal of Indian self-determination. Adams' crucial statement, "we have never been talking about self-determination, but about self-administration" is part of the fundamental reason why the language of self-determination is so important to analyze.[4]

The concept reflects a political ideal, one with a heart of democratic pluralism and political tolerance. Self-determination has entered the American Indian policy vocabulary most forcefully as part of the development of the Indian Self-determination and Education Assistance Act (PL 93-638). A number of authors have added a cautionary note to the assessment of the current policy period. Donald Stull has argued in his study of 93-638 implementation and the Kansas Kickapoo, that while this act "creates a new legal vehicle that Indian tribes can use to control their own affairs . . . it does so within a framework that impedes the achievement of this goal, since it fails to establish concrete mechanisms of implementation."[5] He argues further that this failure is the result of a larger failure of the act to restructure the tribe's relationship with the Bureau of Indian Affairs. He points to the great strides made by the Kickapoo tribe between the years 1976 and 1981: the establishment of a gymnasium, a library-cultural center, a shopping center and, what he argues is the crowning achievement, a community-controlled contract-school. However, he documents the decline of all this growth as soon as the Reagan-administration budget cutbacks took effect. Joseph Jorgensen notes a similar phenomenon in his analysis of the effect of the "New Federalism" during the Reagan Years.[6] He argues that, in the case of the Northern Ute, the "chimera of self-determination" was exposed in 1985 when the tribal treasury was depleted.[7]

Along with the impact of reductions in federal support under the New Federalism, Jorgensen studied how the drop in the world oil price affected the Northern Ute economy. He concluded that "the new federalism and the plunge in the energy market demonstrate that Northern Utes are the dependent owners of resources beyond their control...the roller coaster continues in its rapid descent. It will bottom out and start its climb with the next Federal policy that pumps public sector funds into reservation economies."[8] In Edmund Danziger's study of the Indian response to 1970s reform legislation, he corroborates Jorgensen and Stull's contention that the degree of self-determination is roughly commensurate with the amount of federal funds and resource receipts available to the tribe.[9]

These findings clearly vitiate the contention that self-determination is tantamount to increased independence from federal support for tribal social health. P. Sam Deloria contended that the past fifteen years have been a period when tribes learned a crucial lesson about dealing with the federal bureaucracy. Yet he notes that this also was a period during which tribes were advised to lease their nonrenewable resources for extremely long periods and at unconscionably low rates.[10] He argued that the failure of this policy can be blamed in large part on the Reagan Administration and its policies of New Federalism which have demonstrated how ineffectual self-determination is if funds are withdrawn from the Federal pipeline.[11] W. Roger Buffalohead has said, "the 'tragic flaw' in the tribal consensus surrounding self-determination is because there is so little actual Indian self-determination in Indian country."[12] He argues that the failures are due to fluctuations in national, political and economic trends rather than on the will or needs of Indian people.[13]

I believe that it is correct to focus criticism on the way self-determination may have, paradoxically, encouraged a corrosive and finally politically exhausting form of tribal dependency. Jorgensen, in particular, has been clear to point out the way the failures of self-determination point to the underlying internal colonial relationship of the tribes to the federal government. Indeed, Indian self-determination is a peculiar species of that term. It was generated as part of a vocabulary of "self" referential terms, each of which take on a positive, participatory democratic language which rings rhetorically consistent with the most pluralist dimensions of the self-determination ideal. Hank Adams comments on how "in the past fifty years an unbelievable number of different policy proposals and policy objectives have been 'self' hyphenated."[14] Terms such as "self-help," "self-sufficiency," and "self-rule," all have been used to describe a new direction for Indian people, a direction different from dependency, but also different from the assimilation and termination tendency of mid-century Indian social and education policy.

It is incorrect to say that the weakness of self-determination has been failure to properly implement policy. Nor may its failure be blamed on fiscal or political conservatism. If it is correct to note that the policy is at the mercy of fiscal fluctuation, it is proper to inquire why sovereignty and community-driven development have become secondary considerations.

Rather, the failure of self-determination to deliver on ideals of increased sovereignty, fiscal and political autonomy is the result of the ambiguous relationship between this concept and the managerial liberalism which spawned it. The following chapters are the beginning of an analysis which suggest how the internal logic of self-determination, as a by-product of progressive liberalism, bears a toxin which may be implicated in the destruction of its ideals.

NOTES

1. Umozurike Oji Umozurike, *Self-determination in International Law* (Hamden, Conn.: Archon Books, 1972), p. 3.

2. Steve Talbot, *Roots of Oppression* (New York: International Publishers, 1981), p. 33.

3. Ibid., p. 31.

4. Kenneth R. Philp, *Indian Self-Rule* (Salt Lake City: Howe Brothers, 1986). p. 239.

5. Donald D. Stull, Jerry A. Scholtz, and Ken Cadue, Sr., "Rights Without Resources: The Rise and Fall of the Kansas Kickapoo," *American Indian Culture and Research Journal* 10, no. 2 (1986): 43.

6. Joseph G. Jorgensen, "Sovereignty and the Structure of Dependency at Northern Ute," *American Indian Culture and Research Journal* 10, no. 2 (1986): 75-94.

7 Ibid.

8. Ibid., p. 93.

9. Edmund J. Danziger, "A New Beginning or the Last Hurrah: American Indian Response to Reform Legislation of the 1970s," *American Indian Culture and Research Journal* 7, no. 4 (1983): 69-84.

10. Philp, *Indian Self-Rule* pp. 319-22. Roxanne Dunbar-Ortiz suggests that the prerogatives of Indian social programming must be remembered in light of the very significant material resources held by the tribes. She writes, "Within Indian reservations lie approximately 3% of the total U.S. reserves of oil and gas, amounting to 4.2 billion barrels of oil and 17.5 trillion cubic feet of gas. Estimates of identified coal reserves range up to 200 billion tons on 33 Indian reservations in 11 states, or 15% of the total identifiable reserves of accessible coal in the U.S. Indian uranium reserves amount to 55% of the U.S. reserves, and 11% of the world total, making Indian reservations potentially the fourth leading producer of uranium in the world." See Roxanne Dunbar-Ortiz, *Indians of the Americas: Human Rights and Self-determination* (New York: Praeger, 1984), p. 129. See also her *Economic Development in American Indian Reservations* (Albuquerque: University of New Mexico, 1979).

11. Ibid.

12. Ibid., p. 271.

13. Ibid.

14. Ibid., p. 239.

PART I
Economic Self-help and Self-determination

Between the turn of the century and World War II, movements to reform the Indian Service and Bureau of Indian Affairs worked to shape policy, sending it through periods of changing emphasis regarding the acculturation and education of Indian people. The dominant reform took place during the New Deal and was characterized by efforts to roll back the corrosive results of the Allotment Act, and consequent detribalization, loss of cultural identity, and the loss of millions of acres of tribal land as a result of heirship confusion and land sale by allottees. The Indian Reorganization Act (IRA) of 1934 was the most visible of the reforms developed to counteract the failed allotment policy.

It appears on the the surface that these changes were a direct attack upon the Bureau and the Education Service's traditional policy to assimilate Native Americans into white culture. Indeed, many of the new reformers were optimistic about encouraging the rebirth of Indian societies and communities within a context of the larger polity. However, the reformer's dream, expressed in New Deal social and educational policy, lost much of its revolutionary radiance. These dreams, and the policies which were their shadow, all emphasizing in some degree tribal and community pluralism, did not hold up well during and after World War II. The postwar period began with a resurgent spirit of nationalism that renewed hunger for strategic resources as the cold-war climate chilled.

In this part I will argue that self-determination grew as a response to the moral requirements of reservation development in a political climate of resurgent Americanism after the war. In order to provide an Indian policy which would be acceptable both to Indian people and to the rest of the interested public, it was crucial that the policy be developed with the moral and practical interests of each group in mind. For many non-Indian opinion leaders interested in Indian Service reform, Indian assimilation was the ultimate practical goal. Yet swift termination of reservation status had failed either to encourage this goal or to provide a morally acceptable end to the federal-Indian treaty-bound trust relationship. For most tribal leaders, termination was at best a disaster for tribal social welfare and at worst tantamount to genocide. Yet termination had lurked not far beneath the surface of Indian policy for generations. Especially after the swift termination programs of the early 1950s, Indian leaders were distrustful of any programming efforts.

The development of policy during the latter 1950s and the 1960s was a systematic effort to satisfy the need of liberal reformers for a termination-assimilation policy which also would be justifiable and would work to instill social, cultural and institutional competency as a preparation for termination. Yet this policy was developed to defuse Indian termination suspicion (what came to be called "termination psychosis") by involving Indians in their own social programming, thereby developing a taste for Western European habits and institutions, and by holding out for the promise of increased tribal sovereignty in the bargain.

A second analysis of this development notes how the broadest outlines of policy were carved by a relatively few, elite policymakers. These policy developments were surely influenced by the persistent struggle by Indian people for greater control of their affairs. Yet it is ironic that a policy of tribal self-determination was conceived and designed primarily by closely connected, unelected, policy oligarchies, the commissions and task forces whose operations so characterize the shape and formation of so much twentieth century progressive government Indian policy advisement.

1

Swift Termination and Indian Emancipation

During and after World War II there was great pressure to terminate reservation status for many tribes, and a growing emphasis on the successful assimilation of Indian people and lands into the American social and economic culture. Termination refers to the end of the responsibility of the federal government for the provision of a variety of social, educational and economic services as well as the protection of Indian lands and property held in trust for the tribes. The relationship stemmed from agreements in treaty and in exchange for lands and rights ceded to the United States or colonial territories by Indian people. The arguments that are most often given for the resurgence of an effort to assimilate and terminate after the war are based, ironically, on the success of the Indian GIs and war workers. World War II mobilized a great number of Indian adults who aided the war effort in a variety of ways. At least 25,000 Indians served in the armed forces during World War II.[1] Twenty-two thousand served in the army on the front lines; 2,000 served in the Navy, 120 in the Coast Guard, and 730 in the Marines.[2] The earliest arguments for postwar termination came from those who believed the Indian's war service earned him the right to keep or sell his land as he chose. Indeed, it was argued, the war experience became a tacit evidence of competency, and in recognition of this, Indian emancipation was in order.

During the war, Indian men and women were serving in such a fashion that their contributions would be regarded with note by government leaders and the press. Yet services to Indian people were being cut, and their right to trust entitlements was coming increasingly under attack. Defense spending and the capital requirements of the war effort were eroding the fund for Indian education and welfare. In addition, many people appeared to be questioning the fairness of continued restrictions over Indian property. Some were asking why the Indian should bear the burdens of war, yet not share in the privileges of peacetime - ownership of private property and a standard and style of living commensurate with their fellow white GIs, who by 1946 already had begun to enjoy the fruits of a growing postwar economy.

In June 1946 the Senate Committee on Indian Affairs began hearings on a bill for the "Removal of Restrictions on Property of Indians Who Served in the Armed Forces." This bill was intended to release heirship-allotted lands into the hands of any honorably discharged GI who could meet certain competency qualifications as approved by his reservation superintendent. In addition, the Indian GI faced the irony of a required alien naturalization test, and needed a high school education or its equivalent.[3]

Indian testimony was presented both for support and defeat of this bill. Mr. Henry Ankle of Little Eagle, South Dakota, testified that he thought the emancipation bill would help. He said, "Of course, the boys have spoken of these ex-servicemen of World War II and, of course, they are, as the younger generation, and the advancing generation, (...) we all know that what America wants is educated men to carry out civilization."[4] This and several similar emancipation bills came out at this time and Indian opinion was divided over the impact and consequences of such proposed legislation.

Peter Red Elk, a delegate from the Black Hills Treaty and Claims Council of the Pine Ridge Reservation, testified with regard to three similar emancipation bills. He claimed that the Indians he represented were not in favor of the bills, that if some tribesmen "were given patent fees they would spend their money foolishly. That is the way we lost a lot of land on Indian reservations."[5] The president of the Oglala Sioux Tribal Council came out against these bills, "Well, I want to say in regard not only to this bill but other bills that are pending in regard to Indian matters...and particularly in regard to this emancipation bill—I have given much thought to it and it seems right." He went on to say that it "seemed right" that the men who fought should be able to hold land, but he felt that many of them would sell their allotment because they had "not yet attained the level where they can meet their problems and live like a white man. They just want to take their land, sell it, and then squander the money."[6] Many Indians were fearful of the powerful interests who, their elders had warned, would try to separate them from the land. Floyd Maytubby of the Oklahoma Chickasaw testified that his grandfather warned during an earlier struggle for Oklahoma mineral rights that, "there was too much mineral on these lands, and that the Indians would soon sell the lands and dispose of them because they were allotted this land....As years went by, we find lots of lands were sold even though the value of mineral and oil rights were under the lands."[7]

Throughout the hearings related to these emancipation bills, two things become apparent. First, Indian opinion was not uniformly for nor against the bills. Indeed, much of the controversy seemed to arise not from the differing stands taken on the issue but, rather, from disagreement as to who may rightfully represent the tribespeople at a hearing, with differing factions squaring off against each other. Second, despite the debate, there was no question but that Congress had every power through the Constitution to abrogate its trust responsibility. Speaking at an emancipation hearing before the Senate in 1944, Oklahoma Congressman O. K. Chandler, a Cherokee tribal member, argued that "there can be no serious question of the authority of Congress to remove restrictions upon the alienation of the lands of allottees with or without the latter's consent.[8]

Congress was moving quickly in the direction of a kind of allotment which paid little heed to the readiness of tribes to assume this type of ownership. Issues of demonstrated competency took a back seat to the rhetoric of GI justice and individual property rights which came to dominate policy in the early termination years. Congress was beginning to reassert its power to alter the trust relationship after the liberal social melioration which characterized Indian policy during the New Deal and culminated in the Indian Reorganization Act. With regard to emancipation, many Indians as well as whites were in favor of rewarding the Indian GI upon his return from war. However, feelings were mixed about the wisdom of allotments. Many Indians were experiencing tremendous value conflicts. The value of maintaining the tribal patrimony intact came in conflict with the desire of many veterans who through increased experience and cultural assimilation, wished to establish individual ownership of property.

In the period during and just after the war, policymakers began in earnest a no-holds-barred pursuit of termination of the federal-Indian relationships. The Republican Congress during the early Truman years was growing more and more impatient with expenditures in the Indian Bureau at a time when the country was beginning the postwar recovery and gearing up for its cold war defense posture.

William Brophy was selected by Truman to replace commissioner John Collier, the architect of the Indian New Deal and a liberal reformer whose policies had become less and less desirable in the changing congressional climate and national mood during the war. Brophy came to the bureau with a record as an Indian civil rights advocate who had been successful and personally popular as attorney for the Pueblo Indians. His appointment was supported by many Indians. He also had served the secretary of the Department of the Interior as a special representative for Puerto Rican affairs.[9]

Without Collier and Roosevelt, government officials redoubled efforts to assimilate the Indian into mainstream American life and to swiftly terminate the reservation status of many tribal lands. The involvement of Indian people in the war effort played a significant role in these policy changes.[10] The nation was recovering from the war and the national mood was not sympathetic to pluralistic sentiment. As the nation had unified to defeat a common enemy, it would now unify to begin the task of building the postwar world, both internationally and domestically. It was an easy shift from the wartime industrial mobilization to an expanding postwar economy. Indian resources could play a part, with the availability of a trained or trainable work force. and by the steady subsumption of tribally held material resources - water, minerals, fossil fuels and rangelands.

Even during the early war years, the Indian educational service began to institute a vigorous vocational education effort which was intended to "train students for placement in vocations for which there [was] a demand and those directly related to the war effort."[11] The Indian Bureau educational service pushed for "training that is intensive, thorough and effective, without a waste of time, which will contribute to his ability to participate in the war effort of the nation on the home, agricultural or industrial fronts."[12] The Indian Service set a strong direction to guide the student toward a firmer place in defense-related industry through skills training and attitude education.

"Indian Education," the bureau field letter edited by Willard Beatty, director of Education, presents the positive steps being taken in 1942 to educate recalcitrant Indian youth leadership to a clearer understanding of their potential place in the changing American landscape during the war. "Somewhere in the educational pattern," he writes, "it appears necessary to insert a training period which can be devoted to helping the young Indian understand himself and his racial heritage, the White races and their heritage, and the industrial culture which dominates America."[13]

Bureau administrators were addressing the problem here of how to encourage cooperation from those Indian leaders who often were hostile to the bureau and the government. For the bureau, the problem seemed to stem from, "a tendency to perpetuate that [rebellious] condition because of our reluctance to provide adequate advanced education for young Indians who are aggressive, critical and inclined to be non-cooperative....It is in our power to influence such leaders through education."[14]

During the war the bureau began an effort to align the Indian student with the larger war effort on all fronts. This continued after the war as many servicemen returned looking for meaningful lives and a place to start after their service experience. For Indian servicemen, who for the first time had experienced life off the reservation, this was particularly difficult. Yet this readjustment and its associated cultural and social problems were exacerbated by the renewed emphasis on emancipating the Indian, and especially the Indian serviceman, who the policymakers agreed certainly earned his freedom. Termination of reservation lands was beginning in earnest after the war. Assimilation of Indian people into the postwar recovery economy and American national culture was concomitant to that termination pressure. The bureau would argue that while the boarding school should continue to meet the needs of the reservation student, the public school was better equipped to properly educate the Indian student, for:

> The present policy of placing Indian children in public schools near their homes instead of in boarding schools or even in the Indian service day schools is, on the whole, to be commended. It is a movement in the direction of the normal transition, it results as a rule in good race contacts, and the Indians like it.[15]

Congress and, increasingly, the Indian Bureau began to conceive of the Indian trust status as a handicap rather than a benefit. Holding lands in trust only helped prevent some citizens assertion of their property rights. These sentiments were fueled by returning Indian vets. At the same time that many Indians and whites warned that release of federal supervision would cause another great buy-off of Indian land, Congress was proceeding apace to enact measures to "get the government out of the Indian business" as quickly as possible. It also was at this time that the Indian Claims Commission was created to deal with tribal land claims through payments in cash for lands claimed through treaty.

In Brophy, Congress had found an amenable commissioner, for Brophy had claimed the job of commissioner was to work with Congress in the execution of its mandate on Indian affairs.[16] Yet ill health forced him to hand the responsibility of his office over to Associate commissioner William Zimmerman. While Brophy had accepted the growth in termination pressure, he also had been successful with his advocacy of Indian civil rights issues and had been a relatively popular and trusted commissioner. Indian people were not sure how to react to the acting commissioner. As the new termination policy gained momentum critics were lining up on both sides of the issue. Zimmerman, under congressional pressure, advanced a plan whereby tribes were divided into three separate categories "depending upon what he regarded as their readiness for withdrawal from federal supervision."[17] This policy became known as the Zimmerman Plan, despite the suggestion that Zimmerman himself might have resisted some of its more restrictive elements, and became the blueprint for an ever more vigorous termination policy adopted during Truman's administration under the guidance of Dillon Myer.

Among the first tribes slated for termination were the California Laguna Band of Mission Indians. Brophy concurred with their termination as was suggested in House Resolution 3064, August 4, 1947, and enacted as Public Law 335. He and other federal officials "deemed that trust status hindered the progress of the California Indians as progressive American citizens and viewed the bill as a reform measure to succor the living conditions of these people."[18]

On December 31, 1947, William Brophy resigned as Indian commissioner. His departure and the paucity of reliable and current data regarding the Indian tribes led, in part, to the appointment of a special Indian affairs task force within the Commission on Organization of the Executive Branch of the Government. It was headed by former President Herbert Hoover, to analyze the condition of Indian country.[19] The Hoover report came to loggerheads with government policymakers who wanted to further rationalize the economy and resources through the use of a centralized administrative function such as the Department of the Interior. The Hoover group seemed to be saying that this extension of government policy engineering was too costly to the taxpayer. In its task force on Indian affairs, the commission argued that the function of the Indian Bureau could be made more effective and less expensive if its functions were taken over by specific service agencies outside the Interior Department and that the bureau could therefore be dismantled.[20] The members of this task force were John R. Nichols, Charles Rhoads, Gilbert Darlington and George Graham, chairman.

The group's fundamental argument in its 1949 report was that Indian assimilation is inevitable and should proceed without impediment. However, the Interior Department, in its reaction to the report, issued a persuasive warning with regard to Indian lands and their resource potential. "Any move which would result in transferring the trusteeship of the Indians' 56 million acres of land to an agency not concerned with resource development and use must be viewed as a further splintering of resource functions."[21] The response continued that the Interior Department had not only successfully husbanded Indian resource capital but had gingerly yet efficiently coaxed tribal accommodation with regard to the use of resources. "It has taken continuing effort over the past dozen years to bring the Indians to the point where they are becoming actively interested in planning the development and use of their own resources."[22]

The Interior Department was successful in holding off the assault on its Bureau of Indian Affairs. However, the Hoover Commission Report was to have a substantial effect on the progress of Indian affairs during the postwar years.[23] The findings of the report make clear the intent of policy, one which was harmonious to the ears of a terminationist Indian committee in Congress. Assimilation, it says:

> is recognized as the dominant goal within the Bureau of Indian Affairs. Officials and employees, high and low, in Washington and in the field, agree on this objective. . . . the sentiment in Congress is also solidly behind the goal of assimilation. . . . It is in the public interest and in the interest of the Indian to see that Indian people fit into the economic and social structure of the country."[24]

The Hoover Commission argued strongly for a policy which would remove the responsibility for Indian administration from the U.S. government to the states. While this decentralization could loosen the stranglehold of paternalism, at the same time it effectively released the government from its trust and treaty obligations.

The Hoover task force considered the benefits of emancipation to be commensurate with citizenship and rights, while the treaty-bound trust was considered a hindrance, and stated, "Regardless of treaties and agreements with Indian tribes in which a good many specific commitments have been made as to both educational and economic assistance toward assimilation, the Indian at least deserves a fair break because he is a human being and a citizen of the United States."[25]

With the resignation of Brophy, Truman nominated Hoover task force member John Ralph Nichols as commissioner of Indian Affairs. Nichols, an ex-president of Idaho State College, was serving as the president of the New Mexico College of Agriculture and Mechanical Arts at Las Cruces when he was nominated. However, he served only eleven months as commissioner, during which time he reflected the assimilationist, terminationist mood of the time, stating that the "federal government can and should remove itself as trustee over Indian property and as a service agency."[26] Nichols was transferred in 1950 to another jurisdiction within the Interior Department and was replaced by a man who was to become one of the most controversial commissioners in the history of the bureau, Dillon Myer.

A career government official, Myer had been Director of the War Relocation Authority, the agency chiefly responsible for removal, incarceration and relocation of Japanese-AmericanS and Japanese aliens in the U.S. during the war.[27] Myer was known as an efficient and stern administrator who often antagonized people during his tenure as commissioner.[28] He was an advocate of the position, then gaining momentum in Congress, that Indians be assimilated and their reservations terminated as quickly as possible. At this time, following up on the Zimmerman Plan, Utah Senator Reva Bosone introduced Joint Resolution 490, which "proposed to direct the Secretary of the Interior to study the respective tribes, bands and Indian groups to determine their qualifications to manage their own affairs."[29]

Myer was in wholehearted concurrence with the terminationist mood in Congress. In 1950 he spoke before the National Congress of American Indians stating his belief that Indians, being citizens under the Constitution and Bill of Rights, had a "responsibility as American citizens to become a productive society."[30] Myer not only vigorously pursued rapid termination and assimilation but used his experience on the War Relocation Board to begin the relocation of reservation Indians to urban centers.[31] He tried through support of termination legislation and through "Operation Relocation" to quickly put an end to the trust relationship between the government and Indian people. "Myer stated that federal policy deemed Indians as museum pieces whose lifestyle was no longer viable in the Atomic Age."[32]

His single-minded pursuit of terminationist goals began to draw fire from a variety of directions. The National Congress of American Indians accused Myer of "imposing drumhead justice" on the tribes.[33] Former commissioner John Collier, serving in his unofficial capacity as elder statesman and Indian policy gadfly, charged that Meyer had

> coerced the Indian Bureau into becoming an instrument toward his single purpose of termination.... [According to Collier, Myer had] regressively transformed the Indian groups and personal life, even going so far as to seek the power to make arrests and searches and seizures without warrant, for violation of any of his administrative regulations [and] has doubled the Indian Bureau's appropriations, and sought to have them trebled in 1953.[34]

Opposition to Myer's heavy-handed tactics was also raised by the Blackfeet tribal council. With Myer's tenure weighing heavily, it reminded Eisenhower of his inaugural pledge that Indians would have a voice in the selection of the next Indian commissioner.[35]

Increasingly, Myer's brand of rapid assimilation and termination was running into serious domestic opposition as well as support. Eleanor Roosevelt, in one of her *Washington Daily News* columns, had warned in 1949 that, "The government's handling of Indian affairs should be carried out cautiously and justly because it involve(s) international scrutiny." Ironically, she added, "One of the Soviet attacks on the democracies particularly in the United States, center(s) on racial policies. . . . In recent months the Russians have been particularly watching our attitude towards native Indians of our country."[36] In 1951, Harold Ickes, who had been Interior secretary during the Collier era and the Indian New Deal, wrote in the *New Republic* calling Myer a "Hitler and Mussolini rolled into one . . . so far as American Indians are concerned."[37]

The issue of termination did not end when Myer was forced to resign after the election of Dwight Eisenhower. However, Myer's approach was so roundly criticized that it would need to be reconditioned under subsequent administrations. Myer's answer to the so-called Indian problem was termination with all possible speed. Myer believed that policy must be formed to provide for the quickest possible assimilation of the American Indian into the mainstream of American economic and social life. Clearly, he did not invent termination. He merely became its loudest champion, with the wholehearted support of a terminationist Indian committee in Congress. His failure, however, helped to inform the Indian policy of the following generation. Myer's rapid assimilation plan, which had drawn so much bad press, would be replaced by termination with a human face. Competency and Indian consent to termination would begin to find their way back into the policy rhetoric. There had been only a perfunctory concern for the immediate postwar generation of terminationists who urged the liberation of the Indian veteran and his family. For them, the federal-Indian trust was an impediment to freedom and anathema to their interpretation of the Constitution.

In addition to competency and consent, economic development would take on new meaning for Indian people. Eisenhower's appointment of Glenn Emmons to the commissionership began an era in Indian social policy which would be characterized by the pursuit of termination through an increasingly sophisticated variety of social, psychological and economic methods, leading eventually to the clothing of termination in the cloak of self-determination. The story of this second generation assault on the federal trust responsibility must begin, however, with the nomination of Glenn Emmons, the "warm-hearted country banker, [whose] enlightened policy . . . for the first time offered Indians a future, not as wards of the government, but as full-fledged, self-respecting citizens."[38] The news editor who wrote this was clearly not aware that the goal was not a new one. It was only new, perhaps, through the means by which it would be pursued.

NOTES

1. U.S. Congress, Senate, *Hearings before the Committee on Indian Affairs*, 79th Cong., 2d sess., from a statement by D'Arcy Mc Nickle, in "Bills to Provide for Removal of Restrictions on Property of Indians Who Serve in the Armed Forces" (Washington, D.C.: U.S. Government Printing Office, 1946), p. 2. Also, for important background on the development of New Deal policy between the wars, see Kenneth R. Philp, *John Collier's Crusade for Indian Reform, 1920-1954* (Tucson: University of Arizona Press, 1977); and Lawrence C. Kelly, *The Assault on Assimilation: John Collier and the Origins of Indian Policy Reform* (Albuquerque: University of New Mexico Press, 1983).

2. Donald Lee Fixico, *Termination and Relocation: Federal Indian Policy in the 1950s* (Albuquerque: University of New Mexico Press), 1986, p. 4.

3. U.S. Congress, Senate, 79th Cong., 2d sess., p. 8.

4. Ibid., p. 11.

5. U.S. Congress, House, *Hearings before the Committee on Indian Affairs*, 79th Cong., 2d sess., on H.R. 3680, H.R. 3681, and H.R. 3710 bills concerning the purchase of certain restricted Indian land, removing restrictions on Indian property and for the emancipation of Indians, 13 June, 1946 (Washington, D.C.: U.S. Government Printing Office, 1946), p. 4.

6. Ibid., p. 5.

7. U.S. Congress, Senate, *Hearings before the Subcommittee of the Committee on Indian Affairs*, 78th Cong., 2d sess., in "A Bill to Remove Restrictions on Indian Property Now Held in Trust to the United States and for Other Purposes" (Washington, D.C.: U.S. Government Printing Office, 1944), p. 21.

8. Ibid., p. 116.

9. Fixico, *Termination and Relocation*, p. 24.

10. Ibid.

11. U.S. Department of the Interior, Office of Indian Affairs, *Indian Education: A Fortnightly Field Letter of the Education Division of the U.S. Office of Indian Affairs* (Washington, D.C.: U.S. Government Printing Office, 1943), p. 5.

12. Ibid., p. 6.

13. U.S. Department of the Interior, Office of Indian Affairs,"Selecting Indians for Leadership," *Indian Education*, 79, 1 December, 1942 (Washington, D.C.: U.S. Government Printing Office, 1942), p. 5. The article concentrates on the fact that "if there is any phase of the human relationship problem which government and missionary groups have sadly muffed, it is the selection and training of Indian leaders" (p. 4). It is ironic that the problem of white missionaries and administrators selecting Indian leaders should be addressed in a pamphlet which is entitled "Thoughts on Democracy."

14. Ibid., p. 4.

15. Willard W. Beatty, *Indian Education*, 130 (Washington, D.C.: U.S. Government Printing Office, 1946), p. 284.

16. S. Lyman Tyler, "William Brophy," in *The Commissioners of Indian Affairs, 1824-1977*, eds. Robert M. Kvasnicka and Herman Viola (Lincoln: University of Nebraska Press, 1979), p. 284.

17. Fixico, *Termination and Relocation,* p. 33, See also Tyler, "William Brophy," p. 280.

18. Fixico, *Termination and Relocation,* p. 36.

19. Ibid.

20. "Hoover Commission Recommendation Contained in Report on the Department of the Interior," Recommendation #3, Hoover Commission Report, U.S. Department of the Interior, p. 56650, Dale E. Doty Papers, Box 8, Archives of Harry S. Truman Library, Independence, Mo.

21. Ibid.

22. Ibid.

23. Fixico, *Termination and Relocation,* p. 62.

24. "Excerpts from the Report of the Committee on Indian Affairs to the Commission on Organization of the Executive Branch of Government," October 1948, William A. Brophy Papers, Box 23, Archives of the Harry S. Truman Library, Independence, Mo. p. 7.

25. Ibid.

26. William J. Dennehy, "John Ralph Nichols," in *The Commissioners of Indian Affairs, 1824-1977,* ed. Robert M. Kvasnicka and Herman Viola (Lincoln: University of Nebraska Press, 1979), p. 290.

27. Patrick K. Ourada, "Dillon Seymour Myer," in *The Commissioners of Indian Affairs, 1824-1977,* ed. Robert M. Kvasnicka and Herman Viola (Lincoln: University of Nebraska Press, 1979), p. 293. See also Richard Drinnon, *Keeper of Concentration Camps: Dillon S. Myer and American Racism* (Berkeley: University of California Press, 1987).

28. Fixico, *Termination and Relocation,* p. 64.

29. Ibid., p. 55.

30. Fixico, *Termination and Relocation* (dissertation), p. 68.

31. Ibid., p. 84.

32. Ibid., p. 103.

33. Ibid., p. 69.

34. Fixico, *Termination and Relocation.,* p. 71.

35. Ibid., p. 75.

36. Ibid., p. 13.

37. Fixico, (dissertation). p. 75.

38. Patrick K. Ourada, "Glenn Emmons," in *The Commissioners of Indian Affairs, 1824-1977,* ed. Robert M. Kvasnicka and Herman Viola (Lincoln: University of Nebraska Press, 1979), p. 301.

2

Justifying Termination
Through Competency:
The Roots of Self-determination

Glenn Emmons was appointed commissioner of Indian Affairs on July 28, 1953. At the time of his appointment Emmons was president and chairman of the board of the First State Bank of Gallup, New Mexico. Like other commissioners, Emmons inherited the policy legacy of his predecessors, Dillon Myer and Ralph Nichols.[1] Just before taking office Emmons received word that Congress had passed House Concurrent Resolution 108 (H. Con. Res. 108) and Public Law 280 (PL 280). PL 280 turned the responsibility for law enforcement over to the states rather than the BIA on selected reservations in California, Nebraska, Oregon, and Wisconsin.[2] H. Con. Res. 108 was a far-reaching resolution which showed the determination of Congress to establish a general policy of termination and assimilation and to begin accepting in Congress bills for the termination of specific reservations. The resolution finally stated the assimilationist motive of the 83rd Congress and set in motion the juggernaut of specific reservation terminations. It reads:

> it is the policy of Congress, as rapidly as possible to make Indians within the territorial limits of the United States subject to the same laws and entitled to the same privileges and responsibilities as are applicable to other citizens of the United States, to end their status as wards of the United States, and to grant them all the rights and prerogatives pertaining to American citizenship.[3]

In addition, it gave a list of those tribes selected to be first among those terminated, including the Flathead tribe, the Klamath, the Menominee, the Potowatamie and the Turtle Mountain Chippewa. The major effect of the resolution was the creation of a large number of new specific termination bills which the Department of the Interior had drafted as a direct result of H. Con. Res. 108.[4]

Emmons came out in support of H. Con. Res. 108, claiming that, "like all other friends of the Indians, [he] was particularly pleased by the action taken by the Congress, in wiping off the books or modifying a series of laws which have for many years been a form of discrimination against the Indian people."[5] Emmons's support of the termination policy of the 83rd Congress was clear enough. However, Emmons was more attuned to the competency issue and criticism of Myer's approach. For Emmons, termination would work only if it were carefully engineered and personalized to fit the requirements of specific reservations. "You cannot," he said, "apply the same yardstick to the more than 200 tribal groups in the U.S. each tribe has its own customs, its own set of problems."[6]

Emmons made clear in this same article that while it should be personalized and individualized, termination was still his ultimate goal. "I sincerely hope," he said, "that the day will come when it is no longer necessary for the federal government to serve as a trustee for the Indian."[7] Emmons wanted the tribes on a self-supporting basis, and he pushed a plan which perhaps would make termination more palatable to its critics. He began to support the development of industry on the reservations. These "tribal industries," in his words, "would train Indians in skilled work and make jobs for themselves."[8] His so-called "Emmons Plan" would encourage "light industry" and reclamation of Indian lands leading to increased leasing of farm and rangeland.[9]

Emmons wanted to proceed with these plans without forgetting what he called the "human equation."[10] "The Indian brain," he said, "is just as flexible and intelligent as that of white businessmen, and I have complete faith that Indians will eventually take their place along with whites in everyday American life. Both races will benefit from the association."[11]

Reservation industrial development was being considered partially to cool the growing anti-termination fervor. Yet the goals of the Eisenhower administration were clear. Assistant Secretary of the Interior Orme Lewis summed up the attitude guiding the administration when he wrote:

> Basically [Indians] are Americans and ought to become a part of us for their own good and for the benefit they can give us. . . . I have utterly no patience for those who think more about Indian culture than they do about Indians. The world is made up of people who overran others, as a result of which we have great nations.[12]

Most of the loudest termination criticism came from those who thought that termination was proceeding with little regard for tribal preparation or competency and less regard for tribal treaty and trust responsibility. Two of the most influential private groups with an interest in Indian policy were the Association on American Indian Affairs (AAIA) and the National Congress of American Indians (NCAI). The AAIA consisted mostly of white business leaders, academics, lawyers and others with an interest in Indian affairs. The NCAI was, on the other hand, composed of Indians. The original board of directors of the AAIA included Felix Cohen, preeminent scholar and opinion leader regarding Indian law during the mid-century, and Dr. Philleo Nash, an anthropologist who succeeded Glenn Emmons as Indian commissioner.[13]

Beginning in February 1954, the AAIA began in earnest to oppose a succession of specific termination bills. Their early criticism of these bills was directed at the quality of the termination decisions, not at termination per se. AAIA executive director Alexander Lesser wrote Philleo Nash, stating that while some tribes were ready for termination, others, including those such as the California groups and the Turtle Mountain Chippewa, who were slated in the proposed legislation, were not.[14] Oliver La Farge, association president, and a man who spent virtually his entire career in Indian policy reform, states, "I do think it is important for us to be able to show that we do not automatically oppose any termination bill."[15] His warning here is seemingly full of concern for the political inexpediency of a doctrinaire position on termination. However, it also is evident that AAIA had developed a curious criticism of termination. La Farge viewed termination as a viable option for well-adjusted, economically sound tribal entities, regardless of the desire of the tribe to be terminated. Indeed, the social-philosophic differences between Lesser's and La Farge's position on termination were to have expanding implication for the dialogue of self-help and self-determination later on.

The May, 1957 issue of the *Annals of the American Academy of Political and Social Science* was devoted to "American Indian and American Life." The issue presented the differing perspectives on termination between La Farge and Arthur Watkins, the Utah senator who had been one of the architects of rapid termination during the 83rd Congress. Watkins, a "deeply religious and nationalistic Mormon Senator . . . saw the continuing plight of Indians as the result of their failure to follow the path toward development forged by the nation's dominant culture."[16] Watkins was a firm believer in the plenary power of Congress to unilaterally end trust arrangements—the sooner, the better.[17] For Watkins, "The matter of freeing Indians from wardship status is not rightfully a subject to debate in academic fashion, with facts marshalled here and there to be maneuvered and counter-maneuvered in a vast battle of words and ideas." Watkins saw Indian assimilation and freedom from wardship status as, "an ideal or universal truth to which all men subscribe, and concerning which they differ only in their opinion as to how the ideal may be attained and in what degree and during what period of time."[18]

In turn, La Farge presented a position which was not so much in opposition to Watkins's belief, as it was a critique of method. He wrote:

> In theory, there is a kind of termination which those who believe in Indian progress through Indian integrity do not oppose; it is in fact, the ultimate goal. This is a termination of Indian Status of a tribe when its members have reached a point of competence at which they find they will do better on their own, with full freedom to handle or dispose of their assets, than under established protections or restrictions.[19]

La Farge was not critical here of termination itself; rather, he complained about the lack of competency in some of the tribes slated for termination. He argued for intensified programs to increase social and political competencies in preparation for termination. Yet La Farge was well known, as was the organization he led—the AAIA, as a prime opponent of termination. It might better be said that La Farge, like so many termination critics and "reformers" at the time, was not really in opposition to trust violation; rather, that the violation would come before it was "justifiable" by competence criteria which were more stringent than perhaps would be required by a Watkins or a Myer. To effect compliance with such criteria, La Farge argued for intensified programs to increase social and political competencies in preparation for termination.

In another article in the same issue of the *Annals*, anthropologists Edward Dozier, George Simpson and J. Milton Yinger argued that La Farge differed from those who, like Watkins, pushed for Indian "freedom" through forced assimilation. La Farge, they claimed, differed in that termination must be dependent on (1) a condition of sufficient competence and (2) tribal preference.[20] It is clear that La Farge and the AAIA held an early attack on the technique, if not the fundamentals, of termination policy. La Farge did not see termination as a problem due to its violation of treaty and trust. He viewed the problem as a violation of Indian social and economic welfare. He was reacting to termination proceeding on reservations like Turtle Mountain where Indian people were arguably the poorest of the nation's poor. Termination of wealthier tribes presented less of a problem.

It was to this type of reaction that Emmons and the Eisenhower

Administration had begun around 1955 to prepare a response. He began to initiate interest in reservation rehabilitation and development.[21] Emmons tried at first to enlist the help of business and "envisioned a private organization that would solicit grants from large foundations to finance the resource studies" which he knew would be "a prerequisite to any plan of action."[22] He had limited success in getting funding for resource studies. The Rockefeller Foundation denied him because of a stated policy to donate nothing toward the formation of government policy.[23] His early efforts were aimed directly away from public funding of area economic development. The BIA was not really involved. Emmons pushed toward the development of a plan to incorporate Indians into existing industrial and commercial networks.[24] Thus the "tribal industries" whose development he argued for earlier would be tribal only to the extent they depended upon tribespeople for labor. During this period the language of termination and anti-termination forces is reflected in the educational discourse emerging from government Indian education planning.

Educational plans for Indian children during this period began to reflect more and more the assimilationist, terminationist intent of Congress and the new administration. Hildegard Thompson had replaced Willard Beatty and held the position of education director through Myer's, Emmons' and most of Nash's tenure.[25] Thompson began working to accelerate the movement of Indian children from the boarding to the public facilities, and cooperated with Emmons on the Navajo Emergency Education Program (NEEP). The NEEP made room for an additional 13,000 children. A complex program, NEEP was the most dramatic step taken by the bureau to attack the out-of-school problem. Since 14,000 of the 19,000 Indian children out of school were Navajo, they were given first priority.[26]

Three objectives became uppermost on the Education Division's list of priorities: increasing the enrollment of Indian students, increasing facility use and construction and concentrating on the increased use of the public school as the preferred facility. Programs were to be developed which would meet the growing concern for the type of academic and vocational training required by the new demands of technology.

Table 1 shows the growth in public school enrollment for Navajo students.[27] The public school enrollment increase accounted for much of the total increase. It reflects the urgency felt by the Emmons administration to provide not only a formal education for the Indian student who was not receiving one, but a state public school experience which was widely considered as the best means to assimilate the Indian—in Emmons's words, to "promote good race contacts."[28]

With regard to the renewed vocational emphasis, Thompson en-

TABLE 1

Navajo Growth in Public Enrollment

Year	Enrollment	Year	Enrollment
1951-52	1,846	1960-61	10,250
1952-53	2,393	1961-62	12,879
1953-54	2,847	1962-63	14,067
1954-55	3,900	1963-64	14,183
1955-56	6,581	1964-65	16,452
1956-57	8,317	1965-66	17,367
1957-58	8,531	1966-67	17,072
1958-59	8,181	1967-68	18,201
1959-60	9,791		

couraged post high school vocational training which "meant that the Branch of Education had become, in large part, a job training agency."[29] This new development was part of the bureau's relocation program which was proceeding apace to remove Indians from the reservation to urban service and industrial work. It was also a development growing from the new emphasis on reservation economic and industrial development. This direction proceeded partly through the increased exploitation of mineral and oil resources. The market for resources would grow dramatically after the war. Private developers and the government responded to this change. The developers saw new opportunities for profit, and the government became more aware of the need to rationally organize resource development in order to maximize its availability while maintaining a certain degree of stockpile inventory and control.[30] During this period, educational planning followed the themes of government policy. Educational planning was never a serious critical response to economic prerogatives. Rather, professional educators were thoroughly accommodationist throughout these developments.

In 1957, Secretary of the Interior Fred Seaton released a report titled "Developing America's Resource Base." In it, he tried to show the need for, and the dramatic growth in, mineral and fossil fuel leasing in Indian country. Seaton argued that the growth of a minerals base was vital to both the economic growth of the nation and to its continued military security. In the five-year span between 1952 and 1957, the area of Indian land under oil and gas leases grew from 2,121 acres to 5,835,856 acres. The development of other mineral resources grew from 50,385 acres to 197,673 acres during the same time period. Uranium exploration accounted for most of this latter development.[31]

This concern for development echoed the Interior Department's earlier response to the Hoover Commission indicating the necessity of maintaining the BIA under the authority of its control. The Interior Department saw a vital interest in maintaining control of Indian lands and human capital through the agency of the BIA. Indeed, the mounting termination pressure came mainly from those who were more interested in dealing directly with the tribes on matters of leasing. Without BIA controls and guidelines, minimal as they were with regard to resource use, mineral companies could operate at even less cost and under fewer restrictions due to the inexperience of even the most sophisticated tribal councils.[32]

The development of reservation industry proceeded slowly until 1955 when Emmons was successful in enlisting the cooperation of the National Association of Manufacturers. He called on his assistant Carl Beck to entice industrialists to locate on or near reservations. Part of Beck's claim would stress the alleged manual dexterity of Indians. The implication also was clearly present that reservations would be a resource, not only for minerals and fossil fuels, but also for cheap labor.[33]

Meanwhile, discussion developed over the feasibility of instituting economic development similar to Truman's "Point Four" plan, which was aimed at the Third World in Latin America, Africa, Asia—any locality considered to have political and economic potential.[34] "Point Four" referred to the fourth point which Harry Truman made in his 1949 inaugural speech: "We must embark on a bold new program for making the benefits of our scientific advances and our industrial progress available for the improvement and growth of underdeveloped areas." Point Four was presented as a response to Third World poverty, disease, overpopulation and underdevelopment. However, authors of programs which spun off of Truman's fourth point also were clearly in agreement that Third World development was crucial to U.S. economic interests. These programs would grow out of a concern for "the secure growth of democratic ways of life [and] the expansion of mutually beneficial commerce."[35]

Program emphasis under Point Four was to come mostly from the countries themselves, with the U.S. providing technical advisors. "Economic progress depends not only upon the resources but upon the resourcefulness of the people. It is closely related to their habits and attitudes of work, saving, venturesomeness and adaptability."[36] Economic development clearly could not be successful without a well-orchestrated effort to develop the habits as well as the instruments of industrial society. In Indian country, as in overseas underdeveloped areas, education of a tractable work force would play a crucial role in developing a temperate investment climate, as much as was played by the location of suitable manufacturing sites. Education, however, was not to take place chiefly in the schools, though certainly the increased use of the public school indicated a renewed interest in Indian assimilation. Economic development itself would act as an educative force, imbuing native peoples with habits of work, thrift, acquisitiveness and a growing sense of fondness for the American Way.

Economic planners in the Point Four plan used the availability of cheap labor as an enticement for industry to locate in underdeveloped areas. For many years Puerto Rico had been operating an economic development plan with cooperation between business and the U.S. and Puerto Rican governments. At least since 1934 industrial development was part of the Puerto Rican growth picture. The "Chardon Report" of 1934 presented the details of a study on how to boost the Puerto Rican economy. The report claimed that it was "highly desirable, probably imperative, that a land restoration and industrial development program, combined with a policy of emigration to suitable environments, be fully worked out as soon as possible."[37]

At this time pilot industries were developed to test the program, and planners found that "the Puerto Rican worker is easy to train in new trades and vocations."[38] The report warned that Puerto Rico has limited natural resources and cautioned that only those industries should be developed which can thrive on "cheap and abundant labor . . . since our only great resources are the soil and cheap labor."[39]

In 1943 at a hearing before a U.S. Senate Subcommittee of the Committee on Territories and Insular Affairs, J. A. E. Rodriguez of the Manufacturers Association of Puerto Rico came to the committee complaining about the wartime supply problem. He also presented the consequences should the Puerto Rican needlework industry be forced after the war to compete with China. He noted the impossibility of this since his people were allowed to work only forty hours per week. Yet he complained that the minimum wage law, while "in principal [sic] a very good law" put the Manufacturers Association at a disadvantage in the face of such competition prospects. The minimum wage was twenty cents per hour."[40] He argued for a relaxation of the law until production could match the competition.

Direct parallels exist between the economic development plans in Puerto Rico and those regarding Native America. The BIA, like the Puerto Rican policy planners, was seeking both goals of reservation industrial development and removal of people—relocation. Both efforts were predicated upon the availability of cheap and abundant trainable labor. Both Puerto Rico and Native America were touted as demonstration projects. Neither could technically qualify as Point Four projects since both were integral parts of the U.S. However, they could be and were presented to Third World nations as evidence of the success of economic development.[41]

In 1951 the National Planning Association (NPA) Business Committee on National Policy published a progress report on Puerto Rican economic development which by that time had become labeled "Operation Bootstrap." In this report they presented Puerto Rico as a laboratory for economic reactions:

> Economists are fond of using Robinson Crusoe and his island to illustrate their theories. Here in Puerto Rico we have a much larger island, about two-thirds the size of Connecticut, with more than two million Crusoes, Mrs. Crusoes, little Crusitos on it. Instead of an imaginary laboratory for economic reactions, we have an actual one, filled to overflowing with healthy and active consumers.[42]

The NPA noted the problem of overpopulation—the "Shadow of Malthus" as part of an argument for economic emphasis moving from agriculture to industry. As a way of breaking out of the Malthusian dilemma, the NPA presents the economic development alternative to Puerto Rican economic and population problems. They claimed that economic development would cause population problems. They claimed that economic development would cause the birth rate to fall.[43] They pointed to the fact that Puerto Rico was a good economic bet for social/psychological reasons as well. They noted the difference between Puerto Rico and the Virgin Islands, thirty-five minutes by air to the east:

> The people there seem taller than Puerto Ricans, equally healthy and perhaps even more dignified, but far more leisurely. Few of them seem to take much interest in doing anything about their economic problems, which are considerable. How different in Puerto Rico! Everywhere one goes, even in the high mountains, he sees new enterprise, new construction, new hope . . . indeed, nearly all the stereotypes which people in the North cherish about Puerto Rico tend to dissolve on first inspection. They are not lazy, ill, despairing, mendicant people at all.[44]

Furthermore, NPA argued that Puerto Rico could provide the sort of immunity from ideology which venture capitalists would so desire when doing business in politically volatile underdeveloped areas. An

American engineer noted, "They haven't any ideological principles, or if they have they don't show . . . they are not tied up in either Marxian or free enterprise straitjackets."[45]

All these advantages were augmented by a program of liberal tax incentives offered to the industrialist who would settle in Puerto Rico. And there would be no worry that Puerto Rican leadership would interfere with these sorts of liberal terms, since the cooperation of business and government was very strong. No U.S. federal income tax was to be collected and no property tax—all until 1960. The Puerto Rican Economic Development Administration, known as FOMENTO, was "prepared to furnish your industrial plant a program to: . . . round up, screen, test, and train prospective workers, . . . provide a variety of utilities, transportation, housing, market research functions, and perhaps most important of all assume that you are a friend, rather than a suspicious character with profiteering designs on the people."[46]

All this means "that neither the structure of modern business, nor that of government, necessarily has to prevent friendly cooperation for common goals." The NPA reminds the industrialist of the contrast between this rosy Puerto Rican picture and that on the mainland: "Puerto Rico is farther ahead in such a relation than the mainland."[47] Perhaps relating to this, the report states that "one does not hear much about unions in Puerto Rico."[48] Regardless, FOMENTO warned that the idea of moving industry to the island was not aimed at the promotion of sweated labor. "The idea is a steady increase in productivity, to an ultimate maximum which will still keep a differential for mild climate and other natural factors."[49] It also added that any such drastic economic change must be gradual, indicating that there exist "deep-rooted anthropological, sociological, political and even religious practices. We had better not try to yank people into the best of all possible worlds too fast."[50]

Beginning in the late 1950s and into the 1960s, the BIA cooperated with industry to develop Point Four style economic development on Indian reservations. The reservations were presented to the business community as areas where they would find cooperative tribal and federal government regulation. Labor would be cheap, trainable, and tractable. Liberal tax exemptions were offered. In addition, a feature was added whereby the industries were required to come up with very little capital to open a plant. The government would provide liberal financing, and the tribes were encouraged to provide their funds as working capital.[51]

Many of the provisions just mentioned can be found in Senate Concurrent Resolution 3 and S. 809, two pieces of proposed legislation which were presented to Congress as positive programs for reservation economic development. These bills came before Congress during a period of deepening recession. Sponsored by North Dakota Senator

Richard Langer, S. 809 offered $20 million in loans and grants to Native Americans for the establishment of individual and tribal enterprises or to outside interests for purposes of locating on or near the reservation. Senate Concurrent Resolution 3 was formed as a purported repudiation to H. Con. Res. 108 (the termination resolution) and called for a comprehensive program to raise the living standard of Indian communities up to that of non-Indians.[52] These bills can be seen as an attempt to stimulate Indian economies to a point where reduced federal expenditure could be justified. They also were presented as an opportunity for industry to take advantage of the supply of cheap labor and loans offered by the government during those increasingly lean and competitive business years.

During the hearings on S. 809, participants gave testimony about the merits of reservation industry. William Langer presented the central practical argument. The program was designed so that Indians would become self-sufficient and "not depend any more than necessary upon the services accorded by the state and federal governments."[53]

The Bulova Jewel Bearing plant at Rolla, North Dakota was one of the first facilities to experiment with a reservation labor force. Langer testified at the hearings that turnover at the Rolla plant, which drew mainly from the Turtle Mountain reservation, and employed 150 Indians, was 3 percent. He contrasted this with a similar jewel bearing plant in New England where there was 100 percent employee turnover. He gave no reason for this difference, however.

The *Winner Advocate* of Winner, South Dakota, reported the visit of Emmons's assistant, Carl Beck. It noted the growing importance of the electronics industry, which it claimed was exceeded only by "steel and auto manufacturing."[54] It went on to note again the degree to which Indians, by virtue of their manual dexterity, "a necessary skill in this type of work," were perfectly suited to the electronics assembly industry.[55]

Over and over one reads of the suitability of the Indian for close, tedious, repetitive work which required great dexterity and fortitude. Those whom we find arguing for reservation industrial development often presented a glowing picture of the stoic Indian worker, perhaps to offset the arguments of those who claimed that Indian workers were lazy, shiftless drunks. The counterstereotype emphasized the noble Redman calmly assembling circuit boards against a backdrop of teepees and a russet sunset. Florida Senator James Haley testified for the quality of Indian work he observed during a visit to a West Coast aircraft plant.

When they get a good boss and get started, they are good workmen and certainly many of them have the patience of Job. I saw them in one of the airplane factories and plants out on the West Coast, putting these extremely small wires and so forth on it, and I would not have the patience for it, but they go right along.[56]

He might also have added that they usually went right along at the minimum wage.

Even though these early economic development bills were presented as a partial repudiation to termination, it is clear that they were written from the viewpoint of industries who saw something to gain from the use of Indian labor on reservation land. The arguments presented for the bills do not suggest that termination was a dead policy. Rather, economic development was instituted as a way to prepare Indians; to provide economic and social competencies so that termination could proceed in the good faith that government had done all it could to prepare the Indian for American life. Senator Richard Neuberger commented on the purpose of S. 809, that the bill was a further attempt to establish the "American Indian as an independent and self-sufficient citizen."[57] Policy planners saw the development of industry as a way to wean the Indian away from field and ranch work.[58] Economic development was the newest wrinkle in the plans to provide competency on the road to the termination of trust. Indeed, there was no formal repeal of H. Con. Res. 108 during this period and at the dawn of industrial development, there was no slackening of the "strong pressure . . . on the local and national level to make it easier for Indians to sell their lands. Between 1953 and 1957 Indians had disposed of thirteen percent of their holdings, or 1,600,000 acres of land."[59]

Yet during all this talk of tribal development, the bureau had few provisions for the development of tribal industry. The lion's share of its effort concentrated on the stimulation of non-Indian enterprise.[60] One of the key features of economic development legislation in the 1950s centered on the fact that Indian trust property could be "hypothecated" (offered as collateral) for loans to these non-Indian enterprises as well as to tribal enterprises. The bureau would go to a reservation and suggest that the tribe put up money from the tribal coffers for the construction of a building. By building a facility for industrial rental, the tribe would be more likely to attract an industry which otherwise would be reluctant to put up its own capital. The problem with this was that many smaller tribes would be straining their treasuries to build such facilities and have their success resting on the ability of an outside company to make a profit.[61] The failure of an industry and the inability of a tribe to make good on a bad business loan could endanger tribal trust property, including tribal land holdings.

In May and June 1960, the House met to consider a group of bills, H.R. 7701, H.R. 8033, and H.R. 8590, which grouped together became the proposed "Operation Bootstrap" for the American Indian. They came as the result of the purported success of Puerto Rico's Point Four-style program of the same name. Separately, the bills provided a variety of industrial incentives for industry to locate in Indian country. It was important in the Point Four program for "the major part of capital investment to be financed from sources within the countries themselves."[62] Thus, Indian economic development would progress with the investment of Indian tribal capital. Under the authority of the proposed H.R. 8033, one of the Operation Bootstrap bills, the tribes were given the "authority to purchase, sell, exchange, pledge, mortgage hypothecated property of every description, real and personal, in trust or fee status."[63] This meant that the tribes could use tribal trust property as collateral on loans from the government for the construction of industrial plants. This would allow the government to liquidate such collateral if the tribe should fail to make good on their loans. The danger in this and the threat to tribal holdings already has been noted. John Hart, executive director of the North Dakota Indian Affairs Commission, warned the committee of the danger in the "failure of ventures which could result in tribal income being mortgaged for the next generation and thereby crippling future tribal effort."[64]

William Zimmerman of the Association on American Indian Affairs wondered also whether or not it was wise for a tribe to obligate itself to the United States for money to finance a private operator "who [would] be working for his own profit and whose operations [would] be subject to little if any control by the tribe."[65] Liberal tax relief and loans had been offered to industrial prospects looking at sites in Puerto Rico. However, a bad loan on a Puerto Rican industry did not result in the liquidation of a piece of Puerto Rican territory. A bad loan was absorbed by government. Trust property was not at question. Clearly, the stakes in the industrial development game were much higher for Indian people.

Regardless, it was clear to the committee and committee consultant Robert W. Miller of the American University graduate business faculty that incentives of this type were needed to bring industry into the reservation. He testified that "business is not in business to provide social welfare for a number of people . . . primarily you are going to interest industry on the point of making profits."[66]

In addition to loan security and government/tribal loan support, industry was offered, as in the Puerto Rico Bootstrap program, liberal tax relief. Income taxes would be suspended for ten years from start-up. Liberal property tax relief was offered. In addition, Bootstrap offered a novel payroll relief. For each worker who went from the welfare rolls to the employer's payroll, the employer was allowed to deduct thirty-six times the monthly welfare payment from his gross taxable income for the first five taxable years after the ten no-tax years.[67] This provision left wide open the temptation to fire employees one year after employment and hire more fresh off the welfare rolls.

No provisions in the bill were made for any wage standards. Roger Ernst, the assistant secretary of the Interior, asked, "If an Indian is paid a salary that is little more than a relief payment, will the tax incentives to industry accomplish much in terms of improving the status of the Indian or in terms of improving the Federal Government of a part of its financial burden?"[68]

As in Puerto Rico, favorable labor conditions were counted on to provide results. J. R. Whiteside was president of the Simpson Electric Company of Chicago, whose branch plant at Lac Du Flambeau in Wisconsin was one of the early experiments in the use of Indian labor. He testified that in the plant's fourteen years of operation he had experienced no labor difficulties and had what he considered "to be a very good relationship with [his] personnel."[69] That "good relationship," he claimed, was the reason Simpson could "afford to operate a plant about 400 miles from our main plant."[70] Obviously, the good relationship existed in spite of wages which were significantly lower than those at the main plant. It was clear that Indians could and would work for less and still "had proven beyond any doubt that in any work that required manual dexterity, patience, good eyesight, that they would not only equal other sources of labor, but that they would surpass, exceed."[71]

Part of Miller's consultant report to Congress was taken from a book which was authored by his father and business associate, Raymond W. Miller. Titled *Can Capitalism Compete?*, the book was "underwritten by the Ford Foundation and sponsored by the Harvard Graduate School of Business Administration to examine how we can communicate overseas the fundamentals of American capitalism."[72] It was basically the story of the Rolla Jewel Bearing plant, which produced sapphire bearings for use in guided missiles. Miller wrote the report as a result of criticism from those in underdeveloped nations who asked how America could help them if, as evidenced by Indian poverty, it could not help itself. Miller argued that failure on the reservation would be a "failure in its philosophy of economic opportunity for all. This is a failure with worldwide implications in the field of winning the minds of the world's population to our ideas."[73]

His answer was the Rolla plant, operating successfully and profitably in impoverished country. Clearly, for many, reservation economic development had been a demonstration project to the underdeveloped world. Miller then called attention to the success of the Puerto Rican experiment. This, along with the Rolla success, were evidence for Miller, that "science and progress are race blind. The Puerto Rican with his non-northern European background is no longer merely a helper, a hewer of wood, and a drawer of water. He is a partner in the shaping of his own future."[74]

The Indian, as well as the Puerto Rican, had proved to be a patient, facile and dexterous worker. This was a requirement in the defense ordnance and electronics industries which were among the most likely to locate on the reservation. Reservation industry, as in Puerto Rico, was attracted with the promise of liberal tax incentives and cheap trainable labor. In his support of Operation Bootstrap, congressional sponsor E. Y. Berry spoke in support of the program by quoting a man, "who has been interested in Indian affairs for many years, [who] says, 'a full dinner pail, a weekly paycheck, and a church to attend on Sunday is as essential to the Indian as the non-Indian.' He will lift himself by his bootstraps if given freedom of opportunity, unhampered by Government regulations and controls."[75]

Clearly, then, government protections of tribal trust property would be seen as a government regulation and control. If freedom to hypothecate trust property for loans was seen as a precondition to development, then the liquidation of tribal property to cover a bad loan would most likely be considered part of the price for Indians doing business. Unfortunately for Indian people, that brand of business was continuing ceaselessly during the 1950s to threaten tribal land and resources in the name of economic development.

There were, however, many Indians willing to take their chances for the hope of a real job near home. Over thirty reservation tribal councils passed resolutions in favor of the Bootstrap plan.[76]

Yet Bootstrap was not without its critics. Some warned that by offering such lucrative start-up provisions, reservation development would attract only industries fleeing from labor difficulties elsewhere.[77] Marvin Sonosk, an attorney speaking on behalf of the Shoshone tribe, testified to the Indian committee on the problem of fly-by-night operations. In this case it was a toy factory in South Dakota. The company had come with many questions. They asked about the suitability of living quarters, about where management would live, and about what the tribe could offer in the way of "subsidy in terms of land, buildings and capital investment." The factory came and left after the tribe and the BIA had put up a subsidy and provided vocational training.[78]

When we look at the beginnings of reservation economic development, we must ask the question: In whose best interest was the plan to develop industrial plants designed? Clearly, the liberal subsidies were attractive to industry, as were the promises of tractable tribal governments and labor. In fact, the reservation environment was presented to light industry in much the same fashion as it had been in Puerto Rico. Tax benefits, loans and cheap labor were the attractions. For the Indian people, there was the promise of some jobs but no real tribal development. Senate Concurrent Resolution 3 was presented as a repudiation to termination legislation. It was nothing of the kind. Economic development appeared as a way for Glenn Emmons to soften the criticism against termination by offering development as a comprehensive competency program. Dillon Myer's and Arthur Watkins's draconian form of termination was a political failure. Terminating tribes could not proceed in such a callous manner. But the economic chaos and political fallout of rapid termination could be softened by the new competency program. Industrial development would lead to economic, social, and cultural development which in turn would present an Indian people not only ready but eager to continue without federal supervision.

The Grand Junction, Colorado *Leader* echoed this view in 1960 when it claimed that "Operation Bootstrap would, in our opinion, be the most useful ever devised in emancipating the Indian Wards of the government."[79] Frank Church of the 85th Congress Indian Subcommittee was perfectly lucid in the way he described the problem of "termination." Terminating the federal treaty trust was not bad—the evil came when termination was pursued "as an excuse for selling out Indian lands, selling out Indian assets, in places where that has not been justified because the condition of the people in these places is not yet suitable for termination."[80]

For Church, competency through economic and cultural advancement would be such a justification. Indeed, even Joseph Garry, the leader of the National Congress of American Indians, claimed that termination had become "a fearful thing" to Indian people. "I don't think it should be emphasized as a goal," he said, "but only through natural advancement can we reach the goal of assimilation by natural means."[81]

NOTES

1. Patrick K. Ourada, "Glenn Emmons," in *The Commissioners of Indian Affairs, 1824-1977*, ed. Robert M. Kvasnicka and Herman Viola (Lincoln: University of Nebraska Press, 1979), p. 301.

2. Ibid., p. 302.

3. "Federal Indian Legislation and Policies," prepared by the 1956 Workshop on American Indian Affairs, Department of Anthropology, University of Chicago, Chicago, Ill. p. 25.

4. Ibid., p. 26.

5. Donald Lee Fixico, "Termination and Relocation: Federal Indian Policy in the 1950s" (Ph.D. dissertation, University of Oklahoma, 1980), p. 124.

6. Article in the *Oregonian* by Wallace Turner, Glenn Emmons Papers, Box 1, University of Toledo Library (microfilm). Emmons made clear in this same article that, though it should be personalized and individualized, termination was the final goal he desired.

7. Ibid.

8. *Denver Post*, editorial, 16 July 1953, Glenn Emmons Papers, Box 1.

9. *Gallup Independent*, editorial, n.d., Glenn Emmons Papers, Box 1.

10. *Desert Magazine*, editorial, July 1954, p. 10, Glenn Emmons Papers, Box 1.

11. Ibid.

12. Larry W. Burt, *Tribalism in Crisis: Federal Indian Policy, 1953-1961* (Albuquerque: University of New Mexico Press, 1982), p. 20.

13. U.S. Congress, House, *Present Relations of the Federal Government to the American Indian*, 85th Cong., 2nd sess. (Washington, D.C.: U.S. Government Printing Office, 1959), p. 244.

14. Fixico, *Termination and Relocation: Federal Indian Policy 1945-1960*. (Albuquerque: University of New Mexico Press, 1986), p. 102.

15. Ibid.

16. Burt, *Tribalism in Crisis*, p. 29.

17. Ibid.

18. Arthur V. Watkins, "Termination of Federal Supervision: The Removal of Restrictions Over Indian Property and Person," *Annals of the American Academy of Political and Social Science* 311 (May 1957) #47.

19. Oliver La Farge, "Termination of Federal Supervision: Disintegration and the American Indians," *Annals of the American Academy of Political and Social Science* 311 (May 1957) #41-46.

20. Edward P. Dozier, George E. Simpson, and J. Milton Yinger, "The Integration of Americans of Indian Descent," *The Annals of the American Academy of Political and Social Science* 311 (May 1957):162.

21. Burt, *Tribalism in Crisis*, p. 49.

22. Ibid., p. 50.

23. Ibid.

24. Ibid.

25. Margaret Connell Szasz, *Education and the American Indian: The Road to Self-determination Since 1928*, 2nd ed. (Albuquerque: University of New Mexico Press, 1977), p. 124.

26. Ibid., p. 125.

27. U.S. Congress, Senate, *The Education of American Indians, A Compilation of Statutes*, vol. 1, committee print of the Subcommittee on Indian Education, 91st Cong., 1st sess. (Washington, D.C.: U.S. Government Printing Office, 1969), p. 48.

28. Burt, *Tribalism in Crisis*, p. 52.

29. Szasz, *Education and the American Indian*, p. 137.

30. Fixico, "Termination and Relocation," p. 157.

31. U.S. Department of the Interior, *A Report of the Secretary of the Inte-*

Interior: Developing America's Resource Base (Washington, D.C.: U.S. Government Printing Office, 1957), pp. 34-35, 6.

32. Burt, *Tribalism in Crisis*, p. 31.

33. Ibid., p. 71.

34. Ibid., p. 85. Vine Deloria suggested a plan which would show Native Americans "how to modernize in ways within Indian tradition." Emmons suggested the development of a Point Four program in an article entitled "Broken Arrow," in *Time* 4 March 1957: pp. 48-49. See also Burt, *Tribalism in Crisis* ; p. 153 and U.S. Department of State, *Point Four: Cooperative Programs for Aid in the Development of Economically Underdeveloped Areas* (Washington, D.C.: U.S. Government Printing Office, 1949), p. 13.

35. U.S. Department of State, *Point Four*, revised ed., 1949, p. 2.

36. Ibid., p. 3.

37. "Report of the Puerto Rico Policy Commission" (Chardon Report), 14 June 1934, in William A. Brophy Papers, Box 19, Archives of Harry S. Truman Library, Independence Mo. Brophy, who was deeply involved in Puerto Rican policy during this period and who later served as Indian commissioner, was a part of the 1957 Fund for the Republic Commission on the Rights, Liberties and Responsibilities of the American Indian, the study which attempted to slow down and rationalize U.S. termination policy, through a program of industrial, human, and community development.

38. Ibid.

39. Ibid.

40. Hearings Before Subcommittee on Indian Affairs of the Commitee on Territories and Insular Affairs, S.R. 26, 13 February 1943, in William A. Brophy Papers, Box 14.

41. Stuart Chase, "Operation Bootstrap in Puerto Rico: Report of Progress, 1951," by the National Planning Association, September 1951, p. 7. See also statement of Lawrence E. Lindley, General Secretary of the Indian economic development resolution, "How can we better show the underdeveloped nations of the world the way to improving the standard of life for their people than by a demonstration at home? Where can we accomplish more, with less investment, and with greater rewards than by a 'Point Four' program at home?," in U.S. Congress, Senate, *Hearings Before the Subcommittee on Indian Affairs*, 85th Cong., 1st sess. (Washington, D.C.: U.S. Government Printing Office, 1957), p. 231.

42. Chase, "Operation Bootstrap," p. 1.

43. Ibid., p. 5.

44. Ibid., p. 10.

45. Ibid., p. 41.

46. Ibid., p. 42.

47. Ibid., p. 43.

48. Ibid., p. 49.

49. Ibid., p. 48.

50. Ibid., p. 55.

51. U.S. Congress, Senate, *Federal Indian Policy*, Hearings Before the Subcommittee on Indian Affairs of the Committee on Interior and Insular

Affairs, 85th Cong., 1st sess. (Washington, D.C.: U.S. Government Printing Office, 1957), p. 17.

52. Burt, *Tribalism in Crisis*, p. 90.

53. U.S. Congress, Senate, *Federal Indian Policy*, p. 5.

54. Ibid., p. 4.

55. Ibid., p. 15.

56. U.S. Congress, House, Subcommittee on Indian Affairs of the Committee on Interior and Insular Affairs, 86th Cong., 2nd sess. (Washington, D.C.: U.S. Government Printing Office, 1960), p. 27. "Operation Bootstrap" was the brainchild of South Dakota Congressman E. Y. Berry, who used the Puerto Rican model for this proposed legislation.

57. U.S. Congress, Senate, *Federal Indian Policy*, p. 22.

58. Ibid.

59 Ibid., p. 33. Statement of William Zimmerman on behalf of the Association of American Indian Affairs. It is interesting that Zimmerman is critical here of the bureau's industrial development plans. He is less critical of the terminationist intent of Congress than of their proposed method, which, he argues here and later, should proceed on a community development model. His greatest complaint rests on the case that the Indians were not "competent" to give their informed consent to sale.

60. U.S. Congress, Senate, *Federal Indian Policy*, p. 33.

61. Ibid., pp. 16-17.

62. U.S. Department of State, *Point Four*, p. 39.

63. Chase, "Operation Bootstrap," p. 5.

64. U.S. Congress, Senate, *Federal Indian Policy*, p. 24.

65. Ibid., p. 31.

66. Chase, "Operation Bootstrap," p. 34.

67. Ibid., p. 3.

68. Ibid., p. 12.

69. Ibid., p. 95.

70. Ibid.

71. U.S. Congress, Senate, *Federal Indian Policy*, p. 255, statement by Carl Beck.

72. Chase, "Operation Bootstrap," p. 29.

73. Ibid.

74. Ibid., p. 30.

75. Ibid., p. 36.

76. Ibid., p. 15.

77. Ibid., p. 43.

78. Ibid., p. 50.

79. Ibid., p. 97.

80. U.S. Congress, Senate, *Federal Indian Policy*, p. 244.

81. Ibid., p. 227.

3

The Developing Ideology
of Self-determination

As pressure against rapid termination grew, especially against forced termination, new means were sought to provide the sort of competencies which would produce a justifiable termination through cultural assimilation. The early resistance to forced termination did not come in the guise of a call for increased tribal sovereignty and solidarity. It came in efforts to assimilate Indians into the European-American economic and cultural values through a series of increasingly sophisticated methods. Economic, community and human development were being offered more and more as ways to effect competency and a justification for acceptable termination. The seeds of this development plan, which began under Glenn Emmons with the first halting moves toward industrial development, would grow under the leadership of Stewart Udall as interior secretary and Philleo Nash as commissioner. Special commissions, both public and private, would help accelerate the development of social planning for Indian society for the purpose of increasing their competency toward potential forms of tribal termination rather than tribal development. With these developments would begin the appropriation of the language of self-determination.

Education and industrial development plans reflected a new sophisticated notion of competency development. Competency became the keystone in the development of self-determination. Indeed, the infancy of industrial development on the reservation was conceived as much for its educative, acculturative and assimilative function as for its ultimate lasting effect on Indian economic power. This was the beginning of a pattern in economic and social development which characterized the 1960s under the rubric of economic and social self-determination.

During the late 1950s the policy of swift termination was being plowed under and replaced by the growing ideology of self-determination through community and industrial development. Termination would, however, continue throughout the 1960s to fertilize the growth of this new, supposedly anti-termination policy. The Interior Secretary and the Indian Committee in Congress intensified the effort to develop reservation resources, both material and human. This came as part of the tremendous growth in their desire to precede termination with Indian competency. During the period of rapid termination pressure, the greatest complaints were voiced by those who objected that Indians were not prepared to handle their own affairs. This resistance to termination carried practical as well as moral weight. Many argued that Indians who were released from federal control would fall into the cycle of poverty and would then quickly be back on the federal dole.

Glenn Emmons began the first industrial development program. Point Four-style planning characterized these efforts. The competency development pressure went into full gear during the latter part of Emmons's tenure and accelerated under Interior Secretary Stewart Udall and commissioner Philleo Nash in the Kennedy administration.[1]

In March 1960, near the end of the Eisenhower administration, Secretary of the Interior Seaton announced in a radio speech at Flagstaff, Arizona that reservation termination of special federal protection would not proceed until Indians "themselves are ready, prepared and willing to take on the full responsibilities for managing their own affairs."[2] Seaton's words were one of the first formal admissions at the federal level which made clear the changing tenor of Indian policy. Policymakers were beginning to respond to the failures of rapid, legislated termination, and began to develop plans to enhance the human and physical reservation resource as a part of a comprehensive competency program upon which a "justifiable" termination could be built. To this end, reservation resource analyses were commissioned throughout the late 1950s and early 1960s. Policy planners in the secretary's office continued their interest in locating suitable sites for industry. With equal interest, they began to explore the quality of the reservation's human resource.

As early as 1954, commissioner Emmons had organized the American Indian Research Fund (AIRF) as a way to attract private enterprise support for reservation research studies. Emmons was reluctant to get government directly involved with this type of activity and earnestly hoped industry would finance the projects. His early efforts were discouraged by lack of business interest in AIRF.[3]

Emmons had high hopes that resource studies could provide a basis from which to make decisions about human and industrial reservation development. Emmons sought reservation development for its supposedly salutary effect on Indian assimilation into the dominant culture and economy. "In general," he wrote, "there is a defeatist attitude toward assimilation of Indians into white life. However, I have found that many research groups and foundations are intensely interested in minority groups and are anxious to delve into Indian possibilities."[4]

He went on to discuss the promise of the Stanford Research Institute (SRI) which would later carry out reservation studies aimed not only at discovering material resource potential but would compute "population, birth and death rates, health condition and average age of tribal members. They will even go into such matters as religious ceremonies and social taboos."[5]

"Such matters" begin during this period to take on increasing importance for those interested in reservation development. Increasingly, sophisticated social/psychological methods would be emphasized, both to understand resistance to and to effect change in Indian people. The new yardstick of termination readiness became just that degree to which Indian people could be demonstrably shown assimilated or assimilable into the dominant culture.

Competency would now include psychological and social as well as material determinants before termination could be justified. Indian development was being vigorously sought as a morally and politically justifiable criterion for termination, not as a push for increased Indian control or sovereignty for its own sake. For Emmons and those who followed him, human capital development was crucial in this equation. "The Indians," he said, "must learn not only how to earn money, they must know how to spend it to good advantage." When he was asked whether he favored quick abolishment of the reservations, he replied, "just as quickly as is compatible with Indian welfare."[6]

Indian resource development was a part of a larger move by the U.S. government to aid in the development of poorer nations in general. Growing out of the Point Four initiatives, this policy was a method to further rationalize the U.S. economy by deliberately involving government in programs to curry the favor of new foreign markets. Development did not occur, however, without the aid of sophisticated resource studies used to gauge the investment climate. By 1954, commissioner Emmons had been actively involved in an effort to interest private enterprise in the development of reservation resource development studies. The first studies completed for this purpose were financed by the San Carlos and Jicarilla Apache Councils. They hired the Stanford Research Institute in 1955 to complete the work.[7]

SRI is a private, nonprofit group in the business of providing research data on economic growth potential in the U.S. and abroad. The

Mountain States Division of the institute was interested in fostering the economic growth of those states. It believed, as well, that "high on the list of regional problems is that of a large and increasing Indian population on vast tribal lands throughout the southwest. Activities to improve the economic status of the Indian people and to decrease their dependence on Federal and State assistance are of primary importance in the development of the entire region."[8]

The report is singular for its emphasis on the need to develop the human resources, without which it argued, economic resources could not be mobilized. It argued that the key to development and progress involved the assimilation of Apaches into white culture and economy. This report is similar to other SRI documents in its emphasis upon the human and cultural equation in the growth of an economy.

In October 1954, SRI published a Manual of Industrial Development prepared for the Foreign Operations Administration of the U.S. government. Written with special application to Latin America, the report detailed an analysis of human and material capital potential of Latin America. In this document, human resources play an important part in the investment climate equation, and it made special reference to the availability of a trainable labor force and a stable political climate. The report deliberately put human resources first in what it termed its "inventory of manufacturing resources," and it "recognizes that it is the human resources which shape and control the material resources of industrial development."[9]

Industrial development of the underdeveloped world was continuing as an important goal with both political and economic ramifications in the Cold War climate of the 1950s. In 1957 SRI prepared a paper for the U.S. National Commission for UNESCO. It was titled "The American Citizen's Stake in the Progress of Less Developed Areas of the World." This report presents the argument that economic development of the Third World was not merely salutary but essential to the political and economic health of the United States. It presents alternative development scenarios, but the main theme is the message that development should not be coercive nor be perceived as colonialist. Local community self-help and self-direction emerge as the key to successful development.[10]

The involvement of SRI in the development of the reservations and the interest of the commissioner's office in this activity are testimony to the increasing importance of Indian country in America's economic and resource future. America's reservations, like Puerto Rico and other regions of the less developed world, were viewed increasingly as resource colonies and the source of a cheap and trainable labor pool for light industries and urban relocation.

Interest in the human and material development of the Indian reservations also roughly paralleled the growing political and economic failure of rapid termination. Economic development accelerated in the late 1950s with the aid of scientific research on the quality of the reservation human resource. Glenn Emmons predicated the success of economic development upon the compilation of successful human and material capital resource studies. These studies were conceived as part of an accelerating attempt to rationalize Indian policy by providing a scientific basis for a variety of development initiatives.

Indian economic development was taking root in the late 1950s, its growth watered by pressure from those who argued vigorously against rapid tribal termination. The Association on American Indian Affairs assisted the National Congress of American Indians in the vanguard of the attack on rapid termination and the push for economic development. It is crucial to recognize the nature of the discussion which represented the most important language of resistance to termination through this association. For the AAIA, as represented through its chief spokesperson, Oliver La Farge, development was synonymous with competency, the prerequisite for termination. La Farge had been a vocal supporter of the Emmons nomination. In an address before the annual meeting of the AAIA in May 1954, La Farge supported Emmons. He praised "the new commissioner, whom we have the honor to have here as our guest today, [who] holds views with which we heartily concur."[11]

La Farge agreed with Emmons's desire to develop the reservations' industrial base as an adjunct to urban relocation and as a prerequisite to termination. He also agreed with Emmons on the need to tailor economic development solutions to fit the circumstances of the individual tribes. La Farge envisioned the competency issue as a very complex matter which did not involve simple economic guidelines. He insisted that Indians must be socially as well as economically prepared for termination, and his objections to a number of hasty termination bills reflect this. His opposition to the proposed termination of the Turtle Mountain Chippewas apparently came from his belief that this tribe was "not prepared economically and to a considerable extent socially."[12]

Nevertheless, it appears that La Farge's position on termination was not fully representative of the general will, either within AAIA or between reform groups which were battling rapid termination. La Farge carried on a running skirmish with the National Congress of American Indians. The evidence suggests that the squabbles were not related to policy but to which group was getting the recognition for the reversal of an official policy of termination. There appears to have been a great deal of backbiting with regard to whether NCAI was riding the coattails of AAIA, yet receiving the lion's share of the publicity for reform successes.

Indian reform politics is bitter even in the best of times, and those internecine squabbles can likely be attributed to the scramble for scarce money between similar organizations.[13] Yet the policy divisions behind the scenes in AAIA are not unimportant.

La Farge had a running dispute with association executive director Dr. Alexander Lesser over the issue of termination and the continuance of the federal-Indian trust relationship. This dispute is important for determining the outcome of self-help competency efforts that were to fuel the language of self-determination. When Alexander Lesser was hired as executive director he had moved from academic anthropology into the arena of Indian advocacy. His views also represent a position on tribal survival which characterize one side of a debate regarding the purpose of anthropological research. Lesser was a student of Franz Boas, who at Columbia University had founded a school of historicist anthropology which became extremely influential and had tangential importance for a definition of tribal sovereignty and cultural continuity. Boas - and through Boas, Lesser - was opposed to the presumptions of the functionalist school of anthropology deriving from Malinowski and his students. It is incorrect to oversimplify the differences between historicist and functionalist anthropology; nonetheless, major outlines can be determined and they have an impact on policy formation. For the functionalist, all human institutional structures may be explained by their function within the larger context of society.

Functionalist anthropology, what Sidney Mintz calls "the anthropology of liberal reform," is fundamental to the intellectual argument for social guidance toward a justifiable termination.[14] On the other hand, for the historicist anthropologist, social institutions and minority groups have an "atomic" singularity, a meaning which can be understood separately from the prerogatives of the larger national society. For Lesser, institutional stability, as well as obstacles to change, may be meaningfully understood as "opposition" to the prerogatives of the larger polity. There is a "recognition that many of the obstacles to change which have been attributed to human nature are in fact due to the inertia of institutions and to the voluntary desire of powerful classes to maintain the existing status....the anthropology of liberal reform did not address itself, in any substantive way , to the problem of power."[15]

It is interesting and instructive to contrast the anthropology of Lesser with that of Philleo Nash, who was influential as a member of the AAIA and who later as commissioner of Indian Affairs would help shape the liberal reform agenda during the Kennedy administration. Nash was a student of A. R. Radcliffe-Brown at the University of Chicago, a stronghold of the functionalist approach. Nash also was strongly influenced by the political theory of Harold Lasswell, who will be discussed later and whose theory participates in the general tradition of functionalist social science.

Nash and Lesser both did studies of the impact of the Ghost Dance on tribal reaction to invasion, Nash with the Klamath, Modoc and Paviotso, and Lesser with the Pawnee. [16] For Lesser, the Ghost Dance Hand Game, which he studied, was a way of reclaiming the past, a right way of recovering culture. He argued that it was an appropriate way of conserving revered elements of culture under the impact of white encroachment. For Nash, the manifestation of the Ghost Dance in nineteenth century Oregon was a dysfunctional revivalism and an evidence of general deprivation, not political and social oppression. For Nash, this hybrid cultural practice can be understood only as part of a people's dysfunctional reaction to change, a transitional symptom. Culture adaptation becomes a stage in change toward cultural assimilation. This is consistent with theoretical social functionalism, and given its presuppositions, may be the only interpretation. Minority culture may only be understood as a element in relation to the dominant culture. Its manifestations are, therefore, not ends in themselves, expressing central cultural phenomena in natural adjustment. It is a social rationality which must, by definition, be understood as a subsidiary—indeed, a deficient rationality—to that of the dominant culture of which itself is a part. While not a professional social scientist himself, La Farge expressed agreement with the accommodationism and functionalism of Nash. Indeed, they were intellectually very close throughout this period.

The connections between functionalist social science and developing conceptions of social therapy and social adjustment cannot be underestimated. The liberal social programming which followed the harsh termination period was a study in functionalist social science. Models of cultural deficit, amenable to "guided acculturation" became part of the language of self-determination, rather than pluralist or tribal sovereigntist models. In opposition to this, for Lesser, the reactive character of changing religious practice was forged in the inequality of power relations rather than as evidence of some amorphous "deprivation." La Farge's dislike of Lesser's position on termination erupts in a letter he wrote to Lesser on January 2, 1954:

> One thing that disturbs me very much is that we are moved into termination and competency debates without ever having clarified our fundamental policy. I believe you and I have a profound disagreement on this matter which probably extends through other members of the board. At the risk of boring repetition, I insist that a tribe may reach a point at which it no longer needs the advantages of trusteeship and yet be entirely unwilling to give them up. I

believe that situations can and will arise when trusteeship of trust status for land, should be terminated regardless of the squawks of the beneficiaries. I absolutely will not base an argument for the continuation of trust status entirely upon the wishes of the beneficiaries.[17]

La Farge opposed Lesser on the general issue of assimilation. In a 1961 article, Lesser argued for tolerance of Indian pluralism. He made a distinction between immigrant and Indian assimilation, stating that immigrants arrived willingly and had a homeland to which they could refer. He wrote, "The disappearance of our Indian communities by assimilation has a crucial finality that assimilation can never have for other American minorities . . . our attitude toward the Indians, the stubbornest non-conformists among us, may be the touchstone of our tolerance of diversity anywhere."[18]

For Lesser, Indian people could claim special rights to a sovereignty protected by treaty, on constitutional and moral grounds. For Lesser, sovereignty was inviolable. For La Farge, it was a status to be held only until competency, and achieving that competency was what the government's Indian business was all about.

It is a curiosity that La Farge, who had such little regard for the "squawks of the beneficiaries," should have also built part of his position against termination on the importance of tribal consent to termination. For La Farge, social and economic competency was only a partial prerequisite before termination could occur. Tribal consent was another. Tribes had to be fully consulted and should be in a position to assent to or deny termination. For example, in his letter to Senator Anderson on the Turtle Mountain Chippewa termination, La Farge's "strongest objection, is that the bill was not a government-Indian cooperative effort," citing the tribe felt that "consultation has been a farce."[19]

Clearly, then, there exists a fundamental contradiction in La Farge and in AAIA policy position. Both support *and* revile the importance of tribal will over termination. Both are caught up in the consent issue. At the same time that we hear La Farge require tribal consent before policy initiatives can be taken with regard to termination, we see him denigrating the right of a tribe to use the power of consent if it interferes with his definition of competency.

The final goal for La Farge is termination after competency— justifiable termination. Yet, for La Farge, if Indian people were to be successfully rehabilitated to the point where termination could proceed, development must be much more than economic; it must be social, cultural, and psychological. Indians must themselves see the value of self-support and self-help. The problem for policymakers in the 1960s was this goal of thorough rehabilitation. The squawks of the beneficiaries had become, along with the lack of economic development and Indian poverty, a real problem.

In the end, La Farge's position was more representative of AAIA thinking than Lesser's. In fact, Lesser had become somewhat of an embarrassment to the membership and was soon edged out of a leadership role in the AAIA.

For organizations such as the AAIA and men like La Farge, termination could not easily proceed in this environment. Indians must be developed in such a variety of ways that they will welcome termination. In La Farge's words: "When they are solidly self supporting, masters of our techniques and devices, sound in health, the Indians themselves will abolish the Indian Bureau by rendering it superfluous."[20] The ideology of self-determination has its roots partly in liberal reform of Indian affairs through the special agency of such groups as the AAIA. In addition, economic development, the ethic of self-help, and social/psychological development of Indian communities began to take on greater importance as part of the competency push. This novel change came at the behest of a group of reformers and critics in both business and government. In the creation of total rehabilitation and competence, La Farge and the AAIA were in support of a program to increase tribal control over their own affairs.

As early as 1950, the AAIA had taken the position that "it is the right of tribes to make mistakes. So long as they are anxiously protected from making mistakes, they can never learn to handle their own affairs."[21] Yet while noting this early emphasis on development, it is probably significant that the AAIA included in its membership William Zimmerman. Though he was later to downplay his role in termination policy, Zimmerman was a main conduit for the development of these plans. As acting commissioner of Indian Affairs, he operated in that capacity for the ailing William Brophy in 1946. Zimmerman had supplied Congress with a three-part list of tribes separated according to the tribes readiness for termination. It was this list that was used by Dillon Myer during the darkest days of the rapid termination period in the early 1950s.[22]

ECONOMIC DEVELOPMENT, SELF-HELP, AND SOCIAL SCIENCE

Glenn Emmons was convinced that with the proper competency push, termination could take place. In 1957 he made public a plan which he had developed in concert with Interior Secretary Fred Seaton and

Assistant Secretary of the Interior Roger Ernst. The plan called for gradual termination upon attainment of competency, with all tribes and groups terminated by an interesting target date—Independence Day, 1976. Emmons wanted to drive home the "liberation" theme in time for the bicentennial. To gain support for this plan, Emmons revived the moribund American Indian Research Fund (AIRF). He recruited Col. William Ulman, of the McCann-Erickson Corporation, the nation's largest public relations firm, to serve as executive secretary and renamed the organization the American Indian Development Fund (AIDF).[23]

Under Ulman's direction, and with support of the oil industry, AIDF made a successful start. The first sizable contribution to AIDF came from William W. Keeler of the Phillips Petroleum Co. (Keeler put up $5,000 to get AIDF started). Keeler was to be a key player on this stage of Indian development and rehabilitation reform in the coming years. In 1958 Keeler was both executive vice-president of Phillips and the principal chief of the Cherokee nation. He became a leading spokesman for Indian reform in both the Eisenhower and Kennedy administrations. Touted as a man of both cultures, this unique individual can be found playing a major role as a member of three of the most important Indian policy advisory committees during the late 1950s and early 1960s—The Commission on the Rights and Responsibilities of the American Indian, sponsored by the Ford Foundation Fund for the Republic; the Udall task force in the Kennedy administration; and the President's Task Force on Indian Affairs.

In January 1958, Keeler and Ulman presented a program to businessmen which would work toward termination as mandated in House Concurrent Resolution 108; "Before the end of the month, oil and oil drilling companies had contributed $6,000, almost all in small sums of $25 to $250, and AIDF directors realized the sensitive nature of the fact that all of the money had come from the oil industry and thus naturally did not publicize it."[24]

In 1959 the AIDF was actively involved in the promotion of reservation economic development through the production of human and material resource studies. Using money previously donated by retired oil millionaire Lester Norris, AIDF contracted with MIT professors Everett Hagen, an economist, and Louis C. Schaw, a social psychologist, for an analysis of the Rosebud and Pine Ridge reservations. Their report, "The Sioux on the Reservation," is less remarkable for its direct effect on policy, than for its spirit and intent.[25] It represented a departure from simple economic analysis and entered the domain of sophisticated social/psychological analysis of the tribal mind and its readiness for the merger with white culture and economy. Schaw and Hagen's employment as policy consultants was representative of the growing concern over the problem of Indian social, psychological and cultural adaptability to white economic and political institutions.

Schaw's and Hagen's work reflects the concern over the quality of the reservation's human resource as well as the material reservation resource. Human development would become a dominant theme in Indian policy through the coming decade. Henry Hough writes that "among the resources of any group of people the most important is the 'man-power' of its members and all of the useful work these men and women are capable of accomplishing."[26]

Human development is closely allied to the developing ideology of self-determination. Self-help is a major theme in the work of Hagen and Schaw. The ability of an outside agency to enlist the cooperation of an indigenous people is tightly bound with the ability of that agency to motivate, to recognize and ameliorate social/psychological impediments to change, to enlist not merely the willing, but the enthusiastic cooperation of the local people. For Louis Schaw, social/psychological factors were requisites in the economic development equation. He believed in an interdisciplinary approach to the understanding of economic growth potential, especially the growth of underdeveloped societies. Psychology, sociology, and anthropology would work in concert toward the solution of development problems.[27]

In his book, *On the Theory of Social Change*, Hagen developed an interdisciplinary thesis of effective development by examining "the factors which cause a traditional society to become one in which economic growth is occurring."[28] His analysis led him to conclude that traditional societies could not progress through the mere imitation of Western economic structures. Rather, a climate must be formed in which traditional societies can participate and subsequently create the conditions for economic change. For Hagen, the problem of economic development was fundamentally a human rather than a technical problem. He wrote:

> The technical problem is the easy aspect of technological progress for present-day low income countries. Technological advance requires doing new things; it requires also the creation of new economic, political and social organizations and relationships, or the adaptation to new functions of old organizations and relationships.[29]

In "The Sioux on the Reservation," Hagen and Schaw concluded that the situation for the Sioux was far worse than any they had discovered in the Asian or African developing nations. Hagen emphasized the development of an environment in which the underdeveloped society could create its own conditions for change, rather than have change imposed or to simply provide opportunities for imitation. He also emphasized the maintenance of traditional culture as a seedbed for the roots of change. This was reflective of a growing tolerance for, and encouragement of, the structure and culture of tribal society as a way to maintain morale, initiative and pride, the lack of which was coming more and more to be seen as an impediment to economic and industrial development.[30]

The furor over termination had reached the press and had become a hotly debated issue.[31] The smoldering public furor over termination and Indian poverty, combined with the halting development record under Emmons, prompted the formation of the five person Commission on the Rights, Responsibilities and Liberties of the American Indian. The commission was financially supported by the Fund for the Republic, an adjunct of the Ford Foundation which had been established to support research relating to "two great related needs. The first is the establishment of a lasting peace. The second is the achievement of democratic strength, stability and vitality."[32]

Francis Prucha cites the findings of this group, as reported in *America's Unfinished Business,* as one of the "notable examples of the new mood and outlook"[33] which prefaced the era of self-determination. It would have a significant impact on Indian policy during the coming years and contribute substantially to the growing ideology of self-determination.

William Brophy was selected as executive director of the Commission on the Rights, Liberties and Responsibilities of the American Indian. Brophy had been commissioner of Indian Affairs between 1945 and 1948, while William Zimmerman was acting commissioner during the last eighteen months of that period. Brophy was a logical choice for the post. He had the reputation for being a supporter of Indian civil rights due to his experience as attorney to the Pueblo tribes. He also had experienced the commissioner's responsibilities and pressures. Perhaps equally important was his involvement with the economic development of Puerto Rico. Between 1943 and 1945 he was head of the Puerto Rican Affairs section in the Division of Territories and Island Possessions, Department of the Interior. As we have seen, by this time Puerto Rican development blueprints were being extensively utilized in the architecture of Indian reservation development.

Other members of the commission included W. W. Keeler, chairman of the executive committee of Phillips Petroleum at the time the commission published its report. He was also principal chief of the Cherokee nation. Not precisely a democratic representative of the Cherokee, nonetheless he was appointed to that position by President

Harry Truman. Regardless, Keeler was described in the Commission Final Report as a valuable member, "since he belongs to both cultures he was able to interpret the Indians and the whites to each other."[34]

Arthur Meier Schlesinger, Francis Lee Higginson Professor of history at Harvard, was the third member. Charles Arthur Sprague was editor of the *Oregon Statesman* and former governor of Oregon. The New York *Herald Tribune* called him "the most influential editor in the Northwest," describing him as, "Calvinistic and witty," ...[a] lifelong Republican with liberal tendencies."[35] Karl N. Llewellyn contributed his jurisprudential expertise to the commission. Chairman O. Meredith Wilson was president of the University of Oregon at the inception of the commission. Later, two members were added. Soia Mentschikoff, Dean of the University of Miami Law School, took over for her husband, Karl Llewellyn, upon his death early in 1962. William Brophy also died early in 1962 and was replaced by his wife, Dr. Sophie D. Aberle. She had served as general superintendent of the United Pueblos agency and had been long active in Indian affairs. Both Mentschikoff and Aberle were involved in the work of the commission from the beginning.[36]

The commission set about coming to grips with the problem of Indian poverty and the growing reality of the failure of termination. Their work was part of the effort to approach the "Indian Problem" from more than one direction. It continued the move toward sophisticated social/psychological rehabilitation of Indian America. Its existence was due to the failure of, and dissatisfaction with, termination policy. Yet the commission report left little doubt about the place of the Indian in American society. Schlesinger's idea for a title told the story—"The Indian: America's Unfinished Business." The commission report is one of the early documents which detail the growing liberal ideology of self-help and self-determination. Indeed, the roots of the self-determination movement cannot be really understood without an analysis of this private commission's influence. It was the clearest turning point in Indian social and educational policy since the Hoover commission report.

The commission's goals were congruent with the will of the Ford Foundation and its Fund for the Republic, especially in its belief in planning for economic growth in the postwar years and its concern for the solution of social problems through both economic and social means. The fund's first director, Paul Hoffman, was long active in the production of research relating to the dual goals of social and economic progress in the underdeveloped nations. Hoffman had written on the need to go beyond natural resource surveys to a more sophisticated system. Before capital could be most strategically invested in these areas, Hoffman believed that human capital must be analyzed and developed accordingly.[37]

The commission was an extension of the fund's desire to be a resource base for the establishment of Indian policy recommendations which would carry the stamp of intellectual validity. The commission was a small, privately funded and appointed, elite group of intellectual, media, and business leaders taking time from their private affairs to forge and present policy on a very large, very public issue—the condition of Indian America.

Perhaps the small size of the study group, its elite, academic credentials, ideological congruence, as well as the private mode of its selection, can account for its great degree of consensus on Indian policy issues. Members of the Fund commission were virtually of one voice saying that forms of termination and assimilation should be the ultimate goal in Indian policy. For them, the federal-Indian trust relationship was present, not as an agreement between sovereigns, but as part of a compact made as restitution for tribal dispossession. For the commission, trust remained in force only until Indians were assimilated and competent. Yet the commission was aware that "legislated termination" of the stripe proposed by Dillon Myer and Arthur Watkins was ineffective, both in accomplishing its objective and in garnering public support.

They proposed to attack the problem in a different way. In Chapter 7 of the commission report, titled "Policies which Impede Indian Assimilation," the commission stated its conviction with regard to a method of termination: "To be specific—so long as levels of Indian education, health, and economy are substandard, so long as the Indian's status in practically all areas of life is uncertain, just so long will legislation or other precipitate action fail to assimilate the Indian into the majority of society."[38]

The commission's emphasis on eventual termination also is reflected in the appointmen of its director. As commissioner of Indian affairs, William Brophy was a firm supporter of the plenary power of Congress to rule unilaterally on Indian Affairs. His tenure as commissioner marked the beginning of a period of rapid termination and a "return to a more rapid assimilation of Indians," a policy which received Brophy's full support.[39]

There is no question that assimilation and termination were the ultimate goal for the commission. Yet the methods by which this would be achieved were subtle and indirect, founded in the developing techniques of human social engineering. The commission was aware of this and believed these techniques had their roots in the late 19th century. This commitment is reflected in the following: "Toward the end of the century, under the guidance of the emerging disciplines that we now call the behavioral sciences a clearer view of the Indian problem and the white man's obligation began to develop."[40]

It is far from clear that Indian policy of the late nineteenth century was much of a reflection on the type of social engineering as is represented in the commission's proposals. Its historical genesis appears to be more clearly in the New Deal reforms of the 1930s. Regardless of its place in modern Indian policy history, the commission was carving a place for itself in the late 1950s which was thoroughly in concert with the tradition of liberal social melioration. Yet moves toward cultural pluralism, self-government, and self-determination were more a part of the philosophical underpinning of the policy framework articulated by commissioner Collier during the Indian New Deal. His language, if not so much the effect of his policies, reflected an abiding belief in those values beyond their use as rhetorical weapons.[41]

In the late 1950s, however, tribal self-help, economic, social, and educational self-determination were developed as simple tools toward an assimilation which, for the commission and other Indian policy opinion leaders, made more political and social scientific sense than "legislated" termination. Commissioner Sprague stated boldly in a letter to Sophie Aberle, "American Policy should aim at preparing Indians for self-reliant living in the prevailing social and economic framework. As this is accomplished, tribe by tribe, termination will follow easily and naturally. Then termination would be a proof of success, not a sign of failure."[42]

For this commission, the key to establishing a sound termination policy was the development of social and economic competency to make termination justifiable. But more than that, as an integral part of the competency program, Indian people must begin to initiate and carry through the solutions to their own problems. As commissioner Wilson said, quoting the commission report, "An objective which should undergird all Indian policy is that the individual, the Indian family, and the Indian community be motivated to participate in solving their own problems. Indian-made plans should receive preferential treatment, and when workable, should be adopted."[43]

The Fund commission developed a plan with a double focus. They believed that social engineering could be combined with an ethic of self-help. Human capital could be developed to gain increased competence through the use of social science to bolster industrial economic development. Then with this support, tribes and communities could be enlisted to aid in the solution of their own problems of underdevelopment. Indeed, social engineering and self-help are the conceptual linchpins in the ideology of self-determination. Self-help and self-determination became, during this period, both a motivational tool for the promotion of economic development and a training program in self-government and institutional management.

The Fund commission recognized the power of these techniques in providing a base for motivation. It referred in its report to the success of the Indian New Deal and the Indian Reorganization Act as "evidence that the race wanted community responsibility and self-determination."[44] The commission referred to the Indian New Deal as another era of reform which responded to the failure of an earlier period of termination—that which followed the Dawes Allotment Act in the 1880s. They were aware that, as in their own time, "the realization that conformity cannot be legislated changed the national policy toward Indians."[45] The reaction to this prompted the development of more sophisticated techniques for assimilation, rather than any growth of awareness that something might be wrong with the fundamental notion of assimilation itself.

One of the key building blocks in the total rehabilitation of the reservation Indian centered on the development of morale. The commissioners wanted to find a way to involve the Indian in his own renascence and hoped to aid this effort by encouraging the rebuilding of tribal culture. They referred to the problem of hostile dependence, which Schaw and Hagen also had emphasized in their Sioux study. They realized that "a basic need in successful economic development on reservations is strong motivation. Another is capable leadership. A third is the use of methods and the development of institutions that can fit the Indian thinking and encourage Indian choices."[46]

For the Fund commission, it was an essentially sound social scientific practice to involve the local people in the solution of their own problems. But with regard to Indian people, it was especially important to combine self-help with self-esteem and morale building. Indeed, for them, "to encourage pride in Indianness is not to turn back the clock. On the contrary it is to recognize that the United States policy has hitherto neglected this vital factor as a force for assimilation, with a corresponding loss to our national culture."[47] This is the fundamental paradox within the developing ideology of self-determination.

The program of encouraging Indian culture was presented as a technique which would work toward eventual assimilation. Indianness was designed to effect the eventual disintegration of Indians. And the emphasis on loss of Indian culture was lamented only as its loss became a loss to our "national culture." Ironically, Indians are enlisted to participate in this program as part of a plan to improve their morale.

In all, the commission set about to establish the guidelines of a successful program to include Indian cultural and leadership development, community development and a self-development ethic. In fact, all development was dependent on Indian motivation. "No program from outside can serve as a substitute for one willed by Indians themselves. . . . What is essential is to elicit their own initiative and intelligent cooperation."[48]

In a November 1959 memorandum, Charles Sprague reminded the commission that "more emphasis must be put on Indians helping themselves. We have the word 'responsibilities' in our title . . . . That is necessary not just to get the government out of the Indian business but to get the Indians to assert themselves."[49]

In a letter to Sophie Aberle, W. W. Keeler noted the success of self-help in a Florida program:

> The government at one time made available for the Seminoles, Big Cypress, and Dania reservations some modern housing, which in comparison to their open, thatched roof shelters, represented a big step toward being civilized. I went in some of these new homes with terrazzo floors, TV sets, automatic dishwashers, and the modern laundry facilities. They happen to be people who went to work in their own tribal enterprises which they have also started in the last few years, or through vocational training have managed to get jobs fairly close to the reservations.[50]

Keeler wrote that this program failed, but subsequently the tribespeople began, through repeated efforts, to gain an interest in their own housing development. He went on to note that they had a higher standard of living than Cuban refugees living on the outskirts of Miami:

> I think the only mistake in the program was that the BIA felt they could get the work done by contractors cheaper and better than by the Indians themselves. I believe this fails to recognize that in some respects Indians are no different from any other people, in that they respond to the extent that they are participating in something.[51]

Economic and industrial rehabilitation could not begin in the absence of human resources to support this activity. With a major emphasis on industrial development, the commission was concerned that the lack of a supporting human infrastructure would doom any competency development plans.[52] To resolve this problem, the Indian motivation and morale problem would be addressed in concert with a plan to develop their social and political infrastructure. Community development was the vehicle created to carry the weight of these complex designs. The "Recommendations" section of the commission report stated simply, that Indian motivation should "undergird" all Indian policy.[53]

Thus, the economic, industrial development goals of the commission were dependent upon the solution of some basic problems within both the Indian mind and the tribal social psyche. The commission referred to the development of Indian leaders to direct the community development plans. The report cites the work of Gordon McGregor and his five steps in community development which such a leader must be equipped to direct. These steps include "exploration of internal and external causes of these needs and problems, so the sources of social, psychological and economic difficulties may be recognized . . . a mechanism whereby one undertaking leads to a series of related activities directed toward both economic and social growth."[54]

For the commission, "the economic goals for Indians should be (1) the development of their community and individual resources and (2) the attainment of professional, managerial, and vocational skills comparable to those of their white neighbors, so as to enable Indians to integrate with the non-Indian community on a basis of economic equality."[55]

The commission wanted to put more emphasis on the responsibilities of the Indian. Charles Sprague wrote, "I see no solution to the Indian problem until the Indians themselves develop incentives and enough drive to pursue them."[56] Sprague had less patience with Point Four-style initiatives and appeared to rely more on economic and community development as preparation for "human drainage" to urban centers.[57] Regardless, his is still a plan leading to assimilation and termination.

At the same time that the commission argued for the development of community life in rural, agricultural reservation areas, it was arguing that "Indians should receive manual aptitudes in demand in modern industrial society."[58] As such, community development was to serve as means to an end—competency and termination rather than as an end in itself. For the Fund commission, community development was presented as a transition phase between dependency and termination.

Encouragement of tribal culture and Indian pride were acceptable to the extent they served to build morale. When deep-seated tribal values interfered with industrial efficiency, however, in the words of O. M. Wilson, they were to be "excised" and replaced by more acceptable values. Self-determination was not a species of increased sovereignty, rather it was a sophisticated attempt to provide a successful competency base upon which an argument for termination could be built. Wilson stated, "The Indian should not rate indefinitely as a preferred class of American citizens."[59] Clearly, the trust relationship was defined by the commission as a condition which could and should be cured by an effective competency program. W. W. Keeler echoes La Farge in a letter to Sophie Aberle, reminding her that the trust relationship, far from being treaty-bound, is, rather, dependent only on the extent of Indian dependence. "Some Indians, regardless of any treaty obligation, assume that the federal government should provide them with various services and aids because they are Indians, whether they have a need or not. I am saying that 'need' must get into the picture in some manner."[60]

Self-help and community development were the scientifically sound methods to accomplish this. They also were in concert with a political climate becoming slowly more sensitive to minority issues. Community development fit well with the growing chorus of Indian voices arguing for more control over their own destiny.

The reform fervor of the Association of American Indian Affairs and the Fund for the Republic Indian commission was rooted fast in a policy of humane assimilation. As early as 1950 we hear the AAIA criticizing the BIA's rehabilitation planning for being myopic in its insistence on a land-based economy. For the AAIA the answer was industry—"the great simple need is more income."[61]

The effort to develop communities was to aid in the development of a positive investment climate and to provide the basis for an Indian labor force. The "great simple need for more income" on Indian reservations was becoming very attractive to light industry entrepreneurs eager to make use of cheap Indian labor while taking advantage of tax breaks and numerous other incentives. Industrial development could work as the precursor to increased competency only so long as Indian cooperation could be enlisted and only so long as morale was high and motivation was not a serious problem. The research had shown the success of self-help in providing a positive investment climate in the overseas underdeveloped nations.

Under Stewart Udall, industrial development accelerated in the early 1960s. Unlike Emmons, Udall was not reticent about involving government in the study and rehabilitation of Indian communities as a prelude to development. The commission noted in its final report the promise of a new federal agency created under the Economic Opportunity Act (78 Stat. 508), financed through programs under the Office of Economic Opportunity (OEO) and administered by Indians, while the BIA assists applicants to fill out forms and offers advice.[62]

Indian community development also became institutionalized under the OEO during the 1960s. Community development became a major characteristic of the growing ideology of self-determination. Yet one cannot forget that Indian community development grew up as an answer to the failure of rapid termination and as part of the motivation for Indians to attain the competency upon which a justifiable termination could be built. Arthur Schlesinger wrote:

> For me, the real problem is how best to adapt deep-rooted Indian folkways to the very different ones of the white man. We know, however, that countless thousands of Indians over the centuries have already made the change on their own initiative and have become self-reliant members of white communities. As for the

present and the future, must we not rely on education—and on the training Indians get step by step and reservation by reservation in planning for termination?[63]

Community development, industrial development, self-help and self-determination were all a part of the education to which Schlesinger referred. The recommendations of the commission had a major impact on Indian policy planning during the term of Secretary Udall and commissioner Philleo Nash. Their influence on Udall's task force on Indian Affairs cannot be underestimated. Through OEO, community development and self-determination in educational and economic development were institutionalized and became the hallmark of the Indian reform of the Kennedy and Johnson administrations. Ironically, the war on Indian poverty and Indian self-determination, as part of the sophisticated competency program, became the war on Indian patrimony and, finally, a blueprint for new forms of termination.

NOTES

1. "A History of Indian Policy," S. Lyman Tyler, *Report to the Secretary of the Interior by the Task Force on Indian Affairs* (Washington, D.C.: U.S. Government Printing Office, 1973), p. 186.

2. Ibid., p. 187.

3. Larry W. Burt, *Tribalism in Crisis: Federal Indian Policy, 1953-1961* (Albuquerque: University of New Mexico Press, 1982), p. 70.

4. *Desert Magazine*, July 1954, p. 12, Glenn Emmons Papers, Box 1, University of Toledo Library (microfilm).

5. Ibid.

6. Ibid.

7. Burt, *Tribalism in Crisis*, p. 70.

8. Stanford Research Institute, *The San Carlos Apache Indian Reservation: A Resources Development Study* (Menlo Park, Calif.: Stanford Research Institute, n.d., ca. 1954), p. vii.

9. Stanford Research Institute, *Manual of Industrial Development: With Special Application to Latin America* (Menlo Park, Calif.: Stanford Research Institute, 1954), pp. 68-69. It is interesting to note that according to this report, Puerto Rican women workers also possess the American Indian's fabled dexterity in the assembly of small electronics parts "said also to far exceed that of workers in the U.S." One cannot help but think of the possibilities inherent in an underdeveloped nation's electronics assembly Olympics with dispirited American workers sitting glumly on the sidelines.

10. Eugene Staley, *The American Citizen's Stake in the Progress of Less Developed Areas of the World* (Menlo Park, Calif.: Stanford Research Institute for the U.S. National Commission for UNESCO, 1957), n.p.

11. "Oliver La Farge, 'The Year of Confusion,'" address at the Annual Meeting of the Association on American Indian Affairs, 5 May 1954, p. 2, Philleo Nash Files, Box 77, Archives of the Harry S. Truman Library, Independence, Mo. (hereinafter referred to as the Nash Files), See also Francis Prucha, *The Great Father*, (Lincoln: University of Nebraska Press, 1989). Prucha documents the importance of AAIA as probably the most powerful "anti-termination" voice after the National Congress of American Indians.

12. Letter from La Farge to Sen. Clinton Anderson, 26 February 1954, in Nash Files, Box 77.

13. Nash Files, Box 77, for a record of the tension existing between AAIA, NCAI, and Americans for the Restitution of Old Wrongs (ARROW). On 28 May 1954, Alexander Lesser wrote to La Farge noting that dependency of NCAI on AAIA "is a healthy symptom. It increases the dependency of the whole organization on us and is a demonstration of trust and respect."

14. Sidney W. Mintz, *History, Evolution, and the Concept of Culture: Selected Papers of Alexander Lesser* (Cambridge: Cambridge University Press, 1985), p. 11.

15. Ibid.

16. See Philleo Nash, "The Place of Religious Revivalism in the Formation of the Intercultural Community on Klamath Reservation," in*Social Anthropology of North American Tribes.*, ed. Fred Eggan, (Chicago: University of Chicago Press, 1937), pp. 377-444.

17. Letter from La Farge to Alexander Lesser, 2 January 1954, in Nash Files, Box 77.

18. Alexander Lesser, "Education and the Future of Tribalism: The Case of the American Indian," *Social Service Review* 35, no. 2 (June 1961): 135-43.

19. Letter from La Farge to Senator Anderson, 26 February 1954, in Nash Files, Box 77.

20. Oliver La Farge, "To Set the Indians Free," *New Republic* (3 October 1949): 13.

21. Association of American Indian Affairs, "Restatement of Program and Policy in Indian Affairs," in Nash Files, Box 77.

22. S. Lyman Tyler, "William A. Brophy," in *The Commissioners of Indian Affairs, 1824-1977*, eds. Robert M. Kvasnicka and Herman Viola (Lincoln: University of Nebraska Press, 1979), p. 286.

23. Burt, *Tribalism in Crisis*, p. 108.

24. Ibid., p. 108.

25. Ibid., p. 116.

26. Henry W. Hough, *Development of Indian Resources* (Denver: World Press, 1967), p. v.

27. Everett E. Hagen, *On the Theory of Social Change: How Economic Growth Begins* (Homewood, Ill.: The Dorsey Press, 1962), from the foreword by Max F. Millikan. See also Everett E. Hagen, ed., *Planning Economic Development* (Homewood, Illinois: Richard D. Irwin, Inc., 1963). See also Louis C. Schaw, *The Bonds of Work* (San Francisco: Jossey-Bass, 1968). Schaw used the Thematic Apperception Test as a tool toward understanding the differences in the way traditional societies perceive the significance and experience of work.

Schaw envisioned ways of understanding man's traditional relationship to work which are consistent with the goals of scientific social melioration. Schaw was deeply influenced by the instrumentalism of George H. Mead and John Dewey which he viewed as "the revolutionary creed in the patrimony of the American social sciences" (p. 257). He claims to "have taken Mead's concept of history as an experimental method as a central consideration of my uses of past and contemporary events." His emphasis on the uses of history and science to "motivate conduct" characterize the increasing rationalization of Indian policy during this period.

28. Hagen, *On the Theory of Social Change*, p. 3.

29. Ibid., p. 33.

30. Burt, *Tribalism in Crisis*, pp. 116-17. See Burt's account of army General Holdridge's attempted citizen's arrest of President Eisenhower over the condemnation of Iroquois' land. Holdridge, a classmate of Eisenhower's at West Point, had taken up the cause of tribal sovereignty and "launched a campaign" to help the Iroquois. Along with about a hundred Iroquois and a few Western Indians, Holdridge marched on the White House and demanded Eisenhower's arrest for "permitting crimes against Indians" (19 March 1959) (Burt, p. 117).

31. Ibid., p. 84. The Fund for the Republic is an interesting subject in itself. Thomas Reeves chronicles the relationship between the Fund and its parent, the Ford Foundation. The Fund was established to address "five areas for action." 1. The establishment of peace. 2. The strengthening of democracy. 3. The strengthening of the economy. 4. Education in a democratic society. 5. Individual behavior and human rights. It later became embroiled in a battle with the Joseph McCarthy camp over research it was conducting into the nature and extent of the Communist Party in America. See Thomas Charles Reeves, "The Fund for the Republic, 1951-1957: An Unusual Chapter in the History of American Philanthropy" (Ph.D. dissertation, University of California, Santa Barbara, 1967), p. 3.

32. Thomas Charles Reeves, "The Fund for the Republic, 1951-1957: An Unusual Chapter in the History of American Philanthropy" (Ph.D. dissertation, University of California, Santa Barbara, 1967), p.3.

33. Prucha, *The Great Father*, p.1088.

34. Commission on the Rights, Liberties and Responsibilities of the American Indian, *The Indian: America's Unfinished Business* (Norman, Ok.: University of Oklahoma Press, 1966), p. 229.

35. *New York Herald Tribune*, Sunday Forum, 11 December 1960, in William A. Brophy Papers, Box 23.

36. Commission, *The Indian: America's Unfinished Business*, pp. 230-31.

37. William Platt, *Toward Strategies of Education*, Staff Paper, International Development Center (Menlo Park, Calif.: Stanford Research Institute, 1961).

38. Commission, *The Indian: America's Unfinished Business*, p. 179. According to the report, the termination policy "was characterized by several glaring weaknesses," first of which is that "the basic assumption of assimilation by legislation is invalid" (p. 187). Thus the central concern for the commission was not that the policy of termination was unjust, immoral or

illegal with respect to treaty right, rather it is simply ineffective as a tool for assimilation.

39. Tyler, "William A. Brophy," p. 284.

40. Letter from Arthur Schlesinger to Sophie Aberle, 14 December 1961, in William A. Brophy Papers, Box 22.

41. Commission, *The Indian: America's Unfinished Business*, p. 179.

42. Letter from Charles Sprague to Sophie Aberle, 28 September 1960, William A. Brophy Papers, Box 23.

43. Donald Lee Fixico, "Termination and Relocation: Federal Indian Policy in the 1950s" (Ph.D. dissertation, University of Oklahoma, 1980), p. 372.

44. Commission, *The Indian: America's Unfinished Business*, p. 21.

45. Ibid., p. 180.

46. Ibid., p. 111.

47. Ibid., p. 3.

48. Ibid., p. 4.

49. Charles A. Sprague, memorandum, 29 November 1959, in William A. Brophy Papers, Box 23.

50. Letter from W. W. Keeler to Sophie Aberle, 2 November, 1961, in William A. Brophy Papers, Box 23.

51. Ibid.

52. Commission, *The Indian: America's Unfinished Business*, p. 40.

53. Ibid., p. 23.

54. Ibid., p. 112.

55. Ibid., p. 113.

56. Sprague memorandum, 29 November 1959.

57. Ibid.

58. Commission, *The Indian: America's Unfinished Business,* p. 114.

58. "A Position Paper," treating the problems of off-reservation and non-reservation Indians (William A. Brophy Papers, Box 24). For Wilson, Indian values "are so deeply rooted in the personality and value system of an Indian that their exclusion without careful development of alternative values to replace them creates confusion and instability for him and makes him apathetic when confronted with the difficulties associated with change." Yet, it is the same Wilson who preached unrepentant pluralism when addressing the National Association of American Indians. To this group he called it an "arrogant assumption tonight to insist that American Indians wanted to drop their folkways in favor of the dominant white culture" *New York Times*, 2 November 1957, in William A. Brophy Papers, Box 24.

60. Letter from W. W. Keeler to Sophie Aberle, 13 February 1962, in William A. Brophy Papers, Box 22.

61. Association on American Indian Affairs, "Comment on La Farge Statement of February 8, 1950," 14 February 1950 in Nash Files, Box 77.

62. Commission, *The Indian: America's Unfinished Business*, p. 105.

63. Letter from Arthur Schlesinger to Sophie Aberle, 15 November 1960, in William A. Brophy Papers, Box 22. It is perhaps worth a note that it was Schlesinger who had first suggested the title "America's Unfinished Business" for the report. Unsigned letter to O. M. Wilson, 7 September 1962, in William A. Brophy Papers, Box 24.

4

The Task Force on Indian Affairs

Stewart Udall was an early cabinet appointee after the election of Pres. John F. Kennedy in November 1960. Kennedy's new interior secretary had established a reputation as a conservationist with a long-standing interest in Indians and was an ardent Kennedy campaigner. During his confirmation hearings, Udall had promised the Senate that he would push an "economic development program that will lift [Indian] living standards to the point where they can become full-fledged citizens of the country."[1]

Udall's promise to economically rehabilitate Indian country was consistent both with the current of Indian reform exemplified by the Commission on Indian Rights, Liberties and Responsibilities and with the developing programs in Kennedy's New Frontier. In May 1961 the Area Redevelopment Act (ARA) was passed. This administration sponsored legislation "which provided financial and technical aid to 'pockets of poverty' [and] was filled with references to Indian tribes."[2] ARA was the first concrete step taken by an administration which, with Udall's leadership, would push a no-holds barred assault on Indian industrial underdevelopment.

In spring, 1961, Udall assembled a task force on Indian Affairs. The appearance of the task force coincided with the important Chicago Conference in which 420 Indian leaders from 67 tribes convened to write up a "Declaration of Indian Purpose." Several members of the task force were present at this meeting and no doubt were privy to the insistent call of the "greater Indian participation in Federal Programs."[3]

Udall's task force may have been formed partially in response to Indian leadership cries for greater participation, along with tribal wishes, expressed in Chicago, for human and economic development and an end to the termination policy. However, the task force, far from being a body which represented an effort to include Indians, was not selected with regard to tribal wishes. They were a small group of Udall's private appointees. The members were James Officer, a University of Arizona anthropologist; Philleo Nash, anthropologist and member of the Association on American Indian Affairs who would become Indian commissioner shortly after publication of the task force report; and William Zimmerman, Jr., a key figure in the establishment of termination policy during the 1950s, and acting commissioner of Indian Affairs, and an AAIA member. The task force chairman was the ubiquitous W. W. Keeler, Fund for the Republic's Indian study commissioner.

It is not surprising that the recommendations of the task force would vigorously reflect the will of both the AAIA and the Fund commission. For one thing, Keeler was now not only a man of both cultures but also a man of both commissions.[4] Sophie Aberle wrote to Arthur Schlesinger, saying the "Keeler" task force recommendations "reached substantially the same conclusions that we did, and I assume, since Bill Keeler was Chairman, that our thinking also was influential with the task force."[5] She meant, of course, the managed termination conclusions of the Fund for the Republic study.

The files of Philleo Nash reveal a letter by an unnamed Fund commissioner to O. M. Wilson, also of the Fund commission, citing the tremendous congruity between the task force and what he termed "our commission," as well as with the Chicago Conference "Declaration of Indian Purpose":

> Whatever may be said, all three reports have many parallels and seem to move from the same base, which is fortunate; otherwise the Indians would be confused; in one degree or another, they all say the Indian himself must be the focus, his initiative and intelligent cooperation, not mere consent, must underwrite all programs or they are likely to fail.[6]

Udall clearly intended to assemble a task force which would reflect the conventional wisdom in Indian reform. It was his wish that W. W. Keeler be installed as the task force chairman.[7] This action insured that the recommendations of the Commission on Indian Rights, Liberties and Responsibilities would find a place in administration Indian policy. According to a letter from William Brophy to Keeler, his appointment was evidence of "Udall's wisdom, [and] the acceptance by you is an unselfish dedication to a noble cause. Laying the foundation for the advancement of Indian people, motivated by their own visions and through their own efforts, will bring you great and quiet satisfactions. It is a great day, Bill!"[8]

Indian policy formation was left in the hands of a small group of experts and social scientists, committed now to Indian development and rehabilitation with all the resources of a sympathetic liberal administration behind them. La Farge congratulated Udall in a letter written on February 16, 1962:

> Fine appointments have been accompanied by excellent policy pronouncements. The task force report and the speeches made by you, John and Philleo, reflect the only kind of thinking that can lead to success in solving the grave human problems that beset us in the field of Indian Affairs. With the right policies in effect, sufficient funds available to carry them out, and the right people in Presidentially appointed positions, the job before us is to see that the officialdom down the line understands and carries out these policies.[9]

For La Farge, the Udall task force and the policies it would recommend represented a victory in human engineering of the sort developed by the Fund for the Republic Indian commission. They were equally consistent with La Farge's position on Indian competency development through economic and social rehabilitation.

The activities of the task force were as much an exercise in public relations as they were an effort to accurately determine the tribal will concerning the future of development. In a speech to the National Congress of American Indians Annual Convention at Lewiston, Idaho on September 21, 1961, Philleo Nash, by now commissioner designate of Indian Affairs, spoke of the work of the task force. He referred to the help which tribes gave to Lewis and Clark on their journey to open up the Northwest. "But," he said, "that was the Old Frontier. Let's turn to the New Frontier."[10] He went on to explain the work of the task force and told the delegation that the "report will be a chart for the course to be followed by the BIA during the months and years that lie ahead."[11] Nash then explained the nature of this report. He claimed:

> First, the report itself grew out of consultation with Indian leaders and with the Indian people. We travelled 15,000 miles; and we talked to the representatives of 200 organized tribes. We met face to face with Indians and their friends; and we visited a number of reservations and off-reservation communities. So, although we are the authors of the report in the sense that we wrote the words down on paper, the ideas in this report are *yours*. To be sure, if we didn't agree with them we wouldn't have made the recommendations. But, by and large this is the product of the Indian leaders' own thinking. *We* are merely the reporters who gathered them together and put them down in written forms.[12]

In reality, while the task force may have traveled the miles and met face to face with the Indians and their friends, the intended policy tilt of the task force was set even as the group was being organized, long before any such consultation took place. As early as February 2, 1961, commissioner Philleo Nash, in a memorandum to Udall, suggested a plan of operation which included preparation of a task force report within 90 days.[13] Nash was giving little time for the type of tribal consultation about which he would boast to the National Congress of American Indians. In addition, Nash believed the report could have as much public relations impact as practical utility. He hoped it would be presented to coincide with a special presidential message on Indian affairs.

Weeks before the possibility for formal tribal consultation, and even before the arrival of Keeler, the task force's man of both cultures, Nash would write to Udall to outline the predetermined message which would be carried in an unwritten report by an unconvened commission, "Since the president's and the secretary's stated desires with respect to Indian affairs are to develop human and natural resources of the reservations and of reservation areas where Indians reside, it would seem to me that the basic emphasis in the proposed study should be on economic development."[14]

Four days later, Udall wrote to Keeler thanking him for joining that task force as a consultant without compensation. He made clear that the task force report would follow the general direction of human and natural resource development which had been the hallmark of the Commission on Indian Rights, Liberties and Responsibilities, a goal which Keeler clearly supported. "I want to repeat," Udall wrote, "therefore, that I am pledged to a program for the development of human and natural resources of the Indian reservations."[15]

Planning of the future of Indian policy was left in the hands of a few individuals who wielded great power in this New Frontier for Indian people. The task force was wedded to the Fund for the Republic Indian commission. It is no surprise that W. W. Keeler had a major role to play in both these groups. The influences of La Farge and the AAIA were felt philosophically and practically, given the fact that AAIA members Nash and Zimmerman held task force posts.

The position of the task force accurately reflected many of the recommendations of the Fund commission. They also were in concert with Udall's plans for reservation development. Udall had been fond of sounding, once again, the Jeffersonian echo of anti-federalist liberation. He said, "The proper role of the Federal government is to help Indians find their way along a new trail—one which leads to equal citizenship, maximum self-sufficiency and full participation in American life."[16]

According to the title of an article in the *Christian Science Monitor,* Udall was a man "determined to set the nation's Indian affairs in order."[17] In this piece, Udall is presented as a man who, along with commissioner Nash has "set three major goals in Indian Affairs; 1. maximum Indian self-sufficiency, 2. full participation of Indians in American life and 3. equal citizenship privileges and responsibilities for Indians."[18] Although not popularly elected to the task force nor to his tribal office, the article mentions Keeler as an "Indian leader" and Udall is praised for selecting an Indian to head the task force. The article also refers to yet another group headed by Keeler, the President's Advisory Group on Indian Affairs, which came to Phoenix to consult with Udall on Arizona Indian matters. They had put together twelve points for action. Interestingly, one of the points included the development of:

> a permanent advisory board for Indian Affairs composed of Indians and non-Indians. . . . Its aim would be to focus attention on the most urgent Indian needs . . . and would be a "grass roots listening post" on Indian affairs. It would assist the secretary and the Indian Bureau to set proper goals and move consistently toward them.[19]

What is interesting about Keeler's suggestion here is that he would be paying lip service to grass-roots Indian opinion. Yet he participated in a vital Indian Affairs task force, which established its priorities prior to any consultation with the grass-roots Indian. The membership of this group contained only one Indian, himself, a wealthy oil industrialist, of one-sixteenth Cherokee blood. He had been appointed, not elected, by Harry Truman, just as he had been appointed, not elected, to his positions on virtually every Indian policy advisory committee of the period. It may be an understatement to say that in choosing Keeler the task force was in search of something other than a grass-roots listening post.

Like the Fund for the Republic commission, the task force supported a plan to involve Indians in their own rehabilitation. Like the commission, human and economic development went hand in hand. Along with this developing self-help theme came the ominous cloud of termination. Like the commission, the task force saw self-help and self-determination as part of a competency program leading to eventual termination. In its Statement of Objectives, the task force report cited the departmental aims of the Bureau of Indian Affairs:

(1) to create conditions under which Indians will advance their social, economic and political adjustment to achieve a status comparable to that of their non-Indian neighbors.

(2) to encourage Indians and Indian tribes to assume an increasing measure of self-sufficiency.

(3) to terminate, at appropriate times, Federal supervision and services special to Indians.[20]

Referring to these goals:

> The Task Force [felt] recent Bureau policy has placed more emphasis on the last of these three objectives than on the first two. Indians, fearful that termination will take place before they are ready for it, have become deeply concerned. Their preoccupation was reflected in vigorous denunciation of the so-called termination policy during the many hearings which the task force conducted with Indian leaders. . . . It is apparent Indian morale generally has been lowered and resistance to transition programs heightened as a result of the fear of premature withdrawal.[21]

In this statement the task force recognized the problem of what would be often referred to as "termination psychosis" which was complicating their plans to implement a transition program toward justifiable termination.

In his 1969 study of the Bureau of Indian Affairs, Alvin Josephy described termination psychosis as the "almost ineradicable suspicion of the government's motives for every policy, program or action concerning Indians." He referred to it as a "hobbling theme" in Indian Affairs throughout the Kennedy and Johnson administrations.[22]

Termination psychosis had become an issue earlier in the development of the Fund for the Republic Indian commission report. One commissioner wrote to O. M. Wilson, stating that the commission report had addressed the issue before the task force. Nonetheless, it agreed with the task force that "termination as a goal is wrong, self defeating, impairs Indian morale, generates hostility and limits the effectiveness of development plans."[23]

Indian resistance to termination, the "hobbling theme," was couched in the same therapeutic framework as their social, psychological, and economic rehabilitation. Resistance to termination was approached as if it were a mental illness which could be cured if proper therapy were prescribed. Yet, there can be no mistaking that the task force self-help programs were transitional in nature, designed to take Indians smoothly from dependence to competence to a more justifiable termination.

The following statement succinctly captures the essence of what is an almost cynical ideology of self-help and self-determination:

> The Task Force believes it is wiser to assist Indians to advance socially, economically, and politically to the point where special services to this group of Americans are no longer justfied. Then termination can be achieved with maximum benefit for all con-

cerned. Furthermore, if development, rather than termination, is emphasized during the transitional period, Indian cooperation—an essential ingredient of a successful program—can be expected.[24]

Clearly, it would not take a very psychotic episode on the part of a tribal member to pick up a copy of the Udall task force report, read this section and conclude that perhaps one should be cautious about the intent of government Indian policy subsequent to the task force, especially with regard to termination. Termination psychosis might have better been applied to those Indian people who saw this report and *did not* read termination into every government program.

Tribal self-help and development programs were designed as a way to promote competency and to attack the problem of termination psychosis. If Indians could become, at least in part, the architects of their own rehabilitation, they would be less likely to point the finger at government for creating policies engineered to terminate the trust relationship. In a conference address to BIA superintendents in Santa Fe, Philleo Nash told them that the goals of the Indian Bureau are those of the task force, while mindful of the fact that the Bureau's trusteeship responsibility requires programs for the protection and preservation of Indian property. He reminded them that the task force recommended greater attention to programs of what he termed "group and personal development." He also spoke of the task force goal "to help Indian people attain the education and economic self-sufficiency that gives them full status as participating citizens of this country."[25]

The task force was intent on pursuing the theme of economic development roughly on the same lines as had Glenn Emmons but with greater government support. Once again the industrial development of Puerto Rico was held up as a model to be followed in Indian country. On February 2, 1961, Philleo Nash wrote to Udall arguing that "the successful experience with economic development in Puerto Rico would be studied with a view to its applicability on Indian reservations."[26] Nash then put forth a plan to attract industry to the reservations by holding out a number of attractive investment incentives:

> Long-term low cost loans, tax deferments and holidays, . . . public works planning, . . . vocational training and recruitment, . . . in other words, in the successful Puerto Rican experiment every known device to stimulate industrial development has been used and has been integrated by a single administrative instrument. The applicability of such a program to the Indian country should be very carefully studied.[27]

Nash had taken the Emmons approach to reservation development and carried it into the Udall administration. However, Nash saw the problem of adjusting the Indian psyche to an industrial work-life. He tried to deal with this question as a part of a total theme of human development—attacking the termination psychosis problem and the acculturation/assimilation problem with the mind of a trained anthropologist. In many ways Philleo Nash was an enigma when it came to his relations with Indian people. He has been called the most trusted of all Indian commissioners.[28] He was well liked by an Indian people grown accustomed to distrusting their commissioners. Yet the training and disposition which gave him the ability to understand Indian people also gave him a diagnostic and corrective tool which could be used as part of the engineering design in the rehabilitation and competency plans of the task force.

The Udall/Nash administration approached human development as a concomitant to economic development. In an article in *Indian Education*, a BIA publication, education specialist Edgar L. Wight underscored the importance of human development in the growing climate of self-help. He wrote:

> Some of the most important approaches and principles related to leadership development are related to education and training and in a sense are an engagement in human engineering. This requires a deep interest in and understanding of human values, human behavior, and of course, a friendly interest in the Indian people.[29]

Nash believed that there was a great deal that Indian people could accomplish if they could be trained successfully to adapt to industrial culture. Yet, along with termination psychosis, he thought that "one of the main problems facing all developmental plans in Indian country [was] . . . the problem of motivation."[30] He believed that Indian motivation problems could be solved by a combination of self-help and cultural reorientation.

Philleo Nash was a social scientist whose work would have a significant impact on government administration through the mid-century. In many ways his career was carved out along the lines of John Collier. He came from a well-to-do, politically active Wisconsin family. He was a trained social scientist and activist who, like Collier, went on to ply his trade as an influential policymaker. He was a man who reflected the modern liberal faith in positive social science toward the rationalization of social order. At the University of Chicago he was, according to anthropologist Fred Eggan, greatly influenced not only by A. R. Radcliffe-Brown, as mentioned earlier, but by the political theorist Harold Lasswell, who became a close friend and confidant. Lasswell had done a great deal of work in the study of psychoanalysis and the political process, and the level of his influence on Nash's social philosophy cannot be underestimated, especially in light of the policy developments growing from the Task Force on Indian Affairs. His wife, Edith Nash, emphasizes this influence:

> Philleo and Harold Lasswell became close friends in the summer of 1935 when Harold was teaching at California and Philleo was doing the preparatory work in Berkeley on Klamath, mostly with Cora du Bois. Philleo's view of nativistic movements and his method of analyzing them—an important part of his world-view all his life—was formed during this time and was the underpinning of his subsequent work in solving problems in government at many levels.[31]

Lasswell's social scientist/politician was to be master of symbol manipulation. Lasswell believed in the replacement of "politics" with a technique of public manipulation, through the artful use of symbol, an art to be practiced by an elite corps of social scientists/governors. He regarded the study of politics as the science and art of management. For Lasswell:

> The end of the state, I repeat, is not to make rational beings into brute beasts and machines. It is to enable their bodies and their minds to function safely. Liberty requires that an important role in the power process be played by persuasion. It is not sufficient, of course, to say merely that consent is obtained by symbols rather than violence; it is essential that the symbols function with minimal external inducements and constraints. . . . The freely given consent to power which is constitutive of liberty presupposes education rather than indoctrination.[32]

In an important sense, for both Lasswell and Nash, social science is what Floyd Matson has described as the politics of prevention. Matson argued that Lasswell's influence came as part of a growing tradition of elite scientific control of the political process. He wrote of Lasswell's belief that in a positive social science wherein the "attitude of the analyst [is] much closer to that of the agitator-organizer." [33] This was close to the "applied" and "action" anthropology movement with which Nash was associated. Matson discussed Lasswell's belief that the "overriding problem of world unity, of a universal solution to insecurity and conflict, is that of devising a 'non-rational world myth' capable of commanding the allegiance of men everywhere."[34] Matson calls this the "academic paraphrase of the Grand Inquisitor."[35] It is also quite close to Plato's notion of the "necessary lie" in the *Republic*, that myth which would communicate the necessity of fixed social order, and without which a recalcitrant public might revolt against the prescriptions of such an order. The crucial question remains: who has the ultimate power over the shape and purpose of symbol making? For Lasswell, It would not be the traditional politician. For him, "one skill-group alone stands out as a logical choice. It is that group which is the most skilled in the methods of verbal manipulation and myth-making—namely, the academic 'symbol specialists,' or social scientists." [36]

Pearl Walker McNeil, fellow student of Nash's, contends that "Dr. Nash believed in education as an instrument for the creation of new human values. He was concerned about the thought processes that followed culture contacts and culture conflicts."[37] One of Nash's first important experiences using his social science training in government service is his association with the Office of War Information during World War II. This commission was organized to deal with the problems of race relations as they affected wartime production. Racial conflict during the war was a problem not only in the military but also in plants devoted to wartime production. Nash followed up his research on the Klamath Ghost Dance by extending its generalizations to general issues of racial protest and violence as such might affect industry. He would argue that his contribution to the program was his "deprivation theory"— that the precursor of violence is protest and the cause is deprivation. He believed that violence can be controlled, but in a democratic society, even one at war, the focus should be on the deprivation and not on the protest.

Nash worked with Ted Poston, a black journalist familiar with the urban African-American press. Together they pinpointed potential trouble spots and, by keeping track of rumors, worked to defuse potential racial conflicts. Several episodes were prevented from escalating into major interruptions of work. Thurgood Marshall had once said to Philleo, 'If you'd been at Lincoln's side there never would have been a Civil War...(and we'd all still be slaves.)"[38] Nash was instrumental in the integration of the armed forces during the war and, after the war, served on the Truman Civil Rights commission.

Through the lens of social science Nash interpreted African-American resistance to repression as an extension of his "resistance theory." Resistance becomes a symptom of deprivation, but again, since cultural institutions are only seen in their functional relationship with the larger society, unequal class relations are not a part of the rationality of this phenomenon. Minority resistance becomes by definition, a form of dysfunctional adjustment, which may be controlled by the social scientist's therapeutic technique.

For Nash, Indian culture was not designed to withstand the rigors of industrialization. Indeed, he saw cultural conflicts at the root of the motivation problem. In offering a solution to Indian cultural resistance, Nash employed a concept of, what he termed, "guided acculturation."[39]

In a speech to an education conference in Washington in 1963, Nash tried to explain what he meant by this term:

> While we talk about it here I mean to refer to the process by which individuals or full groups of individuals, societies, sub-societies, are enabled to move from one culture to another—from a culture of one kind to a culture of a different kind. In our case, I will start short-circuiting this thing by saying that I think what we are trying to do or what we are talking about is reservation culture on the one hand as the "from" of it and the culture of the city today as the "to" of it.[40]

Nash expanded his notion of guided acculturation before the conference. He contrasted reservation culture with metropolitan culture in the following outline:[41]

Reservation Culture

Technology:
: underdeveloped resources
great dependency on public assistance
result—idleness
underdeveloped communication (roads, etc.)

Social Structure:
: kinship
weak development of tribal government
factions

Ideology:
: sharing
compensatory religions
hostility
lack of time sense

Metropolitan Culture

Technology:
: very high resource development
maximum communication
machine and factory technology

Social Structure:
: very elaborate division of labor and much speculation
representative government
institutionalized relationships
nuclear family

Ideology:
: education
property
enterprise
ethical values
time-sense

Nash viewed reservation culture as a damaged article from technical, social, and ethical standpoints. Its rehabilitation could be effected only if this so-called cultural deficit was addressed and corrected. Reservation Indian values were regarded here only as a reaction to underdevelopment, not as expressions of cultural difference. Nash saw what he termed Indian "time-sense" only as the *lack* of sense, not as an alternative sense. He said:

> We assume that the values of planning, of giving up short-run gains and thinking about long-run gains are so logical, so rational, provide so much for human need that, of course, the minute we explain it to anybody that they will want it right away. Well, it isn't working very well in our relationships with the new countries in Africa or Asia. I don't think it is working very well as far as our relationships with the reservation people is concerned.[42]

Nash saw the job of the bureau as an effort to supplant reservation culture with metropolitan culture. He saw industrialization and relocation as the ultimate goals which, through guided acculturation, Indians would come to accept. But first, social structure would have to be altered. He wrote, "In order to have machine and factory production, you have to have very elaborate division of labor and much specialization—and actually many of our goals of education emerge as we begin to describe our own social system, because these are things that we are trying to accomplish and bring people to."[43]

For Nash, reservation Indian culture and ideology were rife with traits which were anathema to industrialization. He presented Indian sharing and patterns of generosity as closely related to Christian ideals, yet antagonistic to a spirit of competition which he saw necessary to the development of metropolitan culture. Indian dependency exacerbated those patterns and the reinforcement of "obligations that are traditional and are based upon descent and relationships" in a welfare system in which "there are plenty of instances where the greatest economic asset which anyone can have is a blind grandmother. It doubles public assistance."[44]

In addition, perhaps relating to its use of peyote, and consistent with his position on the Ghost Dance as a nativistic cult, Nash saw the Native American Church only as a compensatory religion, saying, "When you have this kind of general inability to cope with the environment in a significant or meaningful way, I would state it as a general proposition you may expect any time, any place to find great attractiveness in personal religious experiences."[45] The fact that personal religious experiences are at the heart of so much traditional Native American worship seems here strangely lost on an anthropologist of Nash's reputation.

In Nash's speech all these problems were symptoms of maladjustment and impediments to Indian resource development. He spoke of the mistakes of his nineteenth-century predecessors in the Indian Bureau who believed that if you allotted individual Indian plots of tribal land, they would immediately become God-fearing farmers; "that they were going to create a social system which was a duplicate, an imprint of the pioneer frontier as they saw it."[46] In his speech, he pointed to the aforementioned outline on the blackboard and reminded his audience that one of the reasons they were at the conference was due to the failure of both the bureau and "the whole of America to understand the fact which is set forth diagrametrically (sic) in this particular little ideogram here."[47]

Nash went on to argue that relocation programs must be augmented by an "expanded program...bigger and better," aimed at economic development:

> Now if we don't find a method of moving this whole social system forward and moving it together on all sides at once, then my successor and your successors will be coming forward to the Congresses of the United States another 25 years and they will be saying: well just one more generation, a few more millions of dollars.... The history of the back country of the south, the history of the underdeveloped areas of Africa and Latin America . . . indicate that we have no reason to expect that our reservation areas will be any different from them, in the sense that if you do not move them forward as a totality in all aspects of the social system that they will continue as an ongoing society; an ongoing culture, and that they will increase in numbers.[48]

Indeed, it is impossible to separate the racialism and ethnocentrism inherent in the cultural deficit model as it developed into policy in the 1960s. Nash saw Indian cultures and societies as they existed on the reservations as a threat to national industrial progress. However, he believed that guided acculturation through education in and of itself would not solve the problem. The greatest need was "to move the whole economy forward with the introduction of enterprise, with the development of resources."[49] Other anthropologists criticized him for being unmindful of the evils of industrialization. Yet he referred to these critics as members of my profession that want to keep the Indians quaint.[50] To those critics he underscored the fact that industrial opportunity, whether through relocation or reservation development, would retain a spirit of volunteerism.

For Philleo Nash, reservation industrial and cultural development and rehabilitation would go hand in hand with a program of self-help designed to reduce the problem of termination psychosis and to increase motivation. Nash's development plans were consistent with the growing ideology of self-determination, combined with cultural and economic rehabilitation. His views were consistent with the ideas developed through the AAIA and La Farge, the Fund for the Republic's Indian Commission, and the Udall task force. Yet, like La Farge, Nash was both supportive of and hostile to Indian rights.

He was accepted by many Indians as a man they could trust. He represented a move in the direction away from rapid termination, a visible and likeable administrator. He was a part of the New Frontier, giving Indians new hope for economic development. At one meeting of the National Congress of American Indians, Nash "stayed up all night playing the drum and singing. He enjoyed the confidence and respect of [Indian] leaders, one of whom said, 'I always got along well with him because he was more of a human being than a commissioner.'"[51]

Yet we also see his distrust of Indian culture, and values which clashed with metropolitan culture. He appears to have had little patience for a notion of plural Indian cultural or political sovereignty. He had little respect for those who would "keep them quaint."

Yet late in his tenure we see where Nash was at odds with Udall, apparently over the fact that Udall believed industrial development was not progressing quickly enough. The altercation was partly responsible for Nash's resignation.[52]

In 1966 Homer Bigart of the *New York Times* wrote about the problems which had developed in the Udall administration over industrial development. According to Bigart, Udall had been upset with Nash for being too slow with industrial development. Representatives from two of the large garment workers unions beseeched Nash to oppose the proposed Navajo BVD plant. "They had reminded him that other government agencies such as the Office of Economic Opportunity were prohibited from spending money to train workers in industries inclined to 'run away' from unions. What was the use, they asked, of creating a job in Navajo country if it produced a job vacancy in New York."[53]

Bigart surmised that perhaps Nash's reluctance to resist the unions came because he feared his $15 million adult education job training authorization would be endangered in Congress. Whatever the reason, Nash heeded the union protests. Udall "reportedly 'blew up' when he heard Nash had shelved the BVD plans. Because of this, and a general belief that Nash was 'too slow in pushing industrial development on the reservations,' Udall forced Nash's resignation."[54]

Nash, the liberal reformer, is an enigma. In July of 1963, Gil Fates of Goodson-Todman productions invited Nash to be a guest on the popular television quiz program "To Tell the Truth." Fates felt that the "problems of our Indian citizens and the government's methods of coping with these problems would be interesting and prestigeful programming."[55] One cannot help wondering whether the "To Tell the Truth" panel members were not, in fall 1963, the only people asking, "Will the real Philleo Nash please stand up?"

In the meantime, under the guidance of Nash and Udall and the task force recommendations, industrial and human development programs were gaining momentum. Under Udall, industrial development became the centerpiece of a domestic policy projected as a large part of the answer to Indian economic underdevelopment and consequent poverty. Industrial development was presented as a vital part of the human development scheme. Whatever reservations Nash might have had about rapid industrialization, they were downplayed in the wake of this burgeoning initiative. The Area Redevelopment Administration (ARA) was busy during the early 1960s, working with the BIA and business to attract selected industries to selected reservations in a new government sponsored development effort. More vigorous efforts to attract industries to reservation areas were at the top of the list of the task force's recommendations and this was now beginning to be felt in policy.[56]

This type of development was the key to the economic and social competency program and would proceed with little impediment between 1960 and 1969. The task force recommended that a sequence of steps be taken in the process of industrialization: (1) research and analysis of the prospective reservation site, (2) community planning and development, (3) recreation development, (4) industrial contact and (5) on-the-job training.[57]

An emphasis was placed on making reservation sites attractive to prospective industrial clients. Philleo Nash was aware of the difficulty of attracting plants. At the ground-breaking ceremonies for the Burnell Electronics plant at Laguna, New Mexico, in 1963, Nash reminded the audience of their luck in attracting Burnell. He noted that "competition for such plants is keen and constant all over the nation."[58]

Indian industrial development paralleled the growth in the American economy between 1963 and 1969. In addition, defense spending and the needs of the Vietnam war encouraged the rapid growth of defense-related industries on reservations. During that period, approximately three dozen electronics plants, including Burnell, were in the business of making circuits and transistors to be used partly for military purposes. The BIA began recruiting defense contractors and garment and other light industry during this period. The great majority of these industries were off-reservation concerns establishing branch plants. Udall and Nash invited this type of development as part of the plan to ameliorate Indian poverty and to provide a source of jobs. Industrial development grew by leaps during this period, partly to answer "the great simple need for more income."[59] Indian jobs and Indian familiarity with the light industrial workplace would provide a positive step in the direction toward Indian competency and a justifiable termination.

By temperament and inclination, Philleo Nash was sensitive to the problem of culture clash in the typical American workplace. Yet, despite his concerns about culture clash and the need for guided acculturation prior to full capitalization of Indian human and material resources, Nash fully supported the benefits of increased individual Indian income. He addressed the National Congress of American Indians in 1961 and professed his faith in the task force recommendations:

> These programs will provide for the development of people and that, after all, is why we are in business. Ours is not a materialistic approach. We are interested in the wise use of natural resources so that the men, women and children who live on and near Indian reservations may have a better life. That means better housing, better health, more income, more education, better training, more and better opportunity for steady work at better wages.[60]

In reality, the story of industrial development throughout the 1960s is in many respects a study of industrial exploitation and withered expectations of increased Indian income. In 1969 the National Congress of American Indians noted their disappointment with development in a position paper on economic development. According to this document, by December 31, 1968, there were 150 industrial and commercial enterprises established on or near reservations as a result of Indian development programs. Ninety-three percent had been established since 1962. By that time 10,000 new jobs had been created, of which only 4,700 were held by Indians. The report noted that there were 10,699 unemployed Pueblos alone. For the NCAI, "'industrial development off reservations' has often meant economic exploitation of cheap Indian labor for the benefit of white capitalists, leaving in its wake sociological disaster."[61]

Indeed the type, quality and low cost of Indian labor was, along with liberal government loan and tax relief, a major attraction for industry. The BIA conducted a survey of factors which were likely to attract business to the reservation. Labor force availability is mentioned as the top priority.[62] Availability of a labor force was not a problem in the recession years, including the year this report was written. There were thousands of small communities at that time whose chambers of commerce could offer plenty of unemployed workers as well as other inducements. Other factors were working with regard to labor than mere availability.

Industrial development was the keystone of Indian economic development under the Area Redevelopment Administration and its successor, the Economic Development Administration (EDA). Yet by 1967 only about 3 percent of the reservation labor force was employed in such industries, while reservation unemployment remained at 37 percent.[63] Table 2 presents the number of industries to locate on the reservations.[64]

Significantly, Indian employment in these Indian development industries dropped to less than half the work force after 1963. Indeed, the impact on the general problem of Indian unemployment appears to have been minimal. Given the few numbers of Indian workers affected by industrial development, the magnitude of the unemployment problem can be illustrated graphically. In the earliest years of government-aided development, between 1950 and 1960, the number of Indian workers classified as blue-collar operatives rose from 13.1 percent to 21.9 percent. Yet Indian "management" (officials and proprietors, except farmers) rose only .8 percent during this period, from 2.0 percent of the labor force to 2.8 percent.[65] Even the small number of industrial concerns established were able to contribute to the change from agriculture to industrial work.

TABLE 2

Number of Industries Located on Reservations

Year	Established/ Closed	Operating at Year's End	Labor Force	
			Indian	Non-Indian
1957-59	4/0	3	391	171
1960	3/0	6	525	256
1961	4/0	10	702	505
1962	5/1	14	887	600
1963	6/2	18	1,395	1,719
1964	14/7	25	1,668	2,206
1965	21/6	40	2,011	2,479
1966	21/4	57	3,044	3,224
1967	23/3	77	3,730	3,666
1968	36/3	110	4,112	4,375
Total	137/27			

However, it must be said that the greatest reason for the shift must have been due to the effect of the relocation program. As illustrated in Table 3, during the period from 1960 to 1967, when over 100 industries availed themselves of government tax, wage and loan incentives, the Indian labor pool and Indian male unemployment appear to have fluctuated only with the changes in the national unemployment picture.[66]

The development of Indian reservation industry was attractive to corporations for a variety of reasons. The attraction of a job to an unemployed Indian householder cannot be underestimated, and industry found a willing labor force.

The key to reservation location lay in the ability of light industry to turn a profit. The BIA on-the-job training programs offered industry a bargain it could not turn down. While the employer in 1967 was obliged to pay the minimum wage of $1.60, the BIA would reimburse him for one-half that amount paid to each trainee.[67]

The Indian labor force offered other considerable advantages to industry. According to Alan Sorkin, who completed a study of fifteen reservation industries, "One reason many electronics firms have located on the reservations is that the starting wage is $1.60 ($.80 an hour during training), while on the West Coast starting salaries range from $2.00 to $2.25 per hour. In fifteen plants visited on reservations, the average wage ranged from $1.60 to $2.00 an hour, although it was $2.60 for similar manufacturing industries off the reservation."[68]

Sorkin also noted that labor costs were lower, in part due to the virtual nonexistence of fringe benefits accruing to employees. None of

TABLE 3

National Unemployment for Indian and Non-Indian Males For the Period 1961-1967

Year	Reservation Indians (percentage)	Non-Indians (percentages)
1961	49.5	5.7
1962	43.4	4.6
1965	41.9	3.2
1966	41.9	2.5
1967	37.3	2.3

the fifteen firms he visited had medical insurance plans, and only one had an employee life insurance plan. The amount of paid vacation was between three and seven days per year.[69] Another benefit to the industry was the lack of reservation worker organization:

> Only one of the fifteen plants studied was unionized. Since increased unionization would work to eliminate wage differentials and differences in fringe benefits between reservation and non-reservation plants, a manager of one of the plants expressed the opinion that "unionization would deter industrialization on the reservation."[70]

This manager was interviewed at the Fairchild Semiconductor Plant in Shiprock, New Mexico. Sorkin went on to predict from the results of his study that unionization activity would increase. He proved prescient on this issue, since in 1975 Fairchild would be the site of union activity and subsequent violence in a struggle by workers to establish a union at the plant. The manager also would prove to be correct for, with this activity, Fairchild abandoned its branch at Shiprock.

Fairchild is an example of the type of industry which, along with garment operations, would come to dominate the industrial development scene. Once again we hear the Indian reputation for stolidity in the face of the repetition and detail which are required in component assembly. George Schmidt, chief of the Branch of Industrial development, wrote Alden Stevens of the AAIA with regard to the special adaptability of Indians to this type of work. He had conducted interviews and batteries of tests for the Burnell Corporation and found that Laguna Pueblo Indians were "above the national average, in manual dexterity, intelligence quotient and adaptability to training."[71]

In his report on Indian resources development, Henry Hough would reaffirm this claim. The theme of legendary Indian patience and dexterity, which came to the fore in the early industrialization and relocation discussions during the 1950s, continued into the following decade.

The Fairchild Semiconductor Plant in Shiprock was an important site in this period of development. It was the largest and most successful of the plants and was representative of the growing number of Defense Department contractors using Indian labor. In 1975, Fairchild was the largest industrial employer in New Mexico and the largest employer of Indians in the United States. There were 1,000 Navajos employed at the plant.[72]

In April 1970, in an article titled "Industry Invades the Reservation," *Business Week* showcased Fairchild and characterized the Navajo worker. Navajos are called "a vast, little tapped labor pool [who] have woven rugs and worked silver for centuries. Now, nearly 1,200 of them are assembling transistors and integrated circuits."[73] Fairchild is described as boasting of "high profits and high productivity. And the Navajo, after 100 years of near-starvation, has change jingling in his Levi's and a pickup truck at the hogan door."[74]

Business Week noted that along with the "vast labor pool" which attracted Fairchild, they and other U.S. semiconductor and electrical component companies, such as General Dynamics, employing 250 Navajos at Fort Defiance, Arizona, require "row upon row of dexterous women to assemble the microscopic elements of electronic devices."[75]

According to the article, Fairchild's early experience at Shiprock was marred by cultural problems. Many workers spoke only Navajo, and Anglo concepts of time baffled them.[76] What was called a "hardboiled industry attitude" toward these problems caused a number of firings until Paul Driscoll took over as manager in May 1967.[77] The company credited Driscoll for turning their operation into a profitable one by November 1967. Driscoll began by attacking the language and time barrier. Since he found the company used many words which had no Navajo equivalent, he began using substitutes: "Aluminum" became "shiny metal," "circuit" became the Navajo word for "distributor cable," "oscillator" became "tunnel," and so forth.[78] Fairchild also had:

> to overcome a tendency among Indians to mix up electronic compo-
> nents that look alike but are vastly different. The company
> emphasized the importance of keeping them separated by using the
> parallel of a pickup truck. "If you ordered a red truck," the company
> explained, "and the dealer delivered you a blue one, you wouldn't
> take it, okay?; so, if a man ordered a tunnel and you give him shiny
> metal, he would be dissatisfied, too.[79]

The company also addressed the time barrier. "Since Indians do not figure time in multiples of six and twelve,...Fairchild divided the plant clocks into ten sections, painted alternately red and white and numbered each section 1 through 10. Now an employee who spends, for example, 24 minutes on a job can say he has taken four sections."[80] According to Driscoll, after instituting his language and time programs, he found that his, "employees are like employees everywhere.... When I came down here I was told these people were different. You have to find a magic button. After three months of looking for the magic button, I went back to treating people like people, and that's when the world turned rosy for us."[81]

The world would turn less rosy for Fairchild in 1975. *Business Week* had interviewed a manager from the General Dynamics plant who noted one of the advantages of Indian labor was the fact that "they don't have the bad habits people have in more industrial areas. The Navajos have patience, respect for private property [hence a low theft rate], lack of militancy and pride in their work."[82] Ironically, while Fairchild claimed to want the Navajos to "take over every job in the plant," efforts to establish a workers' union would force the plant's closure. *Business Week* noted that it had found "few attempts to organize Indian workers in the area" in 1970.[83] However, when the purported lack of both militancy and "bad habits" gave way in 1975 to an effort to unionize, Fairchild closed the plant.[84] Details of the closure are scanty, but labor unrest had been engendered by persistent low wages and "layoffs before promotions were due."[85] Yet despite Indian worker successes—and production failure rate that was 5 percent in 1974 compared to 30 percent in the company's home plant at Mountain View, California non-Indians were being hired to replace Navajos.[86] The plant was occupied by workers and supporters in February 1975 and gave Fairchild "the pretext to break its lease and leave immediately."[87]

The magazine *Nation's Business* contained an article about Fairchild, ironically entitled "Indian Country is a Frontier Again." It noted:

> Indian tribes welcome only those firms known for their enlightened policies in employee and community relations. They want industries that will relate to the Indian people. When Indian employees feel confidence in their employers they perform skillfully, meticulously and with a personal interest in the company's success.[88]

Fairchild, however, did not want to relate to Indian people about to pick up one of industry's bad habits—organized labor. In its 1975 Annual Report, Fairchild announced the permanent closing of its Shiprock assembly plant due to its "seizure and occupation by a group of armed American Indians."[89] Like their forebears, these new frontiersmen found the Indians less understanding than they had hoped. Unlike their forebears, they discovered the the frontier was moveable—to wherever there was cheap labor without bad habits.

Low wages for Indian workers often were justified by the claim that Indians had never had it so good. P. K. Ferree was the chairman of Saddlecraft, Inc., an Indian novelties company located in North Carolina Cherokee country. Feree noted in a 1967 *New York Times* interview that "you can't measure the Indian's existence by the white man's standards, you have to measure it against the squalid standards the red man once had. . .wages are low and fringe benefits are poor. . .but that's how it is all through Appalachia."[90]

Over and over, Indian labor exploitation was justified by the reasoning that low pay was better than no pay. Yet industrialists complained when labor turnover occurred. Agricultural labor on the Yakima reservation paid $1.75 per hour, while nearby White Swan industries paid $1.60. When Indians left the company for work in the fields at harvest, theirs was called a cultural problem and lack of present-time orientation, rather than a possible interest in fifteen more cents an hour. Similarly, a Papago reservation electronics plant suffered turnover when workers went to work for $2.50 as firefighters during the dry season. Officials were surprised that workers would abandon their $1.60 trainee jobs. Again, they attribute this solely to a problem of culture.[91]

Economic development for Indian people during the Udall administration was purportedly designed to provide maximum self-sufficiency. The task force made a statement which was probably not far afield of the reality of industrial development. Indians were encouraged to participate in these plans so they might "retain their tribal identities and much of their culture while working toward a greater adjustment and, for the further enrichment of our society, it is in our best interests to do so."[92]

Ironically, these programs proceeded for the further enrichment of footloose industries and runaway shops eager to exploit cheap Indian labor and government incentives as long as they both lasted. Lorraine Turner Ruffing pointed out that industrial development has been an effort to provide jobs, not circulating income, for Navajo Indian people. Whatever little money was earned in light industry was used to bolster the income, not of the Navajo people but, of the white border-town merchants.[93] Monroe Price echoed that opinion in a paper for the Joint Economic Committee of the U.S. Congress. He also believed that this type of development "maximizes the opportunity for work rather than the opportunity for income. As a consequence, development plans often have little or no relation to the cultural and political goals of the reservation."[94]

Industrial development clearly did not promote "maximum self-sufficiency." Under the task force's recommendations, Indians were to have "full participation in American life." The exploitation of Indian labor was based on a premise that Indians would settle for low pay and resist organization. Self-sufficiency would have meant greater Indian control of reservation capitalization. It would have meant greater income for Indians as a group, through wages and benefits and through the circulation of capital within the tribe. All these things would have been antagonistic to industries whose interest in Indians extended precisely to the extent which they remained marginally dependent. Indians were encouraged to have "full participation" in the side of

American life which has put a premium on the alienation and disorganization of labor. To this extent, Indian people were able to take part in what had, indeed, become a great tradition. Oddly, Indians often extolled the good fortune of their participation in such a tradition. Henry Hough talked with a "husky Sioux tribesman" at a privately (non-Indian) owned cheese factory. The worker was asked how he liked his job. "Good job" was the answer. Then he was asked if he thought he would like working there any better if the cheese factory were owned and operated by his tribe. "No" was the emphatic answer. "What do you think I am, a Socialist or something?"[95]

Greater Indian participation in policy, self-help and self-determination, and Indian human and economic growth through industrial development—along with an ongoing emphasis on relocation, these are the themes forming the foundation of policy during the Udall/Nash years and the New Frontier for Native American people. These policy pronouncements yield much under scrutiny, however, for in each case the rhetoric appears more certain than the reality. Indian participation in the task force recommendations was negligible at best. Rather, policy was greatly forged in the chambers of a single privately selected group of policy professionals. The growth of self-help was not an end for the Udall task force, but a means to assuage termination psychosis in the effort to secure the bridge from dependency to termination. Industrial development, touted as a plan to provide economic independence, provided social disintegration and exploitation and, in at least one case, when a degree of Indian control actually threatened to raise its head, abandonment.

The task force on Indian Affairs was the administrative crystallization of a line of policy which began in the mid-1950s and received its greatest articulation through the study and recommendation of the commission on the Rights, Responsibilities and Liberties of the American Indian. The ARA and EDA put industrial development in the vanguard of the Indian competency program. Later, the Office of Economic Opportunity (OEO) would enter the effort to institutionalize community development along the lines suggested, once again, by the Fund for the Republic's Indian commission and the task force. Self-determination would be extended by OEO beyond industrial development as a program purported to extend "maximum feasible participation" of Indians over areas such as health care, nutrition and education.

Education must be understood as a crucial theme in this period, yet it must not be thought of primarily as schooling. Philleo Nash's and Oliver La Farge's social philosophy, along with the activities of the task force, exemplify the symbiosis between social science and social education, which was at the heart of liberal reform in this period. Fueled by functionalist social science, Indian policy reform takes a predictable course. It is a reform in style rather than substance. Indian reaction to termination is treated as a symptom subject to a manipulative therapy of symbol change. Replacing the corrosive symbols of assimilation and laissez-faire economics are the reassuring bromides of self-help. Yet while the rhetoric of participation is used, small, interlocked groups of policy power brokers worked to develop policy without much significant community or even tribal government participation.

The fact that policy was forged before any participation was solicited should be no surprise given the faith in the academic/administrative philosopher-kings, whose fundamental rationality was as unquestioned as was their relative lack of accountability. Accountability is only required when the reason of the people can be counted on to inform a decision. The power of the social science experts is in their ability to transcend the need for politics. Expertise is enough to ensure the fundamental rationality of their work. Like Lasswell, Nash would go on to orchestrate public relations manipulation to keep the Indian policy along the correct trajectory. It is this activity taking place on a large scale which is the heart of the education required to replace cumbersome politics for the liberal social reformer.

Schools, and primarily the Indian-controlled contract-school, would become an important aspect of the educational dimension of self-determination. However, these schools played a subsidiary, if supporting role within one of the two major themes which dominated Indian policy during this period—self-help and community development. Both of these themes—self-help/community development and economic/industrial development—were *in themselves* educative programs. Policy in this period was in important ways competency policy upon which to build justifiable forms of termination. The failure of industrial development and the limitations on legitimate self-help and policy participation were evidence of the feeble level of justification being built for new forms of termination.

NOTES

1. Margaret Connell Szasz, "Philleo Nash," in *The Commissioners of Indian Affairs 1824-1977*, eds. Robert M. Kvasnicka and Herman J. Viola (Lincoln: University of Nebraska Press, 1979), p. 311.

2. Ibid., p. 312.

3. Ibid.

4. Ibid.

5. Letter from Sophie Aberle to Arthur Schlesinger, 6 September 1961, William A. Brophy Papers, Box 22, Archives of Harry S. Truman Library, Independence, Mo.

6. Letter to O. Meridith Wilson (unsigned), 29 July 1961, William A. Brophy Papers, Box 24.

7. "Address by Philleo Nash, Commissioner Designate of Indian Affairs," at the18th annual convention of National Congress of American Indians, Lewiston, Idaho, 21 September 1961, U.S. Department of the Interior, News Release, in Philleo Nash Files, Papers of Harry S. Truman, Box 143, Archives of the Harry S. Truman Library, Independence, Mo.

8. William A. Brophy to W. W. Keeler, 26 January 1961 in William A. Brophy Papers, Box 22.

9. Letter from Oliver La Farge to Stewart Udall, 16 February 1962 in William A. Brophy Papers, Box 22.

10. "Address by Philleo Nash," 21 September 1961.

11. Ibid.

12. Ibid.

13. Memo from Philleo Nash to Stewart Udall, 2 February 1961, in Nash Files, Box 148.

14. Ibid.

15. Letter from Stewart Udall to W. W. Keeler, 2 February 1961, Nash Files, Box 148.

16. Quoted in S. Lyman Tyler, "A History of Indian Policy," from *Report to the Secretary of the Interior by the Task Force on Indian Affairs*, (Washington, D.C.: U.S. Government Printing Office, 1973), p. 189.

17. *Christian Science Monitor*, 9 December 1961 (Saturday), p. 5.

18. Ibid.

19. Ibid.

20. U.S. Congress, House, "The Education of American Indians: The Organization Question," *Report to the Secretary of the Interior by the Task Force on Indian Affairs: The Udall Task Force Report*, 91st Cong.,1st sess. (Washington, D.C.: U.S. Government Printing Office, 1970), p. 539.

21. Ibid.

22. Alvin M. Josephy, Jr., *The American Indian and the Bureau of Indian Affairs*, reproduced by the Indian Eskimo Association of Canada, Toronto, Ont., 1967.

23. Unsigned letter to O. M. Wilson in William A. Brophy Papers, Box 24.

24. Ibid. See also *New York Times*, 13 July 1961. Udall also was quoted here saying that placing greater emphasis on termination than on development has impaired "Indian morale and produces a hostile or apathetic response which greatly limits the effectiveness of the federal Indian program."

25. Philleo Nash, "The Indian Bureau and the War on Poverty," BIA Superintendent's Conference address, Santa Fe, 18 June 1964, in Nash Files, Box 146.

26. Memo from Philleo Nash to Stewart Udall, 2 February 1961 in Nash Files, Box 148.

27. Ibid.

28. Szasz, "Philleo Nash," p. 316.

29. Edgar L. Wight, "Indian Leadership," *Indian Education,* no. 394, 1 November 1963 (Haskell, Kans.: Branch of Education, BIA, 1963), p. 3.

30. Philleo Nash, speech before the Governor's Interstate Indian Council, 24 September 1964, in Nash Files, Box 146.

31. Ruth H. Landman, and Katherine Spencer Halpern, eds., *Applied Anthropologist and Public Servant: The Life and Work of Philleo Nash* (Washington, D.C.: American Anthropological Association, 1989), p. 33.

32. Harold D. Lasswell and Abraham Kaplan, *Power and Society: A Framework for Political Inquiry* (New Haven: Yale University Press, 1950), p. 229.

33. Floyd W. Matson, *The Broken Image: Man Science and Society* (New York: George Braziller, 1964), p. 103.

34. Ibid.

35. Ibid.

36. Ibid., p. 105.

37. Landman and Halpern, *Applied Anthropologist.*, p. 30.

38. Ibid., p. 34

39. Philleo Nash, speech at Education Conference, Washington, D.C., 8 January 1963 in Nash Files, Box 143.

40. Ibid.

41. Ibid.

42. Ibid.

43. Ibid.

44. Ibid.

45. Ibid.

46. Ibid.

47. Ibid.

48. Ibid.

49. Ibid.

50. Ibid.

51. Szasz, "Philleo Nash," p. 316.

52. Ibid.

53. "For the Indian: Squalor in the Great Society," *New York Times,* 13 March 1966, p. 1:4.

54. Ibid.

55. Letter from Gil Fates to Philleo Nash, 16 July 1963, in Nash Files, Box 145.

56. Curtis Jackson and Marcia Galli, *History of the Bureau of Indian Affairs and Its Activities Among Indians* (San Francisco: R and E Research Associates, 1977), p. 121.

57. U.S. Congress, House, *The Udall Task Force Report*, p. 544.

58. Excerpts from a talk by Philleo Nash, Laguna, N.M., 13 October 1963, Nash Files, Box 145.

59. Alan Sorkin, "American Indians Industrialize to Combat Poverty," *Monthly Labor Review* (March 1969); p. 19.

60. Address by Philleo Nash, commissioner designate of Indian Affairs, at the 18th annual convention of the National Congress of American Indians, at Lewiston, Idaho, 21 September 1961 (Philleo Nash Files, Box 143).

61. Position paper of the National Congress of American Indians, "Economic Development of the American Indian and His Lands," in *Toward Economic Development for Native American Communities: A Compendium of Papers Submitted to the Subcommittee on Economy in Government of the Joint*

Economic Committee, U.S. Congress, 91st Cong., 1st sess., vol. 1 (Washington, D.C.: U.S. Government Printing Office, 1969), pp. 413-14.

62. Comptroller General of the United States, *Report to Congress: Improving Federally Assisted Business Development on Indian Reservations* (Washington, D.C.: U.S. Government Printing Office, 1975), p. 15.

63. Alan L. Sorkin, "Trends in Employment and Earnings of American Indians," in *Toward Economic Development for Native American Communities: A Compendium of Papers Submitted to the Subcommittee on Economy in Government of the Joint Economic Committee*, U.S. Congress, 91st Cong., 1st sess., vol. 1 (Washington, D.C.: U.S. Government Printing Office, 1969), p. 107.

64. Alan Sorkin, *American Indians and Federal Aid* (Washington, D.C.: Brookings Institution, 1971), p. 81. This is an invaluable source of Indian economic and social data for the postwar period through the 1960s.

65. Ibid., p. 19.

66. Sorkin, "Trends in Employment and Earnings," p. 111.

67. Ibid., p. 113.

68. Sorkin, *American Indians and Federal Aid*, p. 88.

69. Ibid., p. 89.

70. Ibid.

71. Letter from George E. Schmidt to Alden Stevens, 21 July 1965 in Nash Files, Box 142.

72. Roxanne Dunbar-Ortiz, "Sources of Underdevelopment," in *Economic Development in American Indian Reservations* (Native American Studies, University of New Mexico Development Series 1) (Albuquerque: University of New Mexico, 1979), p. 68.

73. *Business Week*, "Industry Invades the Reservation," 4 April 1970, p. 72.

74. Ibid.

75. Ibid., p. 73.

76. Ibid.

77. Ibid.

78. Ibid.

79. Ibid.

80. Ibid.

81. Ibid.

82. Ibid.

83. Ibid.

84. Ibid.

85. Dunbar-Ortiz, "Sources of Underdevelopment," p. 68.

86. Ibid.

87. Ibid.

88. *Nation's Business*, "Indian Country is a Frontier Again," (September 1969): 75-77.

89. Fairchild Camera and Instrument Corporation, Annual Report, 1975.

90. *New York Times*, "Industry and the Indian: The Profit in Progress," 23 July 1967, 111, 1:2.

91. Sorkin, *American Indians and Federal Aid*, p. 95.

92. U.S. Congress, House, *The Udall Task Force Report*, p. 540.

93. Lorraine Turner Ruffing, "Dependence and Underdevelopment,"

Economic Development in American Indian Reservations (Native American Studies, University of New Mexico Development Series 1) (Albuquerque: University of New Mexico, 1979), p. 104. See also Keith Gilbreath, *Red Capitalism: An Analysis of the Navajo Economy* (Norman, Okla.: University of Oklahoma Press, 1973).

94. Monroe E. Price, "Lawyers on the Reservation: Some Implications for the Legal Profession," in *Joint Economic Report*, p. 202. See also Joseph G. Jorgensen, "Poverty and Work Among American Indians," in *American Minorities and Economic Opportunity*, ed. H. Roy Kaplan (Itasca, Ill.: F. E. Peacock, 1977).

95. Henry W. Hough, *Development of Indian Resources* (Denver: World Press, 1967), p. 202.

PART II
Self-determination, Community Control, and School Reform

Education and economic development were both used to increase the utility of reservation lands and quality of human capital. Efficient reservation resource use depended on an available work force and a stable political climate. Much of the activity during the immediate postwar period was an effort to "get the government out of the Indian business." Control over Indian education was included in this effort. The Indian student was encouraged to attend public schools, and curriculum in the boarding schools turned even more toward an emphasis on preparing Native American students for their "place" in society.

The ship of Indian education has rarely strayed from the current of American social and economic development priorities, and the period under discussion was no exception. Wartime economic priority, postwar reorganization, growth of service and industrial economy, the cold war, the development of the American postwar leadership posture: each of these, and other changes had an impact on government Indian education policy

During this period one can note the changes in Bureau of Indian Affairs (BIA) educational philosophy and policy, and can see how the shifts from limited academic to vocational and back to limited academic emphasis reflect the vision of Indian future as prophesied by bureau leaders. Changes in bureau policy showed that the BIA responded to pressure from those who wished, during the 1950s, to get the Indian off the reservation and into gainful employment. The bureau began, in the 1960s, under different but still persuasive forces, to de-emphasize the off-reservation vocational boarding school and to place new stress on public and day school operations and academic curricula.

These are but a few examples which point to some of the clearest generalizations about Indian education. First, for all its diversity of facilities—the off-reservation boarding school, the border-town boarding school, the on-reservation day and boarding school, state public schools, mission schools and community contract-schools—Indian education is remarkably uniform throughout this period. True, facility policies diverge, for example, in the off-reservation boarding school and in the day school. The boarding schools were aimed at students from broken or unstable homes and at students for whom no other school was available. The day schools served a homogeneous local community. The boarding schools were targeted to acculturate reservation Indians whose English language skills were poor. The public schools were entrusted to teach the more highly assimilated pupil. Despite the variety of approaches between schools, the net effect was an institutional monolith. Schools were designated by type as to which would best serve the goal of Indian assimilation into the postwar service and industrial economy—usually off the reservation.

An important focus of schooling within the ideology of self-determination was the development of Indian controlled contract-schools. These were schools originally designed to be an education for the community rather than primarily for the students who attended them. They were an extension of the human development theme, stemming from the earliest reactions to rapid termination. Originating as an Office of Economic Opportunity (OEO) program, contract-schools are, along with contracted Indian industry, the bellwether for tribal self-determination practice. As an offspring of OEO, it was a logical extension in a generation of liberal social engineering and the Indian competency programs. With this parentage, the beginnings of the contract-schools display the earmarks of yet another Indian competency program framed as an effort to increase Indian community control and community tribal sovereignty.

Educational efforts took place during this period as a part of an overall emphasis on economic development. Schooling cannot be understood in its variety of forms without reference to its socializing role, and its role as an instrument of human capital development. Contract schools; extended access to compensatory education; and codification of contracting through the Self-determination and Education Assistance Act: each characterized the visible reforms of this era. Yet, Indian Education entered the 1950s with a full commitment to termination, relocation, a resurgent boarding emphasis and a program of full school attendance to help expedite these goals. This emphasis should not be forgotten as an undercurrent beneath Native American school reform constructed to fit the economic development themes of the period.

5

Primer for Control: Immediate Postwar Indian Education Policy

Termination and relocation were part of a different political climate which followed the war. Returning after the conflict, Indian people saw education as a way to participate in the white world. This nascent cosmopolitan spirit emerged in two forms: first, that Indian people should equip themselves for bigger roles in national economic life, and second, that Indian leadership would now bring a greater sophistication to the negotiating table. As this was occurring, American government was developing a new role in world affairs. To serve as a leader in the postwar economy, the United States needed trained manpower, needed to rebuild markets which could not rebuild themselves, and it needed to find new sources of raw materials for the growth of industry and technology. Indian people could be of small benefit for the manpower requirement, except in some isolated cases where they could be used as a source of intermittent cheap labor. Their land figured more greatly in the enterprise of rebuilding and refueling U.S. industrial might. All this was growing in a climate where the government reacted as counterpoint to the political hegemony of the communist world.

Between the years 1945 and 1948, each report of the Secretary of Interior is a dual warning. First, wary of the threat of an unstable peace, he wrote that America must be warned of the fact that resources have been dangerously depleted. Second, he cautioned that if we did not develop new sources of raw materials, we would be in a precarious position.[1] It was no accident that the year 1946 saw the Indian Claims Commission set up to pay tribes dollar value in exchange for land entitled to them by treaty. It also is no coincidence that this clarion call for resource development was connected to the development of policies to terminate federal supervision of Indian lands and to a return to a policy of assimilation in education. Both programs ostensibly were set up to give Indians full rights and responsibilities as American citizens.[2]

During the later 1940s and the 1950s the boarding school once again began receiving its due share of the credit as the most effective acculturation institution in the BIA education planning. In addition, these institutions were being developed to serve as educational depots between the reservation and labor in urban industry.

> During 1948 a total of 1,335 Navajo students were enrolled in off-reservation boarding.... A special program [was] developed which was designed to give a useful command of English, a basic elementary education and vocational skills within a 5-year period. Careful tests of academic achievement and of English mastery [were] given at intervals. On-the-job employment training opportunities [were] arranged . . . and every effort [was] made to find them permanent placement away from the reservation.[3]

At the same time these relocation education efforts were being made, leases for the development of mineral resources were granted at an unprecedented rate and "accomplished by private enterprise...because Indians have lacked experience and the heavy capital requirements."[4] The secretary felt confident to announce that, "through education...and through the development of community organization [the Indian administration has moved] toward the final objective of bringing Indians into fuller possession and use of their resources and the adaptation of their cultures to the life in modern America."[5] In reality, Indians were being encouraged to leave the reservation at an unprecedented rate and were training for industrial occupation, not for fuller possession and use of their resources.

The work to educate the Indian for cultural adaptation continued apace in the late 1940s. BIA Education Director Willard Beatty wrote that Indians must be taught to appreciate the value and meaning of time. Without that, he argued, they would be forever at a disadvantage in the jobs for which Indians would be trained. While commenting on the day school program he said that Indians would be better for an understanding of what he called "our clockwork civilization" and suggested one possible means to encourage this:

> [It would be interesting] to see what could be accomplished by a dozen inexpensive watches, to promote among day school children the regularity which we consider so important. It is clear that the average boarding school is so slavish to clocks that it does not make much difference whether individual children have them or not."[6]

Regarding the boarding schools Beatty also commented that, the boarding school program emphasized more and more the development of good work habits and desirable attitudes toward work. "Emphasis [is] placed on putting in an honest day's work in a vocation. The equivalent of three-fourths time [is] spent in vocational instruction and in performing the skills of a trade, one-fourth time in related instruction and in the requisites of good living in any community."[7] Curiously, however, employers made it clear to the bureau that vocational education per se was not important.

> Employer after employer seemed to feel it did not make much difference what kind of machine the student had worked. . . . The important thing was not to learn all the possible things that a machine could do but to realize a few things about the nature of machines: (1) that a machine is very powerful, (2) that it operates without intelligence and in accordance with a fixed pattern of performance, (3) that the student, by controlling the switch and other operating gadgets on the machine, can control it; but by neglecting to exercise this control, the machine can become exceedingly dangerous, and seriously injure the operator.[8]

Students were spending three-fourths of their learning time in vocational education programs in preparation for repetitive assembly-line factory work skills which they could be taught in a relatively short time. Indeed, the only serious problem employers had about Indian workers was the fact that they might be forced off the line and onto the disability rolls. The BIA school had gone without a uniform course of study since 1936. The uniform course had been dropped under pressure of reform policy which said such a program did not take the unique aspect of each tribe and reservation into account. With a return to an attempt at assimilation of the Indian student, and in answer to a need for a direction toward relocation, the *Minimum Essential Goals for Indian Schools* was published in 1953.[9]

This program contained nine levels and included content and method recommendations. There was no great hint of the bicultural-bilingual direction taken by the various curricula developed in the late 1930s and the 1940s. In Suggested Activities and Techniques for levels 5 and 6 in the Social Studies, students were asked to know about people who have made significant contributions to America. Among the famous figures were Sequoyah "a mixedblood Cherokee Indian, [who] observing the advantages shared by the whites as a result of written language, devised a syllibary [sic] for the writing of the Cherokee tongue."[10] Kit Carson also was included and children were taught to think of him as a

Carson also was included and children were taught to think of him as a famous scout and pioneer trapper, "He has often been called 'the Pathfinder.' Children will be interested to learn about him as they read adventure stories of that period. . . .They may trace some of his journeys over trails he explored. In some areas it will be possible to visit places that are remembered because of Kit Carson."[11]

No mention is made of the fact that Carson was shown those trails by their great grandparents, and one is left to wonder whether teachers would choose to visit Carson's retirement home in Taos or the canyon from which he rounded up and herded Navajo people 300 miles to four years of captivity at Fort Sumner.

Cross-cultural education never did feature much of this sort of knowledge. More attention was usually paid to indigenous arts and crafts and fostering the development of the Indian's exemplary manual skill. However, the *Minimum Essential Goals* were an even further step toward the assimilation of Indian people through education. What was more significant, there now came a renewed emphasis upon a monolithic curriculum which could accomplish assimilation and accelerated relocation in a more efficient fashion applied consistently to all Indian school children under the aegis of the BIA.

The schooling of the Indian child during the late forties and early fifties was fraught with contradiction. The boarding school population rose. Boarding schools were renascent throughout the country. In 1948 half the number of all (60,000) Indian children in school were enrolled in public school. The Indian Service enrolled the other half, whose numbers were equally divided between the boarding and the day school. In addition, 8,000 Indian children attended mission schools and 22,000 were out of school, largely as a result of the lack of facilities. The majority of this group (15,000) were Navajo students on the vast remote reservation which had always constituted a special problem for bureau educators.[12]

In an achievement study commissioned by the BIA, Dr. Shailer Peterson noted the discrepancy in achievement between the public school group, who scored generally higher, and the boarding school group. He attributed this difference to the variation in language competency between what he termed "mixed-bloods," a large group of which attended the public schools, and "full bloods" who were predominant in boarding schools. He did not attempt to raise the question whether there was an important difference in the quality of education available between these two types of schools.[13] Further on he noted that "the schools enrolling a greater proportion of full bloods (boarding schools) report these children are less responsive to test material based on non-Indian culture."[14] Yet, one must ask, why was this type of test administered if, as stated in the program of the bureau schools, "for the

Indian the primary objectives of Indian schools are: To give students an understanding and appreciation of their own tribal lore, art, music, and community organization, to teach students through their own participation in school and community government to become constructive citizens of their communities."[15]

Clearly, these objectives flew in the face of the fact that relocation and termination pressure was increasing at a great rate. This statement was certainly a product of Indian New Deal reforms, and in the renewed climate of assimilation, it sounds almost quaint. If the Indian Service had not revised the objectives in their education policy program manual, revision in practice was well under way in 1950. The Indian Service employee civil service guide noted that education should aid students in analyzing the economic resources of their reservation and in planning more effective ways of utilizing these resources for the improvement of standards of living.[16] At virtually the same time, the Interior Secretary was pushing for termination of federal responsibility over Indian lands and relocation. When applied to Indians, education for the utilization of resources meant training to increase their self-sufficiency in the pastoral economy or vocational training to become useful factory employees who "know when to shut off the machine." When applied to Indian land, utilization of resources meant in an "expanding economy that calls for steadily increasing production, our Indian citizens must be counted on to contribute their talent and energies to our national wealth."[17] Indian land must be available, and "in the current period of world tension, we must work aggressively to mobilize our resources . . . intelligently to meet any test which may confront us."[18]

In the same report the secretary argued that after fifteen years of economic and community development during the Indian New Deal reforms, Indian family net income was $501 and that many Indian groups found it difficult to gain a decent living from their limited land resources.[19] Certainly, these must not be the same meager resources which on the next page of the report are depended upon to contribute to our expanding national economy.[20] Indian resources development for the national economy and Indian resources development for Indian people were clearly two different things here. The same page in this report began a section on Territories which reads: "Irresponsible propaganda attacks upon the United States as an expansionist power bent on exploiting the peoples and resources of colonial areas receives its most incisive answer in the development of our territories."[21] One can assume that here also development meant the same thing as it did with respect to Indians—there is development for colonial people, and there is development for the capital requirements of a world power. However, the Indian Service education manual states that one of the objectives of education in all BIA schools, in addition to the teaching of tribal "lore" and vocational education, would be "to give the students an understanding of the social and economic world immediately about them."[22]

As the 1950s unfolded, bureau officials attempted an expanded achievement evaluation, to build on Peterson's work of the late 1940s. The results of the test indicate that retarded educational achievement was inversely proportional to the degree of cultural and English language assimilation of the students in question. The extent to which achievement differed between the five types of schools—off-reservation boarding, reservation boarding, day school, public, and mission school—depended mainly on the degree of assimilation of the pupil. "As cultural and educational backgrounds of Indian children become more like those of white children, the more closely will the educational achievement of Indian children match that of white children."[23]

These findings worked to certify the growing emphasis on public school education for partially assimilated children and strenuous vocational, English competency training in the resurgent boarding school programs. The Education Division desire for the day school and cross-cultural/bilingual education became faint echoes of an era whose time had passed.

This new round of achievement testing was completed during the commissionership of Dillon Myer, an ardent proponent of termination and relocation. Beatty, a relic of the Collier era, did not fit into the new image of the bureau, and Hildegard Thompson took the reins of the Education Division.[24] Under Thompson, bureau policy changes which were set in the late 1940s and 1950s continued solidly into the late 1950s and early 1960s. She continued the effort to fit Indian students into a place in the burgeoning industrial, technical, urban community.

After Myer's short tenure as commissioner, the post was assumed by Glenn Emmons. Emmons began a tour of the reservations and sought immediately to end the truancy problem, especially among the Navajo. The Navajo emergency education program involved the building of trailer schools, increased border-town schools and boarding school enrollment. The program entered 8,000 additional students above the 14,000 previously enrolled.[25]

As the Indian education service proceeded rapidly to enroll all eligible students, on the national scene ten years of pressure toward termination of federal responsibility for Indian land was coming to fruition. In 1953 the Eighty-third Congress adopted House Concurrent Resolution 108 which established a policy of terminating as fast as possible the special relationship between the federal government and the American Indian.

Increasing enrollment figures and preparing students for off-reservation industrial employment continued to be the cornerstone of bureau policy in the 1950s and early 1960s. In Table 4, the enrollment breakdown for 1955-56 shows an increasing emphasis on the boarding school at the Navajo agency Branch.

The large enrollment noted in reservation boarding schools came as a result of the Navajo Education Program which was responsible for the construction of several reservation boarding schools, such as the large one at Kayenta. In addition, many students were housed in dormitories near border-towns. Yet, the number of Navajo students enrolled in such schools was kept sufficiently small so they did not dominate the social patterns, on the premise that they would thus make greater use of English and be more rapidly acculturated. In all institutions, winter conditions, student apathy, and movement of parents from camp to camp created a persistent attendance problem, especially in the trailer and day schools, due to their lack of a captive audience and transportation problems. Total boarding school enrollment reached 7,989, yet average daily attendance (ADA) was 6,904. The peripheral dormitories had 1,030 enrolled, with 953 ADA. This suggested a serious runaway problem, which was not addressed in this report. The fact that the percentage of nonattendance was virtually the same for boarding versus day school pupils is quite suggestive given that the boarding schools were often scores of miles from home and that the transportation problems—a factor in day school attendance—are legendary on the Navajo reservation.[26]

Indian education entered the 1960s with a renewed commitment to both the spirit of termination/relocation—and a program of full school

TABLE 4

Enrollment Breakdown and Projection for 1955-56

Type of School	1954-55 Enrollment	1956 (anticipated enrollment)
Reservation BIA Boarding	7,267	7,316
Off-reservation BIA Boarding	1,406	1,575
Day Schools	544	394
Hogan Schools	373	350
Trailer Schools	1,188	1,000
Peripheral or Border-town Dormitories	960	1,295

judicious use of the public school and the development of strong accul-turation/vocational boarding school programs, the Indian school child was well on his/her way to his/her place in the American dominant culture. In accordance with the mission to terminate federal supervision, Indian human and resource capital was being used more efficiently than ever. Indian oil and coal resources were being leased at an unprecedented rate, most negotiated with extremely small royalty benefits. Also, contracts for Indian labor in relocation cities were growing. "Contracts were made by the commissioner's assistant, with numerous industries from New York to Los Angeles. . . . the Navajo tribe managed to attract a manufacturer of baby furniture to employ one hundred Navajo workers in Gallup as a further step toward 'resource development.'"[27]

During the late 1940s and 1950s the change from Indian New Deal policy to that of the termination period was accomplished. By the beginning of the 1960s, the new program's curricula and facilities for education were largely in place. Assimilation of Indian children was occurring through such means as the Special Navajo Education Program, and "there was never any question that placing graduates in full-time gainful employment, usually off the reservation, was the final goal [of this program]."[28] This new development in Navajo education complimented attempts to gain full enrollment in schools for Navajos. New school facilities were built and the program for the 1960s was set.

There was, as ever, significant resistance within the ranks of the Indian leadership and among white reformers, people who had protested termination and were equally adamant about the detrimental goals of the relocation-assimilation policies. In 1944, at the beginning of the drive for termination, the National Congress of American Indians was organized. It was largely due to their efforts and those of their leader Joseph R. Garry (Coeur D'Alene), that termination legislation was not more decisive in this period. Reformers were arguing that termination, while not a poor solution in itself, was proceeding too hastily. Tribes must be given a chance to collect themselves before accepting such a weighty responsibility.[29]

Educational changes, like economic development moves, would begin to reflect the effects of The 1961 Udall Task Force and the Fund for the Republic Commission on the Rights, Liberties and Responsibilities of the American Indian. The American Indian Chicago Conference's "Declaration of Indian Purpose" also had a powerful effect on policy. Another Indian nationalist group which influenced this period of policy was the National Indian Youth Council. This group was designed for the purpose of leadership training, training which had gone into eclipse since the war years.[30]

since the war years.[30]

The action of pressure groups brought a new awareness of the question of Indian sovereignty. Indians wanted more control over all aspects of their lives, including the education of their children. The leadership provided by these people helped to articulate these desires. Statistics for American Indians were bleak, despite years of reform after reform. For example, in 1964, unemployment ran to 40 or 50 percent (seven or eight times the national average); family incomes on the reservation averaged one-fourth or one-third below national average; and average schooling of young adults on the reservations was only eight years—two-thirds the national average.[31] A changing political climate began its response to these grim figures.

The deciding factor weighing in the direction of change for Indian education was the report of the Senate Select Subcommittee on Indian Education, headed by Robert Kennedy, the recommendations of which were guided after his death by Senator Morse, and finally by Edward Kennedy. The Kennedy Report was the most scathing summation of the failure of Indian education since the 1928 Meriam Report, *The Problem of Indian Administration,* whose recommendations, it declared, were as yet unfulfilled.

In 1964 the Office of Economic Opportunity put a variety of Head Start programs into effect for Indian preschoolers. Bureau reaction to this was frosty at best.[32] When OEO funds became available for the development of Indian-controlled schooling, as well as other programs benefitting Indian students, funds totaling 60 to 65 million dollars—over half the bureau budget—the BIA could no longer ignore the power of the Indian leadership in the policymaking process.

Indian educational self-determination grew out of the efforts of a variety of reform-minded forces and as a result, there was a tacit return to Indian education policy which emphasized cross-cultural and community-controlled education. Unfortunately, as the dreams of Indian nationalists and reformers were forged into policy, much of the meaning of the notion of Indian control changed. Indian control, for self-determination and the impulse it represented, was never intended by its key architects to confer to Indian people any legitimate degree of control over their own destiny. Nor were cross-cultural curricula designed primarily as part of an admission that Indian language and culture studies were an end in themselves. Rather, these efforts and the community contract-school which represented them were, very much like their counterpart efforts in reservation economic development, a part of a sophisticated economic and community development model designed to give the appearance of competency to an Indian community.

NOTES

1. U.S. Department of the Interior, *Annual Report of the Secretary, 1945-48* (Washington, D.C.: U.S. Government Printing Office, 1948).

2. Willard W. Beatty, *Education for Cultural Change: Selected Articles from "Indian Education," 1944-51,* U.S. Department of the Interior, Bureau of Indian Affairs, (Washington, D.C.: U.S. Government Printing Office, 1953), p. 42.

3. U.S. Department of the Interior, *Annual Report of the Secretary 1945-48,* pp. 384-85.

4. Ibid., p. 375.

5. Ibid., pp. 388-89.

6. *Education for Cultural Change,* pp. 131-32. Beatty noted that boarding school children were "called in the morning by a whistle or siren, they go to meals at some kind of signal; report to school by another signal; and frequently change classes at similar notification. They should be thoroughly indoctrinated as to the importance of time . . . . As many of our boarding school youngsters do pass out into competitive American life, this is probably a pretty good experience" (p. 132). Beatty noted further that day school students should also have the benefit of this indoctrination in virtue of the fact of their "increasing contact with the non-Indian world" (p. 132).

7. Ibid., p. 476.

8. Ibid., p. 489.

9. Margaret Szasz, *Education and the American Indian: The Road to Self-determination 1928-1973,* (Albuquerque: University of New Mexico Press, 1977), p. 110.

10. U.S. Indian Service: Education Division, *Minimum Essential Goals for the Indian Schools, Levels 4 and 5* (Washington, D.C.: U.S. Government Printing Office, 1949), pp. 37-38.

11. Ibid.

12. Shailer Peterson, *How Well Are Indian Children Educated?,* U.S. Indian Service: Education Division, (Washington, D.C.: U.S. Government Printing Office, 1948), p. 105.

13. Ibid., p. 16.

14. Ibid.

15. Ibid., p. 9.

16. Ibid.

17. Oscar Chapman, Secretary of the Interior, "Resources for an Expanding Economy," in *Annual Report of the Secretary,* (Washington, D.C.: U.S. Government Printing Office, 1950), p. xxii.

18. Ibid., p. vii.

19. Ibid., p. xxiv.

20. Ibid., p. xxiii.

21. Ibid., p. xxv.

22. Kenneth E. Anderson, E. Gordon Collister, and Carl E. Todd, *The Educational Achievement of Indian Children—One Examination of the Question: How Well Are Indian Children Educated?,* (Washington, D.C.: U.S. Government Printing Office, 1953), p. 10. For further discussion of Indian school

achievement at this time, see Robert J. Havighurst, "Education Among the American Indians: Individual and Cultural Aspects," in *Annals of the American Academy of Political and Social Science,* 311 (May 1957). This volume is devoted to American Indians and Indian life during the termination period. It is essential reading for anyone interested in the contribution of scholars and policymakers to this era of Indian affairs.

23. Anderson et al., *Educational Achievement of Indian Children,* p. 77.

24. Szasz, *Education and the American Indian,* p. 121.

25. U.S. Department of the Interior, *Report of the Commissioner of Indian Affairs* (Washington, D.C.: U.S. Government Printing Office, 1954), p. 230. See also Hildegard Thompson, "Education Among American Indians: Institutional Aspects," in *Annals of the American Academy of Political and Social Science,* 311 (May 1957): 102.

26. U.S. Department of the Interior, *Report of the Commissioner,* pp. 234-35, 1954.

27. Ibid., pp. 208-209.

28. L. Madison Coombs, *Doorway Toward the Light: The Story of the Special Navajo Education Program,* (Washington, D.C.: U.S. Government Printing Office, 1962), p. 115.

29. Oliver La Farge, "Termination of Federal Supervision: Disintegration and the American Indians," in *Annals of the American Academy of Political and Social Science,* 311 (May 1957): 41-46.

30. Stuart Levine, and Nancy Oestreich Lurie, eds., *The American Indian Today* (Deland, Fl.: Everett/Edwards, 1968), pp. 64-66.

31. Ibid., p. 68.

32. Szasz, *Education and the American Indian,* p. 152.

6

Community Action and the Development of the Indian-controlled Contract School

The ideology of self-determination took shape in the postwar years as the result of efforts to encourage Indian competency, in the wake of the failure of rapid termination. These plans were developed through the influence of a cadre of academic and business elites with the support of private foundations, such as the Ford Foundation, and benevolent associations such as the AAIA. Their work was crystallized through administrative fiat during the tenure of Stewart Udall in the Kennedy administration.

The developing theme of self-determination must be understood in its variety: self-help, community economic development, morale building through culturally sensitive programming, tribal consultation. These themes and others were developed for their usefulness in reducing Indian hostility and apathy toward social programs which they believed to be designed for termination. Social science had shown that underdeveloped peoples could be encouraged to cooperate with outside forces if they could be given an opportunity to form and implement policy. And, indeed, given this opportunity, programs, whether they were agricultural, industrial development, health or educationally related, could flourish.

Reformers and social planners during this postwar era believed that the "Indian problem" would not disappear without Indian cooperation, and a change in Indian attitude toward government policy. Without such cooperation, changes in the Indian competency profile would never come about.

Virtually all Indian social policy development in this period is an effort to provide a basis for such competency. As such, all programs—including economic and industrial development and social services—

were increasingly educative in nature. No Indian social or economic program can be understood apart from its use as an educative institution. For example, industrial development was designed, at least partly, to augment Indian wage earning, yet it cannot be treated apart from its function as a trainer of Indian social habits and values, from values of hard work, punctuality, thrift and saving. Acquisition of such characteristics was essential for the Indian to fit into the dominant society and economy.

With the development of these action social science competency programs, references to termination were actively avoided. Indeed, policymakers were in the business now of preventing the spread of termination psychosis which was such a block to their efforts. Termination had not been abandoned as the ultimate result of all Indian policy.

In its report to the Interior Secretary, the Udall task force argued that the objective of termination of federal services to Indians had been overemphasized in the past and argued, instead, for developmental programs "to assist tribal groups to advance socially, economically and politically to the point where special services are no longer justified."[1]

In its 1961 report, the Udall task force reaffirmed the plenary power of Congress to "repeal, abrogate or amend Indian treaties even though they are the supreme law of the land. It has been hard for some tribes to accept this conclusion."[2] The object of Indian social policy during the 1960s was not to end the threat of termination. In the words of President Johnson, the object was first and foremost a goal that "ends that old debate about termination of Indian programs and stresses self-determination; a goal that erases old attitudes of paternalism and promotes self-help."[3]

Self-determination developed as an effort to end the "old debate," not the specter of termination with all that implies, including wholesaling of Indian lands. Yet in his presidential message on Indian affairs, Lyndon Johnson sounded words which rang with promise. His goals, outlined in his message, were summed up by "a policy of maximum choice for the American Indian; a policy expressed in programs of self-help, self-development and self-determination."[4] Community development, in addition to economic development, the focus of the previous chapter, was becoming more and more greatly emphasized in the 1960s.

The Udall years and the Task Force on Indian Affairs brought a series of programs to Indian America which to a great extent represented the thinking of the Ford Foundation Fund for the Republic. On a larger scale, American social policy, begun during the 1960s, was shaped by a group of social scientists who were influential in the Kennedy and Johnson administrations. Policy initiatives in Indian country reflected the impact of rationalized public polic planning toward the solution of a wide variety of social ills as they were perceived by these social scientists and policymakers.

"Community action" was the term for the approach to social problems and poverty, in which the poor themselves were invited to participate in problem solving. It is very similar in theme and character to the applied anthropology referred to earlier. Daniel Moynihan referred to the influence of social scientists in this effort as a part of a movement toward the "professionalization of reform."[5]

During the 1960s, Indian poverty, like the poverty of the urban ghetto, was presented as a cycle, which, with adequate human cultural development and the active participation of the poor, could be broken. Community action was that portion of the plan which was to involve the local community in the solution of their own problems, thereby reducing the alienation stemming from outside administration of programs.[6]

The central feature of the Community Action Anti-Poverty Program was to be the "maximum feasible participation" of the poor.[7] The Office of Economic Opportunity, which evolved from the 1964 Economic Opportunity Act, developed the principle of maximum feasible participation through its community action programs, which could be found in most of the larger urban areas as well as in two of the largest rural poverty pockets in the United States—Appalachia and Indian America.

Much of the emphasis on community action appears to have been partly a response to the growing concern of social science in the 1950s and 1960s with the failure of community. Community change and disintegration is an old theme in American intellectual life, with its roots in the concern over the anomie and rootlessness of modern industrial life. The advent of Community Action and the War on Poverty was not the first time social scientists, concerned with the problem of community, sought to impact public policy. Many programs of the New Deal, and much of the liberal social thought which led to it, were a response to the problems of the cities and the disintegrating rural society in the Depression. However, the War on Poverty/Community Action Program was, perhaps, the first time such a large-scale effort was made to solve the problem of poverty through rational manipulation of community structures.

One of the most powerful influences on social policy after the war came from private philanthropy. In particular, the Ford Foundation had a great influence on social programming and policy. Ford began in 1950 to develop as a nationwide philanthropy, and between 1950 and 1963 distributed almost $2 billion in grants, much of that money going to institutions for the creation and administration of social policy. Ford helped to crystallize the concept of community action as a method to ameliorate conditions of poverty. Indeed, we have seen the development of this effort through the ministrations of their Fund for the Republic during the late 1950s.

The Fund for the Republic policy language had argued vigorously for the revitalization of Indian communities and for economic development as a solution to the Indian Problem. The Udall task force and the Area and Economic Development Administrations worked to provide economic development by working with light industrial corporations. This was augmented by the community development efforts of the OEO Community Action Programs. Indeed, from information gleaned in a 1966 study, Ford Foundation alumnus and OEO official Richard Boone was found to have originated the concept of maximum feasible participation, the concept which would have a profound effect on the Indian community control movement.[8] It is no coincidence that community development played such a major role in the recommendations of the Fund for the Republic, the Task Force on Indian Affairs, and now in the OEO. The social interventionism of the Ford Foundation can be found behind each of these associations, both through intellectual and financial influence. Ford's urban *gray areas* program of the early 1960s was one of the first efforts to "experiment with ways of improving the social conditions of the central city."[9]

Whether community and human capital development could help break the cycle of poverty was a source of academic debate, even as the Office of Economic Opportunity was developing and instituting programs. As always, the stakes of the game in Indian country were different. For the poor of black and white America, the question was whether or not social, cultural, and educational rejuvenation and participation would cure poverty. However problematic, this was the question for Indian people as well. Yet social scientists saw the solution of poverty for black and white poor as an opportunity for those groups to culturally and economically assimilate into mainstream white America. For Indian people, this type of success meant competence and the justifiable termination argued for by the Fund commission and the task force. Community Action was added to the industrialization efforts of the Udall administration. Community involvement and participation would bring cooperation and dilute termination fears.

Maximum feasible participation was the key to program success and local cooperation. Herbert Striner, writing for the Joint Economic Committee of the Congress, with regard to Human Resources Development on the reservation, said "There must be a policy that substantial Indian participation is involved or must be involved at both the national and local levels when any new proposals or programs are contemplated concerning improvement of Indian education, training and employment or the economic development of Indian tribes."[10]

Again, the best-known political strategy associated with the EOA is the stipulation that community-action programs should be "developed, conducted and administered with maximum feasible participation of residents of the areas and members of the groups served."[11] Sar Levitan and Barbara Hetrick, who wrote about the impact of OEO on the reservation, claimed that it was this agency which gave impetus to self-determination.[12] Local participation was to be the blueprint for self-determination. They argued that Indians in the 1960s were demanding control and should be given it, in accordance with EOA guidelines. They also mentioned that cultural differences should be protected from erosion, that living conditions should be improved, that economic development must occur, and that Indians must be given the option of maintaining their separateness rather than being forcibly integrated into the dominant society.[13]

This emphasis on avoidance of forced assimilation is inseparable from the developing notion of self-determination. For central to the concept is the willing participation of Indian people in their social and educational programming, participation and "control" which in themselves work to engender trust that programs are Indian, not government, programs which had, since the war, been tainted with the stench of termination.

In his 1969 study of the Bureau of Indian Affairs, Alvin Josephy, Jr., wrote that in 1961 Indian leaders of 67 tribes at the Chicago Conference had pleaded for control of social programming. Their "Declaration of Indian Purpose" was only partially incorporated into The Udall Task Force Report. Now, with OEO they saw their dreams coming true. The promise of community control would release them from the patronage of the BIA. Josephy said Indian people saw OEO as a momentous breakthrough.[14] Yet with all this, the essential goals of the Udall administration had not changed. It was Udall's belief that "while we should test our thinking against the wisest Indians and their friends, this does not mean that we are going to let, as someone put it, the Indian people themselves decide what the policy should be."[15] Indeed, Josephy himself recommended, in his report on objectives that were consistent with the goals of the Udall task force, to "shift Bureau emphasis from termination to social and economic development."[16]

Community, social and economic change was designed to maximize local participation in development in order to minimize the negative effects of the underlying move toward justifiable termination. This is not what the Indian leaders of the Chicago Conference had in mind when they expressed their desire for more control.

Community development and community control became identified nationwide with OEO. OEO and its Indian Community Action

Programs may not have been the "origination of 'sel-determination' [but] there is little doubt that OEO's Indian program gave strong impetus to the approach, and OEO pioneered in making grants . . . directly to Indian groups."[17] By 1969 there were sixty-three Community Action Programs, serving 129 reservations, with a total budget of $22.3 million in 1968.

Both the Udall task force and the OEO Indian Community Action Programs responded to the same chord in their pronouncements and programming. We can hear the Ford Foundation Fund for the Republic sound its chord: economic development, community and human development, self-help, morale building, etc. The current of human capital development runs through all this. Some were seeing self-determination and community control as the beginning of a new spirit of planned community, as social science creating the conditions for a better, more prosperous age. Yet we cannot ignore the voices of those who would use local cooperation, not as the beginning of a resurgent Indian community sovereignty but, as the foundation for the moral, social, and economic conditions for termination. Whether termination is desirable or not, its presence under the rhetoric cannot be denied.

The Udall recommendations were subsumed under a much larger national effort to alleviate poverty. The chorus of voices came to sing praise to the new effort. BIA Commissioner Philleo Nash claimed that:

> The war on poverty, articulated through the new Economic Opportunity Act, gives us a starting point. . . . It calls for community action . . . for the Indian people, this means that they must be willing to assume a more active part in the shaping of their own future. They must design and carry out the programs for their own economic and social advancement.[18]

Indian people began to gear up for a host of organized efforts to solve the blight. The *Navajo Times*, the nation's largest tribal newspaper, wrote in 1966, "Indians Lead in Anti-Poverty War," citing the variety of new programs, including Vista, Job Corps, Head Start, Youth Corps and, of course, Community Action.[19] Nash touted the OEO model as an answer to the persistent problem of motivation. He echoes the Fund commission on the problem and its solution in Indian country:

> Helping people help themselves is a cliche—you will find it in many government and private agency reports, in particular you will find it appears a number of times in the Economic Opportunity Act of 1964. . . . The question is *how* do you help people to help themselves? This has been asked all over the world and a whole new field of social science has come into being as an answer—this being the discipline called "community development."[20]

Indian community development could be a perfect panacea to an old competency problem, the lack of European-style bureaucratic institutional organization. For Nash, "what is important is the learning by the people of the techniques of organizing, of finding out the facts in a situation of coming up with plans and carrying them out."[21] Yet the guiding spirit of the OEO approach to poverty was that poverty came as the result of cultural deficit. Cultural deficit was supposedly found in such symptoms as malaise, lack of motivation and apathy. These conditions were not seen as the result of poverty but, rather, were presented in large part as its cause. Community development was a comprehensive method of addressing this model of cultural deficiency which was supposedly the cause of such institutional anemia.[22]

The Indian programs of the Office of Economic Opportunity presented a comprehensive attempt to develop human capital on the reservation. OEO provided a source of additional funds as well as a variety of new programs to the existing economic development efforts of the Economic Development Administration. The OEO community action was designed to increase the effectiveness of developing projects by encouraging community participation. In 1967, the EDA issued a statement which underscored the importance of local initiative and cooperation, saying, "It cannot be stressed too strongly the essential aspect of the success or failure of EDA's program is that Indians themselves must be brought into the initial planning process. The tribal attitude toward change will in the long run, determine their progress and allow them to move toward self-sustained economic growth."[23] Indeed, "the current of belief within OEO was that the community development worker rather than economic development expert may prove to have more valuable skills."[24]

Programs were being expanded to inlude a wide variety of opportunities for human capital augmentation. Resource and economic development initiatives were beginning to be pushed beyond the encouragement of reservation-based light industry. Given the large role played by schooling in the socialization of Indian people, it is not surprising that schooling should become a major focus in this new climate of broadening reform. Indeed, the Bureau of Indian Affairs went on record at this time arguing in favor of a broadened definition of development to include its traditional bailiwick—schooling. The BIA outlined "steps that have been found effective as a systematic approach to economic development [and these include] establishment of priorities for development—taking into account not only resources to be developed, but schools, homes, medical services, recreational services, etc."[25]

The OEO collaborated with the BIA in the development of an approach to schooling which emphasized the principles of economic and human development via community action. It was at the Rough Rock

Demonstration School, thirty miles northwest of Chinle, Arizona, where the first large-scale experiment in community action schooling occurred. Rough Rock and the Indian community contract-school movement which it led, was the flagship in the movement for what became identified as self-determination in Indian education. At Rough Rock, Indian schooling was melded with Indian social development through community action. The result was a demonstration, an experiment, which was to show that Indian people could and would work to control their own education and, in the process, would develop to a point where proof could be offered for similar experiments in other areas of Indian country.

The Rough Rock experiment had potential to have a great impact in the schooling of indigenous peoples worldwide. In the first year and a half of operation at its remote site, seventeen miles from any paved road, in the heart of the most remote and traditional area of the Navajo nation, Rough Rock had 12,000 visitors from forty-two states and eight foreign countries.[26]

Robert A. Roessel, Jr., was the first director and a guiding force in the development of the school. Roessel had a long record of experience in schooling and community development at the Round Rock and Low Mountain communities on the Navajo reservation. When he assumed directorship of the school, Roessel was the head of the OEO Indian Community Action Center at Arizona State University at Tempe. In his book on the Rough Rock Demonstration School, Roessel gives credit for the success of the school to several other individuals in the OEO community development hierarchy. He credited Ford Foundation alumnus Richard Boone, the man who gave vision and drive to the community development concept. He cites Boone's "friend and cohort Sandy [Sanford] Kravitz, who ended up being responsible for Demonstration and Research Projects under Community Action. It was Sandy who wanted to support demonstrations in Indian education."[27]

He also credited "a former Peace Corpsman, Tom Reno, under whose leadership the earliest attempt at Navajo involvement and control broke the ice and paved the way for the Rough Rock Demonstration School."[28] While Kravitz provided the funds for the project, Reno guided the development of the school at Lukachukai, Arizona, in 1965-66. Because both BIA and OEO administrators were attempting to run that operation, Lukachukai failed, but the lessons learned led directly to the establishment of Rough Rock at the site of an old BIA school built in 1935, at the foot of Black Mesa. Roessel also cites the influence of Allen D. Yazzie of the Navajo Tribe and Graham Holmes and Buck Benham of the BIA. The cooperation between this triumvirate—OEO, the BIA, and the Navajo tribe—led to the establishment of a funding agreement between OEO and the BIA for the operation of a locally controlled school.

Roessel also mentions the influence of Robert Kennedy, whose Chairmanship of the Senate Subcommittee on Indian Education led to an indictment of the quality of Indian education in 1967, setting the stage for experimentation.

Indian control and self-determination in education appears to come from two contradictory sources during this period. On one hand, community control often was presented as an antidote to the mediocrity, ethnocentricity, and paternalism of BIA education. Community control would hold the line on the assimilationist efforts of bureau education and on the increasing use of the public school for Indian students. On the other hand, we have seen the genesis of community development as an aspect of the type of social programming for Indians which uses local participation as a method, a means to another end. Community development, as we saw it coming through the Udall task force recommendations and the admonitions of the Fund for the Republic commission, was to be part of a transitional phase in Indian life between dependency and a termination which that program would work to help justify.

In his work on the Rough Rock project, Roessel accentuated the first argument for community control much more than the second. For him, there appears to be nothing transitional in the nature of the project. Instead, he argued for the right of Indian people to take control of their education, even to the extent of what he would emphasize as their "right to be wrong" without fear of BIA intervention. Roessel wrote:

> The time has long since passed when Indian people will be content to allow officials in Washington or anywhere else to make decisions affecting the future of their children and the future of their communities. The words of an old World War I song are appropriate in amply highlighting the impact of Rough Rock on Indian people: "How can you keep them down on the farm after they've seen Paree."[29]

Roessel appears to argue that community control is the result of Indian people demanding their release from Bureau paternalism. He outlined his conception of the essential nature of the demonstration in a series of statements intended to highlight the move toward a renewed pluralist vision of Indian education: "Navajo people are directly and actively involved in the operation of the school . . . the policies and programs at Rough Rock are the result of action—initiated by the Navajo people. The creation of the most successful programs lies with the community—not the professionals."[30]

He also highlighted the importance of the bilingual, bicultural curriculum efforts. These were offered as evidence that Navajo culture and language are important for their own sake. He included mention of the Navajo curriculum center which worked to develop elementary school bilingual, bicultural learning materials. He summarized the Rough Rock mission by saying:

> First, the Rough Rock Demonstration School is guided by the philosophy that the Indian can, and should, be educated to retain his identity with his native values and culture while at the same time learning to master the Anglo culture and to take his place in the Anglo world, if he so desires. Other schools established for the Indian have followed in the past the theory that he should be separated from his natural heritage, that he should forsake his culture and traditions in favor of the way of life of the dominant Anglo society.[31]

Finally, Roessel highlighted the community-development efforts at the school. He mentioned the fact that the school was the chief source of employment for the community; that adult education in basic skills and arts and crafts was a keystone to local development. He discussed the variety of auxiliary services offered by the school to the community—shower facilities, recreation programs, a toy factory, adult driver education, English language instruction and several other adult education and employment opportunities that were created with the school.[32]

Through all of this, Roessel placed great faith in the wisdom of the local Navajo school board to oversee the demonstration and its administration. He argued that this board, composed of seven of the area's prominent leaders, was the soul of the efforts at local control, since they represented the will of their constituents, the people of the Rough Rock area. Roessel argued vigorously for the strength and virtue of democracy, even among an uneducated people. He believed strongly in the virtue of experience. He wrote, "It is refreshing, if one believes in the principles of democracy, to see a community like Rough Rock with its almost non-existent economic base, its relatively uneducated school board, and its isolated location practice democracy in a most successful, visible and magnificent fashion."[33]

The Rough Rock Demonstration and contract schooling have been supported as a revolutionary approach to education which attacks the problem of BIA control. However, there is no denying the *genesis* of community development as a part of a transitional strategy toward forms of eventual tribal termination, not as a move toward strengthened cultural and political sovereignty.

Bilingual, bicultural education, community control of local institutions, arts and crafts development and maximum feasible participation, all were used in earlier arguments as required parts of a successful transition program. The Fund for the Republic commission argued for each of these programs citing the effect they would have on reducing

Indian apathy, increasing motivation, and thereby increasing the chances for a successful, justifiable termination built on a foundation of competency rather than legal fiat.

While director of the Indian Education Center at Arizona State, Roessel corresponded with Nash in 1962, discussing the question of Indian community. This came long before the advent of the Economic Opportunity Act and suggests that community development was in the wind prior to OEO. In his letter, Roessel indicated that he and Nash had discussed hearing Hildegard Thompson, head of the BIA education branch, and James Officer, a member of Udall's task force, "speak for programs which several years ago would never have been attempted."[34] Roessel then went on to say he was, "interested in Mrs. Thompson's suggestion that 'functional schools' be established in various parts of the Navajo reservation on a pilot basis. These schools would attempt to meet the total educational needs of the local community and would serve as a true community school."[35]

Day schooling was not a new thing in Navajo education, but the concept of total community development through an educational facility was. It is interesting to see the genesis of this concept as Roessel heard it coming from Thompson, a Nash staff member, in 1962, long before OEO. Yet, the community development ideal, with which Roessel had become enamored, was presented earlier by the Fund for the Republic commission and by the Udall task force. However, its purpose was antagonistic to the reasons for Roessel's enthusiasm; it was not community democracy for the sake of the ideal, but for the sake of embattled Indian morale and as a cure for termination psychosis. Bicultural curriculum was not presented for the reason that Indian culture and language simply should be taught to Indian students, as a belated recognition to their hegemony and nationhood, but for the salutary effect it would have on embittered communities—whose apathy and demoralization stood in the way of a justifiable termination.

Indeed, some of the programs which were developed at Rough Rock bear the marks of the transition theme. One of the interesting things about Rough Rock is that it was a *community* -action program which first needed to create a type of community different from the one which actually existed. The school became the focus of an area which had been a loosely scattered organization of camp settlements near the site of a BIA school. There had not even been a chapter house (county-like) government recognition by the Navajo Tribe for the Rough Rock area.[36] The self-help ethic, a hallmark of the Udall task force and fund committee recommendations, is everywhere in evidence at Rough Rock. Navajo participation in their children's schooling is certainly consistent with an ideal of self-determination.

It is important to note that fostering arts and crafts development also was an aspect of the Fund commission's recommendations. It had a dual role of building morale while building an economic base. Following this, the local toy factory and arts development are interesting adjuncts to the early Rough Rock experiment. Bilingual, bicultural education was a highlight of the demonstration. Yet Roessel seemed to be arguing that this was mainly part of an effort to build morale and "self-image," not as an end in itself, "Education must enable our Navajo students to acquire positive feelings about themselves and to establish a pride in their own culture and heritage. This can be accomplished in incorporating [into the curriculum] the reading and writing of the Navajo language and studies in Navajo social living."[37]

Roessel was understandably interested in cooperating with parents who wanted their children to be "proud of their heritage as Navajos." Perhaps this is what he meant by asserting that "at Rough Rock, the primary involvement is in the development of a positive self-image."[38] However, Roessel seemingly assumed here the cultural deficit model which was adopted for use during the War on Poverty. Yet his interpretation also fell in line with the reasoning of those who saw community development and cultural education as essential during this transition in order to increase Indian morale and cooperation as a prelude to an argument for competency and termination.

Roessel believed it was crucial that "what the people want is to be able to say 'This is my school'."[39] He was fond of quoting the differing names given by the Navajo people to the various attempts to educate them:

> Navajos called BIA schools "Wa'a shindoon bi'olt'a" or Washington's schools. They call public school "bilaga'ana Yazzie bi'olt'a" or little whiteman's school. Mission schools are "eeneishoodi bi'olt'a" or the schools of those who drag their clothes . . . a fourth kind of school has now appeared. Its English name is Rough Rock Demonstration School. Navajos call it "Dine' bi'olt'a," or the Navajo's school.[40]

As for Roessel, it is not clear from his writings whether he was altogether aware of the full impact of the control issues at stake, except in that he was responding to Indian desires for less BIA paternalism and more Indian knowledge in the curriculum. Yet the evidence does suggest that the success of a Rough Rock and the genesis of education for community development becomes the quintessential misuse of ideology—the involvement of a people and their wholehearted support of a program whose real purpose, if it were known, would be reviled, not welcomed.

Vine Deloria warned of the problem of ideology in Indian social programming. At a 1967 panel discussion, he separated the means to educate from the intention. The means were, "actual appropriations, what the dominant society is willing to put into Indians or any other minority group. The [intention] is the ideology behind why we do it—and so I don't believe you can talk about Indian education without talking about the place of the Indian in American society."[41] He went on to argue that any study of Indian education has to challenge the ideology behind the education.

Achieving willing involvement of Indian people in social development programs was the culmination of a desire to blunt termination psychosis and apathy. Self-determination through community control and development assumes the quintessential purpose of ideology—the active involvement of a people in their own exploitation. Whatever the honorable intentions of community development during the war on Indian poverty, and there were many, the parentage of Indian community development is undeniable. Since World War II, social scientists had argued for the direct involvement of indigenous and underdeveloped peoples as a way to ensure economic and social support for development projects.

These ideas did not simply surface in 1964. Their genesis can be traced back through the administrators and social scientists who had influenced a more scientific approach to the Indian problem since the war. A premonition of the Rough Rock experiment come up as early as 1950 in interior department communiques. A manuscript from the papers of Assistant Secretary of the Interior Joel Wolfsohn argued for development of Indian communities along the Truman "Point Four" model:

> If the federal government is to terminate its special relation to Indians . . . the Indians must be helped to establish the kinds of *institutions* which are found in American life generally: . . . for example, before Indians can take over responsibilities for operating schools, Boards of Education, patterned after those of the State in which they live, must be authorized and established.[42]

In this manuscript were listed eleven types of institutions which it argued needed to be developed among Indians before their political and economic life could be integrated into the general American culture. Further on it read, "Many of these [tribes] will maintain a distinct cultural tone for many years, which I think will be good to prevent demoralization by too rapid assimilation."[43]

"Demoralization by too rapid assimilation" had become the major problem for Indian policymakers and a problem which was to be alleviated by the establishment of culturally sensitive institutions. Yet these institutions also would mimic those found in the mainstream of white America. The following statement by the 1948 Hoover commission serves as a preface to a generation of Indian policy planning. It operated and was effective whether one looks at the hard termination of the 1950s or the anti-poverty Indian programs of the 1960s:

> Assimilation is recognized as the dominant goal within the Bureau of Indian Affairs. Officials and employees, high and low, in Washington and in the field, agree on this objective. The feeling is as near unanimity as is possible on any issue of domestic policy . . . if Indians, officials and legislators were all opposed to assimilation it would still have to be accepted as a controlling policy. . . . Assimilation cannot be prevented. The only questions are: what kind of assimilation, and how fast.[44]

The answer given is couched in terms concomitant to the growth of new developments in social science:

> The thing that has been most lacking and most needed is Indian motivation. For 150 years policies have been imposed by the government. The policies have been Indian policies, not the Indian's policies. . . . It will not be easy to arouse Indian initiative and enterprise, but there is evidence that it can be done if the Indian people are drawn into the program building process themselves. . . . The Indian people of the reservations can be drawn into program building, and if they are drawn in they will have something to contribute. The biggest gain, however, will be their emotional commitment to the program and the increasing revival of hope, initiative and drive. If this can be done the largest obstacle to the success of an Indian policy will have been removed.[45]

This statement could have been written to apply to the community development movement in the 1960s. It is almost as if policymakers of the Udall years had finally found the correct time to create and implement the policies which were germinating after the Hoover commission recommendations of 1948.

The advent of the community-controlled school movement originated with Rough Rock and OEO, and continued with the development of over fifty other schools and Indian-controlled community colleges. Yet they were not originally designed primarily to increase Indian sovereignty but to "improve the *sense* [italics mine] of sovereignty."[46] Indian self-determination through community control of education was a continuation of the dominant conception of "reservation as campus—to be terminated when the graduates all attained a sufficient degree of civilization."[47]

NOTES

1. U.S. Congress, Senate, *The Education of American Indians: The Organization Question*, "Department of Interior Position Paper," 91st Cong., 1st sess., prepared for the Subcommittee on Indian Education of the Committee on Labor and Public Welfare (Washington, D.C.: U.S. Government Printing Office, 1970), p. 654.

2. Ibid., p. 459.

3. Ibid., p. 655.

4. U.S. Congress, House, Message of the President of the United States on the American Indian, 6 March 1968, 90th Cong., 2d sess., included as supplement to *The Education of American Indians: The Organization Question*, 91st Cong., 2d sess. (Washington, D.C.: U.S. Government Printing Office, 1970), p. 852. Also, see S. Lyman Tyler, "A History of Indian Policy," in *Report to the Secretary of the Interior by the Task Force on Indian Affairs*, (Washington, D.C.: U.S. Government Printing Office, 1973), p. 200.

5. Daniel P. Moynihan, *Maximum Feasible Misunderstanding: Community Action in the War on Poverty* (New York: Free Press, 1969), p. 22.

6. Ibid., p. 79.

7. Ibid., p. 87.

8. Ibid., pp. 35-36. Also see Charles Brechner, *The Impact of Federal Anti-Poverty Policies* (New York: Praeger, 1973), pp. 36-37; and Joel Spring, *The Sorting Machine: National Educational Policy Since 1945* (New York: David McKay, 1976), pp. 186-229.

9. Moynihan, *Maximum Feasible Misunderstanding* p. 36.

10. Herbert E. Striner, "Toward a Fundamental Program for the Training Employment and Economic Equality of the American Indian," in *Federal Programs for the Development of Human Resources* (Washington, D.C.: U.S. Government Printing Office, 1968), p. 296.

11. Brechner, *The Impact of Anti-Poverty Policies*, p. 80.

12. Sar Levitan and Barbara Hetrick, *Big Brother's Indian Programs—With Reservations* (New York: McGraw Hill, 1971), p. 90.

13. Ibid., p. 192.

14. Alvin M. Josephy, Jr., *The American Indian and the Bureau of Indian Affairs* (reproduced by the Indian Eskimo Association of Canada, Toronto, Ontario, 1967), p. 9.

15. Ibid., p. 16.

16. Ibid.

17. Sar Levitan, *The Great Society's Poor Law: A New Approach to Poverty* (Baltimore: John Hopkins Press, 1969), p. 264.

18. Speech by Philleo Nash, commissioner of Indian Affairs, delivered before the National Conference on Poverty in the Southwest, 25-26 January 1965, in Nash Files, Box 146, Archives of the Harry S. Truman Library,

Independence, Mo.

19. *Navajo Times* (17 March 1966): 10.

20. Speech before the Governor's Interstate Indian Council by Philleo Nash, 24 September 1964, in Nash Files, Box 146.

21. Ibid.

22. U.S. Department of the Interior, Economic Development Administration, Department of Commerce, "Indian Development Program," in *Toward Economic Development for National American Communities,* vol. 1, a compendium of papers submitted to the Subcommittee on Economy in Government of the Joint Economic Committee, 91st Cong., 1st sess., Vol. 1 (Washington, D.C.: U.S. Government Printing Office, 1969), p. 369.

23. James J. Wilson, "The Role of Indian Tribes in Economic Development and the Efforts of the Indian," in *Toward Economic Development for Native American Communities,* vol. 1, (Washington, D.C.: U.S. Government Printing Office, 1969), p. 373.

24. Bill King, "Some Thoughts on Reservation Economic Development," in *Toward Economic Development,* vol. 1, p. 71. King was the director of the Office of Community Development, Bureau of Indian Affairs.

25. U.S. Department of the Interior, Bureau of Indian Affairs, "Economic Development of Indian Communities," in *Toward Economic Development,* vol. 1, p. 352.

26. Broderick H. Johnson, *Navajo Education at Rough Rock*, foreword by Robert A. Roessel, Jr. (Rough Rock, Az.: Rough Rock Demonstration School, DINE, Inc.,1968), n.p. in foreword. Also, for a good overview of the development and progress of the Rough Rock community, see T. L. McCarty, "School as Community: The Rough Rock Demonstration," *Harvard Educational Review* 59, no. 4, (November 1989), pp. 484-503.

27. Robert A. Roessel, Jr., *Navajo Education in Action: The Rough Rock Demonstration School* (Rough Rock, Ariz.: Navajo Curriculum Center, Rough Rock Demonstration School, 1977), p. 4.

28. Ibid.

29. Ibid., p. 13.

30. Ibid., p. 9.

31. Johnson, *Navajo Education at Rough Rock*, p. 15.

32. Ibid., p. 11.

33. Ibid., p. 32.

34. Letter from Robert A. Roessel to Philleo Nash, 26 February 1962, in Nash Files, Box 143.

35. Ibid.

36. Roessel, *Navajo Education in Action*, p. 15. A "chapter" is a political division of the Navajo tribe, somewhat like a "county," which serves as a community meeting house and focus for tribally distributed local programs. While new chapters are in the process of forming, at the time of this writing there are 102 chapters in Navajoland.

37. Roessel, *Navajo Education in Action,* p. 19.

38. Ibid., p. 21.

39. Robert A. Roessel, Jr., panel discussion, *Proceedings of the National*

Research Conference on American Indian Education, Pennsylvania State University, 24-27 May 1967 (Kalamazoo, Mich.: Society for the Study of Social Problems, 1967), p. 79.

40. Johnson, *Navajo Education at Rough Rock,* p. 9.

41. Vine Deloria, address in *Proceedings of the National Research Conference on American Indian Education,* Pennsylvania State University, 24-27 May 1967 (Kalamazoo, Mich.: Society for the Study of Social Problems, 1967), pp. 88-89.

42. Unsigned document in Papers of Joel Wolfsohn Box 27, Archives of Harry S. Truman Library, Independence, Mo. (hereinafter referred to as the Wolfsohn Papers).

43. Ibid.

44. Ibid.

45. Ibid.

46. Monroe E. Price, "Lawyers on the Reservation: Some Implications for the Legal Profession," in *Toward Economic Development, vol. 1,* p. 199.

47. Ibid., p. 212.

7

Self-determination and Education Assistance Act: The Illusion of Control

Community contract schooling began as a thoroughgoing experiment along psychosocial lines that had been established in the decades since World War II. It was an attempt to use Indian participation to increase motivation and an attempt to educate Indians in their culture to prevent alienation and encourage self-image. It was an attempt, also, to inculcate a sense of sovereignty in order to mitigate termination psychosis. There were those, Indian and non-Indian alike, who had been drawn to the ideal of self-determination through the contracting movement. Many believed deeply in a commitment to Indian cultural, linguistic and political renascence. The record of the times provides, however, a more realistic framework within which to understand this movement.

In 1975 self-determination was codified as official policy language. Indian control of education and economic development was codified through the Indian Self-determination and Education Assistance Act (PL 93-638). This act provided the legal base upon which to regulate the existing practice of Indian people developing contractual agreements whereby the government would pay the local community to provide a variety of services, schools, clinics, tribal enterprises, public works, legal services, and so forth.

Much of the impact of PL 93-638 falls on the developing institution of the Indian contract-school which, after its start at Rough Rock, had grown considerably to include a number of primary, middle and high schools, and Indian-controlled community colleges. PL 93-638 was greeted with the same laudatory comment as Rough Rock had been in its first experimental months.

Margaret Szasz, who has written the only full-length treatment of contemporary Indian-education policy, concluded that community control, as it was formally conferred through PL 93-638, was a "remarkable achievement [and] would mean that the Indian people, after so many years of denial, had finally achieved the right to determine the education of their own children."[1] She claimed that through the process of hammering out legislation and applying political pressure during the difficult years after World War II, Indian leaders had learned a valuable lesson in how to gain control of education for their children.[2]

Education writers often view PL 93-638 with an optimism uncharacteristic of professionals accustomed to viewing federal Indian legislation with a jaundiced eye. Robert Cooper and Jack Gregory wrote that "we now stand on top of the mountain, about to walk down the other side into a valley of sunshine, with a new ray of hope called Indian self-determination."[3] Robert Havighurst, who has written extensively on Indian education policy issues, also concluded that self-determination was a great success and holds much promise. He wrote, "All in all, educators and planners in the U.S. can take some satisfaction in having developed, at long last, flexible and effective long-range policies for the Native Americans. Problems are still there, of course, but Native Americans are beginning to feel that they can control their own destiny."[4]

This chapter argues that the ideal of self-determination and community control of education, as authorized by PL 93-638, has been severely compromised by the nature of the language in which it was written and developed. Both the language of the law and its implementation severely limit legitimate self-determination. Indeed, the act works as much as a rhetorical device as an instrument to provide real opportunity to run a successful program. It offers Indian people an opportunity to show that Indian people can run their own institutions, yet it does not provide the flexibility or resource availability required for the efficient operation of a school. In addition, it allows the BIA bureaucracy to maintain indirect control and thereby some of the bureaucratic functions upon which its machinery depends. In PL 93-638 we can see the codification of a series of Indian self-help schemes intended to provide not only the illusion of control but the illusion of competency. Self-help has been reduced to a struggle for survival. Yet the problems endemic to contracting under PL 93-638 have not greatly harmed the rhetoric; rather, they have served to create it.

Basic to the idea of self-determination, as stated early in the body of PL 93-638, once again is the notion of control. Indian people are to have, through an "orderly transition from federal domination of programs for and services to Indians...effective and meaningful participation by the Indian people in the planning, conduct and administration of those programs and services."[5] The United States Code of Federal

Regulations, which guides the administration and implementation of PL 93-638 contracting policy through a variety of program guidelines (under the authority of federal law), states, "In carrying out its Education mission, the Assistant Secretary for Indian Affairs through the director shall...ensure that Indian tribes and Alaska Native entities fully exercise self-determination and control in planning, priority setting, development, management, operation, staffing and evaluation in all aspects of the education process."[6]

Stated this way, and carrying such concomitant definition, "control" is interpreted as having both power and broad community discretion. Yet analysis of the legislative records shows clearly that this kind of control is severely compromised. Self-contradictory language within the statute and implementation problems which have occurred since its passage both speak to the serious damage done to any legitimate conception of self-determination.

The Bureau of Indian Affairs' interpretation of the meaning of self-determination, and the extent of control which is thereby conferred through PL 93-638, lies at the root of problems in the implementation of the act. In addition, we can see upon careful examination of the legislative language that with all the purported sharpness of its aim toward increased Indian influence, there are key areas which Congress kept firmly in the grasp of the BIA.

The most representative example of the purported legislative intent of PL 93-638 is found in the form of the community-controlled contract-school, where the greatest expression of Indian control of education was to be located.[7] Implementation and contract compliance problems for these schools have multiplied and caused great difficulty for contract-school communities as the result of this language. Bureau education policy and procedure related to school contracting has ranged, in general, from obfuscation and inertia to administrative sabotage. Indian control of education, basic to the legal and historic meaning of self-determination, has been hamstrung by the high degree of discretion which the BIA still holds under PL 93-638. Its authority to decline contract applications is extensive and allows for little redress. Distribution and amount of funding is a persistent problem, which places contract-school operations in jeopardy time and time again. Payroll, hiring, job and supply security are a constant worry and a drain on administrative energy and time. Finally there are serious problems with the amount and quality of technical assistance for contracted operations which PL 93-638 says will be provided to the tribe/community by the bureau.

These difficulties suggest a reevaluation of the problem of conflict of interest in which the bureau may interpret any successful contracted operation as another example that the BIA itself is unnecessary. Any notion of self-determination which has more than rhetorical intent and which has legitimate self-rule at its root implies at least that tribal entities and communities would be taking responsibility now for program inauguration, continuation and progress. These programs would act partially without dependence on bureau control and thus would work to lessen the need for the bureau to act in its traditional patronizing capacity.

The problems which have arisen in connection with the implementation of PL 93-638 suggest that we analyze the progress of Indian community education contracting. The following is an attempt to begin such an analysis first by sketching highlights in the genesis of the school contracting movement, then by addressing specific problems faced by contract-school operations.

The emphasis on community control began as part of the growing cry for Native American self-determination in social and educational policy. From its start at Rough Rock, through the intensive codification of contracting procedure through PL 93-638, control of education and the call for greater self-determination have been taken up by a number of Indian school communities. They all owe a debt to the beginnings of the demonstration at Rough Rock during the early years of OEO and the War on Poverty, the central aim of which centered on the involvement of local communities in the solution of their own problems.[8]

Following these early experiments, other schools began to contract with the government for school construction and/or operation funds and technical support. In 1971 there were five contracted schools in operation. By 1975 there were fifteen, and by 1978 there were thirty-four.[9] Today there are more than fifty schools which have contracted for all or part of their operations in the United States, including Alaska.

In a July 1970 message to Congress, President Nixon called for a new Indian policy of "self-determination without termination."[10] The message encouraged the contracting of federal, social education and other services to the tribes and Indian communities themselves. Indians were to actively take part in the solution of their own problems and to control their destinies without government patronage, yet without the fear of abandonment. The traditional trust relationship between the tribes of the federal government was not to be altered despite this new reduction in patronage.

On January 5, 1975, following a string of legislative moves directed toward increased self-determination through community control, the passage of PL 93-638 signalled a supposed milestone in the move toward self-determination for Indian people. Title I of this law simply "provided for maximum Indian participation in government programs for Indian people."[11]

Though it had been hailed as a new direction in Indian policy, self-determination requires a closer examination. Robert Roessel himself warned in 1978, more than ten years after Rough Rock's beginning, that the method the BIA uses in allocating funds to support contract-schools makes only the strongest and most fearless communities want to enter such a financially uncertain funding arrangement. There is no doubt that there would have been many more contract-schools on the Navajo reservation if the method of funding such schools had been adequate and certain.[12]

Counter to these warnings and other systemic problems, which will be cited later, the rhetoric of self-determination in the text of PL 93-638 virtually rings with the promise of increased Indian control over the planning and administration of contracted operations. It is purported to be an act:

> to provide maximum Indian participation in the Government and education of the Indian people; to provide for the full participation of Indian tribes in programs and services conducted by the federal government for Indians and to encourage development of human resources of the Indian people; . . . to support the right of Indian citizens to control their own educational activities; and for other purposes.[13]

The act claims to be recognition that "parental and community control of the educational process is of crucial importance to the Indian people."[14] Further:

> The Congress hereby recognizes the obligation of the United States to respond to the strong expression of the Indian people for self-determination by assuring maximum Indian participation in the direction of education as well as other federal services to Indian communities so as to render such services more responsive to the needs and desires of those communities.[15]

With the passage of PL 93-638, the rhetoric of self-determination closed like a steel trap upon the imagination of contemporary writers and policymakers in American Indian Affairs. It has closed with as much power upon the Indian communities which have tried to create programs workable in the best spirit of self- determination.

The analysis contained here will be restricted to an examination of educational programs under the purview of PL 93-638 and concurrent BIA regulations regarding the contracting with the federal government of education services by Indian communities and tribes. By taking a first glance at the statements of purpose which form the first part of the text of the act, it would seem that this legislation was a revolutionary step away from government paternalism. However, a brief analysis of the specific provisions which follow in the text, as well as the documentary and testimonial record surrounding the statute's implementation, suggest that this, clearly, was not the case.

DISCRETION

Problems with the meaning of self-determination were not lost on those who reviewed Senator Henry Jackson's Senate Bill 1017, which preceded PL 93-638. The bill came under immediate fire for being unlikely to achieve the purpose for which it was apparently designed—increased local control. Funding and planning were kept under the purview of the Interior Department and the Department of Health, Education and Welfare (HEW). These departments would retain control through the judicious application of their discretionary power throughout the planning, procurement and operation stages of a contracted school operation.[16]

Congress received testimony from legal consultant Michael Gross during hearings on S. 1017. He argued that "the provisions of this bill would work to entrench and strengthen present systems for educating Indians rather than reform them." He continued on to cite the problem as it centered upon the notion of discretionary power. It must be recognized that the BIA's infrastructure has an interest diametrically opposed to Indian self-determination, for the latter will inevitably mean placing administration of Indian programs in Indian hands, thus making the BIA's over-blown bureaucracy largely superfluous.[17]

Gross noted that trying to implement legitimate self-determination through the Interior Secretary's discretion WAS likely to produce precisely the opposite effect than that intended. Instead of giving Indians control over their lives, the language quoted in the bill probably would serve to preempt the self-determination policy by giving "hostile elements in the Federal government control over the pace and characteristics of its implementation."[18]

The "Congressional Findings" and "Declaration of Policy" sections which form part of the preface to Titles I and II of the act as it finally took form, give the impression that control over Indian education would take a dramatic turn; that control clearly would now be directed by Indian people rather than the BIA. Yet the broad discretion which remains with the Interior Secretary later in the text of the act works to belie the early promises. The act says, "the Secretary may decline to enter into any contract requested by an Indian tribe if he finds that: (1) the service to be rendered to the Indian beneficiaries of that particular program or function contracted will not be satisfactory."[19]

Thus, the secretary retains the right to decide to his satisfaction, and without consultation, except such as shall remain avisory on the part of the contractee, what are the dimensions and characteristics of a fundable program. This is clearly far away from a notion of self-determination which included a right for Indian people to decide which program would be supported and which would not. While the preface to the act argues that the government will actively encourage self-determination, this discretionary power only outlines criteria for dis-couragement— criteria provided by the Interior Secretary through the BIA.

This federal discretionary power is expressed partly in the treat-ment of negotiation which lies at the heart of a true contract. Mel Tonasket, then president of the National Congress of American Indians, elaborated on this problem in 1977 when he testified at the Oversight Hearings on PL 93-638 that, "according to the Indian Self-determination Act, a negotiating process between an agency and a tribe is required. In reality negotiation never actually occurs because most programs have predetermined budgets....Funding levels are not negotiated."[20]

Wayne Holm, director of the Rock Point Community School, which began contract operations shortly after Rough Rock in a community thirty miles to the north, testified that BIA discretionary power was in fact strengthened by PL 93-638, making it more difficult for smaller communities to contract than had been the case prior to the act.[21]

In the development of this legislation, there is one clear case where we can point to a successful attempt by the BIA to strengthen and consolidate its discretionary power. In the 1973 hearings on S. 1017, commissioner of Indian Affairs Morris Thompson attempted to work language into the bill which would greatly increase the discretionary power of the BIA over contracting procedures. Section 106 (d) of the bill and the present statute provides that a contracting body may retrocede the program to the government should it find itself unable to carry out its programs. Thompson referred to this provision as it stood as "indirect" and argued for a more "explicit" approach.[22] He wanted to add a new section (109) which would allow the secretary to rescind a contract "in any case where he found that a tribe was operating a program so as to endanger the health, safety or welfare of any persons or so as to demonstrate gross fiscal negligence or mismanagement."[23] Although he added that he was "primarily referring to contracts with HEW in the health field," the language, as it is found now in section 109, makes no stipulation as to the limit of its intent.

Indeed, one could not argue against the sense of terminating a contract whose operation endangers health, safety or welfare. However, since there is no clarifying language in the law, the interpretation of danger here is left entirely up to the secretary, or more specifically, to his contract officers in the field. Furthermore, section 109 now reads that in such cases the secretary should, under regulations provided by him and after notice and a "hearing," have the discretion to terminate the contract immediately. This provision has developed without local participation in the decision except in the form of a hearing. It appears to effectively limit the scope of community control by virtually excluding Indian participation in a retrocession except a retrocession initiated by the secretary in which the provision then places Indian communities in an advisory rather than a bargaining capacity.[24]

The broad discretionary power invested in the secretary of the interior is evidence that Congress was less interested in a definition of self-determination which mandates self-government and more interested in allowing contracting to take shape without greatly altering the power and influence of the BIA. One of the other ways this power is exercised is in the criteria developed upon which an attempt to contract may, with broad powers retained in the Interior Department, be declined.

DECLINATION

PL 93-638, Title II, Part A, section 202 (sec. 4) reads:

> The Secretary of the Interior shall not enter into any contract for the education of Indians unless the prospective contractor has submitted to, and has had approved by the Secretary of the Interior, an education plan, which plan, in the determination of the Secretary, contains educational objectives which adequately address the educational needs of the Indian students who are the beneficiaries of the contract.[25]

In this way the educational criteria for the establishment of an Indian controlled school must be criteria which are acceptable, not necessarily to Indian parents and educators but to the Secretary of the Interior and the BIA. Yet, in the implementation hearings of 1977, Senator Melcher of the Senate Select Subcommittee on Indian Affairs inquired about the extent to which services delivery could be checked in the field. Replying to this, Mr. LaFollette Butler, acting director of the commissioner's self-determination staff, said:

> Senator, the difficulty that we have is that the contract proposal is often a great deal different than the operation the Bureau has. . . .
> So the standards and criteria for the program operation are really the tribe's. Whether or not the results will be better than an operation by the Bureau under its standards and criteria would be very difficult to arrive at.[26]

There are several problems here. First, the claim by Butler that declination and evaluation criteria are explicitly "the tribe's" is not to be found in PL 93-638. Rather, these guidelines exist in the Code of Federal Regulations, which, though growing out of the law, are subject to periodic revision without legislative review. The Code of Federal Regulations is a published set of documents which federal agencies use to implement the statutory mandate of Congress. These regulations are voluminous, usually covering hundreds more pages than the statutes from which they derive their authority. In all, they are developed within agencies such as the BIA, and as such are often more reflective of the needs of a particular agency and are more susceptible to alteration than the statutes themselves. Indeed, since they are the interpretation of the letter and spirit of congressional intent, subject to easier review and alteration than statutes, and the handbook by which the agency administers programs, they are extremely important documents. They carry much of the real weight of the law between their covers.

Relegation of this mandate to maximize Indian criteria for program quality to the flexible Code of Federal Regulations is reflective of the lack of confidence in self-determination. Furthermore, a violation of the code is not a violation of the law; it is rather simply a disregard for another administrative regulation whose enforcement is overseen by BIA administrators, not Congress. The power of declination criteria in the law lies firmly in the hands of the secretary of the interior. The criteria, as seen in the law and not the Code, are more clearly those of the Secretary, not the tribes' and communities'—the beneficiaries of self-determination.

Declination of contracts has, however, been the exception rather than the rule.[27] The bureau declination authority has been exercised largely in cases where the commissioner's office has decided that insufficient funds were available for the proposal. While not stated in the legislation as a declination issue, funding insufficiency has been used as a criterion for declination. Again the determination of sufficiency or insufficiency is made solely under the authority of the commissioner's office. Community/tribal involvement is not a part of the decision.[28]

Still, the declination threat is always there. According to testimony submitted by Birgil Kills Straight, secretary of the Little Wound School Board in Kyle, South Dakota, "BIA personnel are advocates for the government in terms of negotiating for the government and determining declination issues."[29] Again, according to Wayne Holm of Rock Point School:

> [While] PL 93-638 went a long way in reducing the number of
> reasons why the Bureau could decline to contract . . . as part of a
> trade-off, however, they appeared to raise the requirements for an

initial proposal. . . . New Boards must either start at the place it has taken existing boards several years to arrive at, or . . . decide contracting is simply too complicated and too risky. Too many boards have decided just that.[30]

FUNDING

The control, amount, and disbursement of funds to contract-school operations is a serious obstacle to legitimate community control. One of the most serious roadblocks to running a contracted program exists in the inability of the BIA to disburse funds in a timely manner such as might encourage the operation of orderly administrative procedures. Funds are not provided by advance payment each contract period. Rather, they operate on a cost reimbursable basis. Thus, any delay in the process of administering payments at the agency, area or bureau level results in a shortfall of cash at the site. A problem at any level can result in frozen paychecks, late bills, default and any number o distribution problems which keep staffing and supply in a constantly tenuous position. Community schools often are forced to run their accounts from the authority of letters of credit while waiting for reimbursement. According to Birgil Kills Straight of Little Wound School, cash flow problems are endemic to contract-school operations. Thus, not only the amount of funding remains tenuous but also the pace with which it is disbursed.

The problems faced by contract-schools in receiving funds are built with a purpose into PL 93-638. Section 106 reads that payments may be made either in advance or by reimbursement, as the secretary "deems necessary to carry out the provisions of this act."[31] Yet the secretary would have no real authority to pay in advance and must choose the cumbersome reimbursement method if he is to honor the intent of the next line of the statute. It reads, "The transfer of funds shall be scheduled consistent with program requirements and applicable Treasury regulations, so as to minimize the time elapsing between the transfer of such funds from the U.S. Treasury and the disbursement thereof by the tribal organization."[32] This provision was included in the act on the recommendation of the comptroller general in order to minimize the interest which would be lost to the Treasury by delaying payment of contract support funds until the last possible moment before the tribe or community must distribute its own payments.[33] This is clearly a provision pursuant to more general governmental contracting guidelines which state: "The government's basic policy in procuring property and services is to do so in a manner 'calculated to result in the lowest ultimate overall cost to the government'."[34]

Thus, following the spirit of maximum feasible participation, Indian communities are also allowed to participate maximally in the effort to save the government interest money. This comes, unfortunately, at the expense of running their schools with convoluted accounting, a constant risk of default, and closure. The alleged self-determination has been won at the price of administrative anxiety, staff insecurity, and thus low morale. In the Oversight Hearings, Wayne Holm commented on this problem. "Contract schools are already rather precarious places to work. Many good people are reluctant to work at a contract-school, not because of the generally lower salaries but because of real or potential problems in getting paid."[35]

However, insufficient funds are clearly as great a problem as their insecure disbursement periods:

> The BIA budgeting process takes care of raises and promotions for BIA administered programs but makes no provision for tribally contracted programs (638 funds are indiscriminately lumped with BIA administration and general funds). The consequence is that the BIA is unable to account for expenditures or demonstrate flexibility in negotiations with tribal governments. BIA negotiators tend to bully tribal negotiators into accepting lower funding because of the vaguely defined funds.[36]

Edison Laselute, governor of the Zuni Pueblo, stated that the "greatest problem is budgetary limitations." He saw BIA civil service pay climb while budgetary limitations imposed on the contract operation by the BIA caused the contract pay plan to "deteriorate."[37]

Clearly, the lack of meaningful input on BIA budgeting by tribes for contract support is evidence of the weakness of the claims for self-determination.[38]

CONFLICT OF INTEREST

Complaints about problems relating to PL 93-638 implementation have come from all corners of Native America. Writers sound a central theme concerning conflicts of interest between the tribes and the BIA over the implementation of this fact.[39] One of the loudest complaints centers on the lack of bureau accountability for the use of money earmarked for the provision of technical assistance to the tribes for contract operations. Too often this money goes toward the hiring of more bureau employees and too much is being spent on the operations at the area, rather than local level—the complaint being that the area is "too distant and too ignorant of most tribes' concerns to provide the kind of technical assistance [they] need."[40] Contract operations that run through the few scattered area offices cannot be as responsive as the local agency. For example, the area offices in Phoenix and Albuquerque, while supporting Navajo regional affairs, are far removed from the localities and special problems with which these localities must deal.

Much of the strength of PL 93-638 clearly is used to shore up the bulwarks of BIA control. Tribes which contract a program such that it is operated in an identical manner to the bureau-operated program it is replacing, displaces no bureau personnel, and operates to have the bureau run the program while working within predesigned BIA budgetary guidelines at the level of funding determined by the bureau: This type of program is the kind most likely to succeed.[41]

An advisory relationship has characterized much of the association between Indian communities and tribes and the BIA, that agency entrusted to carry out the provisions of PL 93-638.[42] Charles Johnson, from the Bering Straits Native Association, testified that:

> [While] the intent of Congress is most admirable for its attempt at providing some "self-determination" . . . the truth of the situation is that our "self-determination" is restricted by PL 93-638 because of its basic weakness of allowing BIA and HEW the latitude of making determinations as to the intent of the law. The Rules and Regulations written by these agencies only serve the bureaucratic purpose of extending their control over activities."[43] Johnson goes on to call PL 93-638 the "BIA self-perpetuation act."

Juanita L. Learned, chairperson of the Cheyenne-Arapaho Tribes of Oklahoma, cut to the heart of the jobs issue and conflict of interest. She testified that "in the BIA self-determination means job insecurity. If BIA employees are to truly develop Tribal capacity and allow Tribes to control services through contracting, then there should be a lot of people either working themselves out of a job or coming over to join us."[44]

The meaning of control has been severely compromised in the operation of self-determination as it has come to mean through the codification and implementation of PL 93-638.[45] Certainly, there is a problem when an agency is put in charge of the program which would, should it succeed, spell the beginning of the end of that same agency. The bureau may see no self-interest in increased Indian self-determination. Russel Barsh and Ronald Trosper have argued that the BIA has chosen to interpret the intent of PL 93-638 such that minimal damage will be done to the extensive control of the BIA. They write that two major reasons exist for failure of self-determination to confer increased local control: "(1) The flexibility that the act brings to contracting with tribes involves preserving substantial federal discretion to refuse to contract and to renege on contracts; and (2) the bureau interprets the reference to "trust responsibility" in the law as a mandate not to delegate any of its powers to regulate tribal resources."[46]

The secretary of the interior is given the power to refuse to contract if, in the opinion of the secretary, "adequate protection of trust resources is not assured."[47] Yet the fog shrouding the meaning of trust resource is thick indeed. While Indian people generally want their treaty-bound trust resources protected, there is no clear agreement on the meaning of this concept, despite the attempts—beginning in 1975—of the American Indian Policy Review Commission to define the limits of the trust. The issue is clouded in controversy, its meaning varying with the interpretation of the current administration in Washington.

The fact, however, that tribes are concerned that the government keep its promise to hold its resources in trust to protect natural and, some argue, human resources from harm, abuse or neglect, raises serious questions about the ultimate legitimacy of a policy of self-determination interpreted fully as the operation of self-rule, community control and legitimate sovereignty. This definition runs, perhaps, the risk of abrogating the federal responsibility to provide services for the protection of the trust. All of the issues raised here have profound consequences, not only for the interpretation of the meaning of self-determination but for the concept of trust which lies at the foundation of the U.S. government- American Indian relationship.

Returning to self-determination, however, we see that Indian leaders have disagreed on whether the concept is in itself an abrogation of the trust responsibility. Some will argue for more control over funding and administration of the contracted programs and, while loudly decrying the problems of PL 93-638 implementation, stand firmly by the concept of self-determination as a step in the right direction. Self-determination, through whatever means it is expressed or implemented has, for many Indian people, become a welcome addition to the policy language.

Perhaps they believe that the rhetoric will harden into something tangible, that the betrayal of faith in legitimate sovereignty and self-rule will one day fade away. They believe, perhaps, that the concepts of community control, self-rule and sovereignty one day will be fully realized in a subtle balance with respect to the crucial and sacred treaty agreements which established the present trust accord, and that self-determination will one day be raised from its present status as a vocabulary word. Indeed, the acting director of the Association of Navajo Community Controlled Schools testified: "We must constantly fight to maintain community control efforts, because we strongly believe in self-determination. It is not a fad with us. It is here to stay."[48]

Yet Indian educators and tribal leaders cited here are together in a chorus indicting the language, and especially the implementation of PL 93-638. There are always, however, disagreements within Indian communities as to the dangers inherent in the intent of any Indian policy legislation. Any turn-back of responsibilities of Indian education, welfare and resource development has been seen by some as the beginning of a new move to abrogate treaty-bound trust responsibilities and terminate federal reservation status once Indians have assumed sufficient control. Still, others have resisted contracting local operations because these tribal members also were BIA employees. People have feared loss of jobs when "massive RIF (reduction in force) meetings were held by BIA agency offices when tribal contracting of services became imminent."[49]

For some, the concept self-determination has become the watchword for the beginning of a great new era of local control. For most, PL 93-638, which is the vehicle that carried the concept into the policy arena, is the beginning of a new series of problems in the long history of government-Indian misadventure.

Self-determination has been used most often with an emphasis on its rhetorical rather than its realistic possibilities. It has continually worked as a part of attempts to signify the separateness, indeed, the claimed state sovereignty of roups and peoples within nations. More often than not, the cry for self-determination arose from the throats of those bereft of the benefit of political recognition and legitimate sovereignty. It did not appear often in the parlance of those describing a state of legitimate sovereignty already enjoyed. Self-determination is best understood as the language of the politically and jurisdictionally undernourished.

If we view the Indian Self-determination and Education Assistance Act in light of a definition of self-determination which works to maximize Indian community self-government and local conrol, we can begin to understand the support of those who value this as a fundamental human right. Many of those who supported this law were working to retain power for Indian people which had previously been usurped and held by the federal government through the Bureau of Indian Affairs.[50] Self-determination is a part of the long and convoluted history of reform which had sent U.S. policy toward Indian people through a series of convulsions—major changes in Indian policy: the Dawes Act allotting lands in severalty to individual Indians; the Indian Reorganization Act and Indian New Deal; and the period of termination during the 1950s nd early 1960s. All have come as a result of the real or perceived need of policymakers and opinion leaders to redress the purported wrongs, perpetrated by the then current policy. Yet, as Barsh and Trosper claim, "all major Congressional Indian programs, however well intentioned, have increased the power of the BIA. Each increase in the power of the bureau has decreased Indian welfare."[51]

It is common for policymakers and opinion leaders to be critical of programs and for these criticisms to emerge later in the shape of program alterations or full-scale reform. It is less common for those who are interested in, and who write about, Indian social and education policy to place criticism at the doorstep of reform itself. Yet, bound by administrative precedent and an overweening bureaucratic posture aligned for self-preservation, self-determination through PL 93-638 has become a design for stunted community control, marred by administrative intransigence.

Some may view a move toward Indian self-determination through the implementation of PL 93-638 as the beginning of an attempt to terminate federal trust dependent status, or may see it as a hope, a beginning of a new, stronger era for tribal and Indian community sovereignty. Yet, whatever the dreams of reformers or the nightmares of the reformed, the policy of self-determination grinds on. For all those who have envisioned its promise, still they must listen to Albert Trimble who held no deep confusion about the policy when he said:

> Do you know a few years ago, when I worked with the Bureau, there was one of the individuals [referring to a person who sat in a high echelon in the BIA] who said, before this contracting ever came out, he said, "just drop this on them and watch them die. Let them prove they can't operate these contracts."[52]

For Trimble, the illusion of control is no illusion at all.

The Self-determination and Education Assistance Act has provided the machinery for Indian control, but has given neither the flexibility nor the funds to insure truly successful programming. It has allowed the Bureau of Indian Affairs to keep contracted services in their bailiwick, yet does not interfere in the bureau's extensive bureaucracy. We could ask whether the extensive control of the bureau is an effort to protect Indian trust property and to insure that the responsibility to educate is properly dispatched. However, the problems inherent in running a school under these provisions greatly lessen this possibility.

We can attempt to understand PL 93-638 as the end of the line in a theme of competency development leading to termination. As such, PL 93-638 falls into a pattern, along with the light industrial development efforts on the reservation. In both cases, dual goals were involved—economic and social development. Both efforts were an attempt to remove some of the Indian welfare burden from the back of the government. They were also attempts both to inculcate values of self-sufficiency and to provide European-style institutional frameworks within which Indians could operate and which could provide a solid competency foundation. Both programs operated in the interest of a controlling entity. With industry, it was in the interest of the corporate hierarchy to hire inexpensive trainable Indian labor under liberal start-up provisions. With regard to contract education, the BIA maintained control of a program whose design prevented true Indian control from becoming very extensive. In addition, the programs were not able to really succeed. Funding and other limitations keep the contract-school on the periphery in the world of Indian schooling.

Both industrial and community-controlled school development were presented as a way to socialize Indian people. Yet socialization in both cases was more of a show, an attempt to create an illusion of competency. Neither have proven to be more than limited successes—for purposes of real change nor for propaganda. Yet they have had their impact. If nothing else, both have shown the flimsiness of design in the self-determination tapestry—where both control and competency are illusory. Nonetheless, it is often just this type of illusion which forms the basis of arguments for change, for renovation, for reform.

NOTES

1. Margaret C. Szasz, *Education and the American Indian: The Road to Self-determination since 1928*, 2nd ed. (Albuquerque: University of New Mexico Press, 1977), p. 197. See also Hildegard Thompson, *The Navajos' Long Walk for Education* (Tsaile, Ariz.: Navajo Community College Press, 1975).

2. Szasz, *Education and the American Indian,* p. 114.

3. Robert Cooper and Jack Gregory, "Can Community Control of Indian Education Work?," *Journal of American Indian Education* 15 (May 1976): 9. Written in 1976, Cooper and Gregory could not have been expected to see implementation problems coming, except as this policy was an outgrowth of the history of dysfunctional Indian education policy in general. This article is a call for Indian people to take a firm hand on the opportunity given through self-determination to gain control of education. Those who followed this advice during this period would discover that achieving self-determination under PL 93-638 was like trying to climb a greased pole.

4. Robert Havighurst, "Indian Education: Accomplishments of the Last Decade," *Phi Delta Kappan* 62, no. 5 (January 1981): 331. See also Robert Havighurst and Estelle Fuchs, *To Live on This Earth: American Indian Education* (New York: Doubleday, 1972).

5. U.S. Congress, Public Law " Indian Self-determination and Education Assistance Act," PL 93-638, 88 Stat. 2203, Sec. 3 (b).

6. See U.S. Code of Federal Regulations (25 CFR), Sec. 32.4 (c), p. 78.

7. See Curtis Jackson and Marcia Galli, *A History of the Bureau of Indian Affairs and Its Activities among Indians* (San Francisco: R & E Research Associates, Inc., 1977), p. 138. See also Margaret C. Szasz, *Education and the American Indian,* "Indian Controlled Schools," pp. 169-180.

8. Jackson and Galli, *A History*, p. 5. Also see Havighurst and Fuchs, *To Live on This Earth*, pp. 252-59. Havighurst and Fuchs discuss some of the early contract experiments: Rough Rock, Rock Point, and Ramah, on the Navajo reservation, and Rocky Boy in Montana. They present the importance on Rough Rock as the bellwether for these other later experiments in community control.

9. Thomas P. Flannery, "The Indian Self-determination Act: An Analysis of Federal Policy" (Ph.D. dissertation, Northwestern University, 1980). Flannery shows that the growth in contracted operations in schools slowed after the passage of PL 93-638.

10. Szasz, *Education and the American Indian, p.* 198.

11. Ibid., p. 201.

12. Robert A. Roessel, Jr., *Navajo Education, 1948-1978: Its Progress and Its Problems* (Rough Rock, Ariz.: Rough Rock Demonstration School, Navajo Curriculum Center, 1979), p. 200. Roessel found other inequities and wrote that "the present system of prioritizing school construction for Bureau of Indian Affairs schools is extremely unfair to contract-schools." He cites the lack of interest in contract-school construction on the part of consultants hired by the BIA, p. 201.

13. PL 93-638 (prefatory statement of purpose).

14. Ibid., Sec. 2 (a) (b) 3.

15. Ibid., Sec. 3 (a).

16. U.S. Congress, Senate, *Hearings of the Subcommittee on Indian Affairs,* 93rd Cong., 1st sess., (Washington D.C.: U.S. Government Printing Office) 1973, p. 238, testimony of Dillon Platero, Director, Navajo Division of Education.

17. Ibid., pp. 230-31, statement of Michael Gross, legal consultant.

18. Ibid. It is appropriate to note that some of the recommendations contained in this letter can be found as revisions to the final bill, whether it is as a direct or indirect consequence of this correspondence is not known to the author. For instance, attorney Gross argues that sections 102 and 103 of the bill—which reads, "The Secretary of the Interior is authorized in his discretion and upon request of any Indian tribe, to enter into a contract or contracts...to plan, conduct and administer programs" (see Stat. 1017, 102)—should read, "The Secretary of the Interior is authorized and *directed,* upon the request of any Indian tribe or organization supported by a majority of the Indian community affected, to enter into a contract or contracts..." (see p. 233). The emphasis *directed* is found in the final form of the bill; however, the suggestion that "organization supported by a majority," etc., is not a part of the act in this section.

19. PL 93-638, 88 Stat. 2203, Sec. 102 (a) (1).

20. U.S. Congress, Senate, Select Committee on Indian Affairs, (Oversight Hearings, 1977) 95th Cong., 1st sess., on the implementation of the Indian Self-determination and Education Assistance Act—PL 93-638, 7 June and 24 June, (Washington, D.C.: U.S. Government Printing Office,1977), p. 267.

21. Ibid., p. 471.

22. U.S. Congress, Senate, *Hearings of the Subcommittee on Indian Affairs*, 93rd Cong., 2d sess., (Washington,D.C.: U.S. Government Printing Office,1973), p. 36.

23. Ibid.

24. Ibid.

25. PL 93-638, Part A, sec. 202 (sec. 4).

26. U.S. Congress, Senate, *Oversight Hearings, 1977*, p. 35. Also see 25 CFR, Sec. 271.15, for the elaborated guidelines for declination criteria, where more explicit definition of self-determination is left in the administrative purview of the bureau, not Congress.

27. U.S. Congress, Senate, *Oversight Hearings,1977* p. 41. Through the first half of the fiscal year 1977, the BIA entered into $126,620,000 in contracts. Of this, Education accounted for $41,040,000; Social Services $34,389,000; Employment Assistance $3,622,000; Law and Order $4,639,000; Housing $2,284,000; Natural Resources $3,525,000; and Forestry $1,502,000; Indian Action Team Program $19,500,000.

28. Ibid., p. 29.

29. Ibid., p. 253.

30. Ibid., pp. 478-79.

31. Ibid., p. 256.

32. See PL 93-638, Sec. 106 (b).

33. Comptroller General of the United States, *Controls Are Needed Over Indian Self-determination Contracts, Grants, and Training and Technical Assistance Activities to Insure Required Services Are Provided to Indians* (U.S. General Accounting Office, 15 February 1977). Statement of the Comptroller General who advises, "see section 203 of the Intergovernmental Cooperation Act of 1968, PL 90-577, 82 Stat. 1101 and Treasury Department Circular No. 175 (3rd revision), 1973, 31 CFR 205."

34. U.S. Congress, Senate, *Hearings on S. 1017 and Related Bills*, 93rd Cong., 1st sess., (Washington, D.C.: U.S. Government Printing Office, 1973), p. 271; statement of Arthur Lazarus, Jr., representing the Navajo Tribe, Oglala Sioux, Nez Perce, Laguna Pueblo, Salt River Pima—Maricopa Indian Community, Hualapi Tribe, and Seneca Nation. See also 41 CFR Sec. 1-3.801 for general government contracting regulations.

35. U.S. Congress, Senate, *Oversight Hearings, 1977*, p. 478.

36. Ibid., p. 266.

37. Ibid., p. 466.

38. Ibid., p. 330.

39. U.S. Congress, Senate, *Hearings of the Senate Subcommittee on Indian Affairs*, 95th Cong., 1st sess., (Washington, D.C.: U.S. Government Printing Office,1977), p. 424, Statement of Caleb Pubgowiyi, President, Bering Straits Native Association and Kawerak, Inc. He writes: "Our region is 25,000 square miles, 85% of the total population is Eskimo. With that large a plurality, it would seem that we could control the politics, the economy, the education of our children and our destiny. Yet, that is not true. We are under the control of the merchants, the BIA, and the education system that is imposed on us....Now we

have a 'self-determination act' that looks like it is intended to allow us to determine our own course. But the joke is on us because it won't work unless changes are made that take the arbitrary choices away from the BIA" (p. 424).

40. Ibid., p. 449, statement of Cheyenne-Arapaho tribes of Oklahoma. See also testimony of Miccosukee Tribe of Indians of Florida. "BIA should be required to provide real TA (technical assistance) and not just add personnel to its own staff" (p. 349). In 1978 the Comptroller General issued a report indicting the BIA for inadequate "control over contracts, grants, and training and technical assistance (TA) activities." Ironically, this indictment did not argue the poor quality of TA as it affected the tribes, but as it reduced the effectiveness of the BIA to control the very programs whose control 93-638 had relegated to the tribes. See report of the Comptroller General of the United States, *Controls Are Needed.*

41. U.S. Congress, Senate, *Hearings of Senate Subcommittee*, 1977, pp. 268-69, testimony of Joseph De La Cruz, president, Quinault Indian Nation.

42. Ibid., p. 257.

43. Ibid., p. 426.

44. Ibid., p. 444.

45. Ibid., p. 328. Albert Trimble, president of the Oglala Sioux tribe writes, "The promised technical assistance from the BIA and the Federal government has failed to materialize, to the point that programs contracted for are constantly jeopardized by delayed, drawn out fundings, delayed vouchering for funding expended...in other words, BIA technical assistance has become a circus of complicated procedure that the bureau never experienced itself, when they managed the same programs" (p. 298).

46. Russel Lawrence Barsh and Ronald L. Trosper, "Title I of the Indian Self-determination and Education Assistance Act of 1975," *American Indian Law Review* 361 (1975): 364. Along with the intractability of contracting procedure, the authors argue that despite its "contractual" relationship, the onus for contract compliance lies squarely on the tribes. There is nothing in the law which makes the bureau or the government responsible for neglecting or ignoring fiduciary or procedural responsibilities of the contract.

47. Ibid., p. 366.

48. U.S. Congress, Senate, *Hearings before the Senate Select Committee on Indian Affairs,* 96th Cong., 2d sess., 1980. Statement of Mary Helen Creamer,

49. U.S. Congress, Senate, Hearings of Senate Subcommittee, 1977, p. 308, Testimony of Albert Trimble.

50. Barsh and Trosper, "Title I," pp. 361-95. See also Russel Lawrence Barsh and James Youngblood Henderson, *The Road: Indian Tribes and Political Liberty* (Berkeley, Calif.: University of California Press, 1980), for issues surrounding the development of tribal sovereignty and discussions of trust and treaty obligation.

51. Barsh and Trosper, "Title I," p. 362.

52. U.S. Congress, Senate, *Oversight Hearings, 1977*, pp. 346-47. Statement made by Albert Trimble from a discussion with Sherwin Broadhead who worked with commissioner Louis Bruce in the bureau.

PART III
Native American Dialogue and Impact

The three chapters in this part work toward an analysis of dialogue by Native Americans who directly affected and whose discourse changed and was changed by this policy during the late 1960s and early 1970s. At stake is the question of whose definition and whose vision of self-determination would prevail. The crucial issue of who, if anyone, may univocally represent Indian America would cause great strife in the 1960s and 1970s. A number of groups emerged with claims on a legitimate vision of Indian destiny. Aside from the issue of representation is the question of what a legitimate vision of self-determination would look like and to what needs self-determination policy would respond. Indeed, the conflicting visions have responded to the multifaceted potential of the concept as it has been mobilized to generate policy. While self-determination can be seen partly as a rhetorical device toward manipulative ends, it has always existed ideally as a claim on the right of native peoples to effect economic programs designed for development toward a strengthened sovereign claim, not eventual termination. A central issue here is the problem of consensus development, which would make challenging a politically powerful and unified stand on issues of sovereignty as it affects education and development. Since the early 1960s, tribal governments have been attempting to work out a consensus on the issue of self-determination. W. Roger Buffalohead has argued that what consensus does exist "provides only a thin veneer over reservation communities deeply divided by competing groups who often work at cross purposes....in the last two decades the Indian self-determination consensus has become dangerously dependent upon the federal dollar for its power and survival....Furthermore, this consensus has fended off anti-Indian thrusts at the local and national level and worked out compromises or stand-offs with con-frontational groups."[1]

This part also will attempt to treat the conception of trust as it serves to define the notion of self-determination. For to understand self-determination, we must be aware of the conceptual framework within which the federal-Indian relationship has been molded. In the historic nature of intergovernmental relations between the U.S. and Indian nations, there are certain limits put on the notion of Indian sovereignty upon which self-determination depends.

The trust relationship is a special one, yet we must be aware of how tenuous this relationship is. While Indian land is held in trust, this trust is very different from that notion of a trust which comes to us in the law, that it is a fiduciary relationship in which one person (the trustee) holds the title to property (the trust estate or trust property) for the benefit of another—the beneficiary. The question raised here is how self-determination is, in its usual manifestation, compatible with the trust relationship as history has taught us to comprehend it.

NOTE

1. Kenneth R. Philp, *Indian Self-rule: First-hand Accounts of Indian-White Relations from Roosevelt to Reagan* (Salt Lake City: Howe Brothers, 1986) p. 271.

8

Sovereign Self-determination

During the 1960s, in the heat of developing rhetoric over self-determination, various groups and individuals claimed to represent the will and interests of Indian people. Vine Deloria, who was present and active as an opinion leader and critic during these crucial years of policy development, locates the keystone of self-determination policy development in the Area Redevelopment Act (ARA) in 1961. The tribes were made eligible to receive federal funds under this act, later re-authorized as the Economic Development Administration (EDA), and it financed many community centers and tribal headquarters. Perhaps more importantly, the ARA-EDA included tribal governments on the same basis as county and local government, greatly increasing the emphasis on another leg in the table of self-determination, self-government of local tribal entities.[1] Economic development became and remained the focus of this policy, yet Native America was not unified as to the scope or purpose of development. In 1967 a clash in purpose occurred between opinion leaders and policymakers in Indian America. This conflict highlighted the tension surrounding the perceived meaning and educative purpose of self-determination policy.

Following the early success of ARA-EDA, the Johnson administration had promised to move forward in self-determination policy. Interior Department officials developed what was called the "Indian Omnibus Bill" of new economic legislation. Presented to Congress as the "Indian Resources Development Act," the bill received a poor welcome by many Indian leaders. Yet its main spokesperson was himself an Oneida Indian from Wisconsin, then commissioner of Indian Affairs Robert Bennett. Bennett would argue strenuously for economic policy which deemphasized relocation of reservation people for work in major industrial cities.

Instead he encouraged the on-reservation development of capital enterprise. He argued his case before the Indian Rights Association, a
Philadelphia-based Friend's Society Indian advocacy group, claiming
that Indian people "gain a comprehension . . . as to the nature of the
national economy and the means they must take to benefit from our
continuing economic growth. . . . The American Dream of the good life,
the active life, the life of self-determination should be the fire to rekindle
in the hearts of the first Americans."[2]

Bennett, who was the first Indian commissioner since the Grant
administration, and arguably the most powerful Native American, was
not the author of the Omnibus Bill, but became its spokesperson. In
February 1967 a group of Indian leaders were called to Washington to
react to the developing legislation. Conference leaders Norman Hollow,
Earl Old Person and Roger Jourdain signed a statement which reflected
the fears and distrust developing in Indian communities regarding the
intent of such development plans. Bennett's panegyric to the American
Dream notwithstanding, the conference participants noted their objection to the key point of the bill. Capitalization of Indian economic
development was to be leveraged by mortgage hypothecation of Indian
lands. This meant, in the words of the committee, that

> Implementation of certain of the managerial techniques of the
> proposed legislation affecting mortgage, hypothecation and sale of
> Indian lands, would render the Indian people immediately vulner-
> able to subversive economic forces, leading inevtably and inalterably
> to the prompt erosion and demise of the social and economic culture
> of the American Indian.[3]

The clash in vision between Bennett and this committee lies at the
real and metaphorical heart of both the issue of Indian representation
and the true direction of Indian social and economic and cultural destiny.
Economic development here meant the future participation of the Indian
in the American economic dream from which he had been previously
excluded. For the committee it meant the beginning of the end of Indian
life, because economic failure would cause the foreclosure on mortgaged
lands. Indeed, economic development could come to mean just about
anything, with little reference to the history or culture of people or land.
For example, in 1969 the Four Corners (Arizona, Utah, New Mexico,
Colorado) Regional Development Commission, along with the U.S.
Commerce Department and the four corners states, commissioned
Westinghouse Electric for a proposal to develop a self-contained partly
domed city on the Navajo reservation. "Our idea," said W. D. Brewer,
federal co-chairman of the Four Corners Redevelopment Commission,

"is to bring the twentieth century to the Indian, instead of forcing him away from his lands into faraway big cities." These plans, however, "foresee that the majority of the new population will come from throughout the U.S."[4]

Plans also ignored the Navajo traditional life in the area and the scarcity of water. Though somewhat unusual, this idea shared a common theme with other economic development plans. All envisioned accelerating modernization of Indian life to coincide with labor and industrial needs; all required Indian land and labor, but few, despite the rhetoric of self-government and self-help, acknowledged permanent Indian sovereignty in perpetuity over the pace, style, and nature of development structures. Indeed, meaningful self-determination, which would be incomplete without this sovereignty, was continually opposed by powerful timber, mining, cattle, and petroleum interests.[5] The development of light-industrial concerns, accelerating during the 1960s, was no different in this respect.

Perhaps due to the reaction of Indian opinion leaders, the Indian Omnibus Bill died without being enacted. More and more Indian people struggled during the 1960s to devise a coherent, if not completely pan-Indian strategy for advancing their peoples. Along with reservation industrial development came the host of education and community development programs of the War on Poverty. It is during this time that Indian people developed more strongly than ever a bifurcated awareness both of their cultural heritage *and* their political and legal rights. On one hand, their participation in generic minority poverty programs identified them more strongly as another American domestic racial minority. Programs were purchased at the price of this status.[6] However, at the same time Native Americans were redefining the importance of unique tribal rights to treaty-won domestic sovereignty within the larger national sovereign.

This changing consciousness would serve to waken a large portion of Indian America from the anesthetic of false self-determination to the possibility of utilizing the structure of this ambiguous policy to enforce a definition which would serve economic and social development goals without raising the specter of termination. Indeed, this changing view would serve as catalyst for the reversal of terminated lands and the reopening of treaty based land claims.

As it developed through official government policy, self-determination would be the practice of placing competency education structures in the hands of Indians, with the outcome being the same—termination.[7] As it developed along with new sovereignty and treaty obligations claims, self-determination emerged as a weapon both against government paternalism and eventual termination.

During the 1960s and early 1970s, Indian people gained increasing awareness of their powerlessness and poverty and of their inherent rights to freedom and happiness, guaranteed not only to all Americans by the Constitution but to Indian people alone as the heritage of their treaty based rights. The knowledge of both these realities would result in hundreds of demonstrations of disapproval by Indians from coast to coast, in Alaska and by native people in Canada as well, with similar grievances and frustrations.

The occupation at Wounded Knee, and subsequent death and imprisonment of many of its leaders, was perhaps the loudest thunderclap in a continuing storm which also included the occupation and sack of the BIA headquarters at the end of the Trail of Broken Treaties caravan to Washington, and numerous standoffs and violent confrontations in the Pacific Northwest over fishing rights. Yet during this period of intense conflict over basic sovereign rights, the policy of successive administrations in Washington saw the access of Indians to their treaty rights as a prize, in the words of commissioner Morton during the Wounded Knee occupation, to be won "by the Indian himself climbing steadily rung by rung from a base of opportunity unmatched for any group in the society of the world."[8] In some ways like Booker T. Washington urging newly freed slaves to develop economic power in service to white capital as a method of gaining political power, Morton and others wanted Indians to struggle for economic access to rights which have no price. This ideology of self-help proceeded to fill out the picture of self-determination policy from the quieter years of the War on Poverty to the strife torn early 1970s.

In October 1966 George McGovern, then Senator from South Dakota and member of the Senate Indian Affairs Subcommittee, introduced a Senate resolution which highlighted increased desire that Indians should participate in decisions concerning their development. Self-help and self-determination went hand in hand to emphasize the new direction of policy. President Johnson had led with a speech in March of that year which attempted to allay the persistent Indian fears of termination but managed to obfuscate the point enough not to alarm powerful pro-termination members of Congress. In that speech he proposed "a new goal for our Indian programs; a goal that ends the old debate about termination of Indian programs and stresses self-determination; a goal that erases old attitudes of paternalism and promotes partnership and self-help."[9]

This language, while it encouraged lawmakers like McGovern, must have been cold comfort to Indian leaders who knew that "the old debate" on termination policy was the only thing that kept it from happening wholesale. They knew the old debate also was not really about termination of programs but about termination of responsibilities to protect lands and resources from sale to whites. And few Indians, no matter how traditional or radical, have hated paternalism more than termination. Much later, in opposition to Nixon in his bid for the White House, McGovern would chide the man who made self-determination policy a legal reality, if not a household word. He claimed the Nixon policy was long on promises but short on performance.[10]

The rhetoric of self-help, with its ambiguous relation to competency development and termination, collided in the 1960s with Indian theoreticians who would carve out a more meaningful interpretation. Melvin Thom was one of these early leaders. He spoke at the American Indian Capital Conference on Poverty in May 1964 and represented what would be the beginning of the influential National Indian Youth Council (NIYC). Thom, a Paiute from Walker River, Nevada, was president of this group when he spoke. He recognized the need to alleviate poverty but stressed that development not occur which would compromise a future as Indians with sovereign rights. He said, "Our recognition as Indian people and Indian tribes is very dear to us. We cannot work to destroy our lives as Indian people."[11] He recognized that Native American culture and traditions brought tribal peoples through the period in which they were practically annihilated and it is this which would be the essence of their survival. So, as early as 1964, Thom and others expressed a renewed theme of cultural and tribal sovereignty which had existed since treaty days to support Indian community and political existence. For the NIYC, Indian poverty could not be bought out at the expense of Indian sovereignty and cultural survival.

Thom was expressing a vision of sovereignty which was radically different from that which developed as government self-determination policy. Felix Cohen, who was the legal architect of the Indian Reorganization Act (IRA), commented on the nature of Indian self government in 1949. He argued it is not something that "friends of the Indians" can confer upon them. It is a sovereign right. Cohen reminded us of the lessons Jefferson and Franklin learned about self government from the Iroquois. He emphasized a definition of self-government which would be prosecuted by those most closely affected by its decisions. As it turned out, the tribal governments which he helped form would become the object of criticism by traditional grass-roots Indians who complained during this period that tribes mainly served the interests of white corporate power, not, as W. E. B. DuBois had phrased them, "those most nearly touched" by law.[12]

The problem of the Indian polity lies at the heart of the problem of self-determination. Indians during the 1960s were becoming painfully aware that tribal government could operate successfully without the participation of all community members. The representative nature of tribal government was a radical departure from the more participatory nature of traditional consensus based decision making. In fact, the problems which were re-identified during the 1960s—poverty, job discrimination, tribal jurisdiction confusion, religious persecution, reservation labor exploitation, bad education, hunting and fishing rights violation, resource exploitation—all were identified as problems which could be solved by more self-determination.[13] Yet these problems continued despite the European style tribal governments established in the 1930s under the IRA. The IRA had radically changed Indian life and put a stop to wholesale allotment. However, persistent inability of the majority of Indian people to flourish during this period led to widespread dissatisfaction with tribal governments as representatives of the Indian people and their interests.

For the time during which Indian people occupied Alcatraz during the early 1970s, the people who made that gesture did so on the grounds that Native American sovereignty lay in the traditions of the people and their heritage. These they felt were not well represented by European style tribal governments or schools. Indeed, the chief activity in the occupation was the practical and symbolic act of teaching—teaching specific and pan-Indian educational, political and spiritual activities. The Indian radicals who took the island realized, as well as did the architects of termination, how important education is to the prosecution of any political policy. Yet the emphasis for the developing Indian nationalist movement was education in sovereign self-determination, not self-help and economic competency.[14]

The Indian nationalist definition of self-determination emphasized tribal control of resources and economic development and the restoration of treaty lands. Many of the earliest struggles of the 1960s centered around fishing rights on the Northwest Coast, principally in Puget Sound and the middle Columbia River. Indian fishing camps were bulldozed and armed conflict ensued along the rivers between tribal members and state officials.[15]

These early "fish-ins," styled after the civil rights resistance, were the beginnings of large scale public awareness of the nationalist movement. But they were not the first recognition nor resistance on behalf of treaty rights and Indian sovereignty. Such leaders as Wallace "Mad Bear" Anderson, a Tuscarora, struggled during the 1950s for the same ends. In 1957 he helped the Mohawks fend off the New York State income tax on the grounds of sovereignty conflict. He led a group to the St. Regis county courthouse where he proceeded to tear up summonses which were about to be issued to tax delinquents. A struggle ensued and Anderson was spirited away by a group of Indian women who were present in support of the action. In 1958 he fought New York Power Authority chairman Robert Moses' plan to build a reservoir after the state had condemned 1,383 acres of Indian land. Anderson and others blocked surveyors' transits and deflated tires. When the Power Authority tapped leaders' telephones, Tuscaroras switched to speaking their tribal language. Impoverished Indians were offered $3 million for the land and turned it down. In 1959 the Federal Power Commission said the Indians did not have to sell, and the tribe didn't. The *Buffalo Courier-Express* wrote that "Mad Bear, more than anyone else, was responsible for the tribe's decision."[16] A considerable volume could be devoted to the career of Wallace "Mad Bear" Anderson. Suffice it to say, he and others in the postwar period were among the developing forces who were willing to fight or be jailed in support of their sovereign nationhood and treaty rights.

Tribal control, for the early Indian nationalist movement, could have little meaning without greater tribal sovereign recognition. Extended themes of Indianness and tribal development continued efforts by Indian groups to gain fundamental control of their resources and the destiny of their people. Resource control and educational control developed into key themes toward legitimate self-determination. Yet these areas both developed in ways that would divide the Indian community with respect to the goals of the tribal sovereign. For example, 1975-76 was a crucial year both for Indian educational control and natural resource control. During this time the American Indian Educational Assistance Act was codified, officially establishing guidelines for tribal and community control of schools. Yet we have seen that despite their successes, many Indian people and leaders saw the effect of this act as a method of locking Indian contracting for school services further in the stranglehold of the Bureau of Indian Affairs.

In 1970 Helen Schierbeck, a Lumbee who directed the U.S. Office of Indian Education, would speak confidently of the need for more tribal control of education and more community cultural education. She wrote partly in response to the upswell in nationalism. "The need is apparent," she said, "and if Alcatraz and Littleton are indicative, the hour for action is growing late."[17] The form of control which developed, however, during the 1970s would severely restrict the goals to which she addressed herself.

Similarly, in 1976 Indians had established the Council of Energy Resource Tribes [CERT]. It developed as a method by which the council, consisting of the tribal chairmen of major resource holding reservations, could better control the use, leasing and development of the tribes' resources. Yet through its development CERT, the "Indian OPEC," was criticized by Indian opinion leaders for its insensitivity at best, and at worst, for its collusion with corporate America, in a new sellout of Indian land and power. Oglala Sioux attorney, P. Sam Deloria, cited how CERT was quickly embraced by "federal agencies, corporations and foundations, and has become the spokesman for Indian tribes, not only on energy issues but on many other issues only tangentially related to energy."[18] He also claimed that CERT staff often acted to represent Indian interests in Washington when no such representation existed. Thus, he claimed that "federal policymakers have effectively delegated an important part of the federal trust responsibility to a private agency CERT, out of reach of and unaccountable to the vast majority of Indian tribes."[19]

Indeed, frustration over the failure of efforts like CERT to materially effect grass-roots Indian life have led to continuing, if diminished, resistance on the part of Indian nationalists. Dissatisfaction with the level and quality of Indian control through the contracting process and PL 93-638 fueled the Indian Survival School movement, which used community and alternative education funds during the 1970s to establish schools with a radical vision of Indian individual and tribal personhood, with curricula and teaching methods adhering to cultural values *and* an emphasis on tribal sovereignty and nationhood in a unifying vision.[20] During this period Indian voices were being heard in support of strengthened sovereignty through such periodicals as *Wassaja*, published by the American Indian Historical Society, and *Akwasasne Notes,* a digest of Indian political issues taken from news outlets across the country and published by the Mohawk in New York. The first issue of *Wassaja*—January 1973—placed a statement on self-determination as its opening editorial. In this the editors claimed self-determination must include greater economic development, health and welfare, but these must not be discussed separate from resource control and tribal treaty rights which lay at the heart of sovereignty.[21] Dedicated to this goal, *Wassaja* and *Akwasasne Notes* represented an increasing mobilization of Indian intellectual leadership, acting in a critical capacity to identify the problem of a political philosophy—self-determination, developing without its crucial catalyst for meaningful expression, treaty-bound sovereignty.

Four months later the editors of *Wassaja* would print an editorial entitled "Fake Self-determination." This piece catalogued the frustration of continued BIA paternalism and token Indian participation. It also reiterated the theme that Indian intellectual leadership should control the pace and content of policy development. Finally, the article recounted the frustration of seeing continued human and material resource development which was counterproductive to meaningful tribal life.[22]

Indian critics developed in opposition to Indians who were loyal to the BIA and the administrations in power during this period. For them, self-determination was a tool used by the powerful white interests to manipulate illusory Indian compliance with policy, again, by involving some Indians. Policy, however injurious to tribal interest, could be justified on the grounds of "democratic, community participation." Vine Deloria, speaking of Interior Secretary Morton in 1973, argued that the "present administration [Nixon's] has closed its doors and ears to all but a small clique which is under the control of Robert Robertson, director of the National Council on Indian Opportunity." He went on to indict the Nixon administration Indian office as the most closed in his memory. It is further irony for the administration which had passed self-determination legislation in 1975.[23]

The Teton Sioux and others who occupied the Wounded Knee site during part of 1973 issued a statement which clearly defined their position on the purpose of "fake self-determination." They claimed that their tribal chairmen acted as government stooges, selling out rights and resources without which self-determination is meaningless. In the "Teton Sioux Manifesto," they wrote, "Again we must emphasize that we do have brains and fully understand why the Nixon administration supports the tribal chairmen, even while many of them commit criminal acts against their own people."[24]

Sovereignty and its protection remained of paramount importance to these and other critics of self-determination policy. Without sovereignty it is meaningless, a competency scheme. Tribal councils, while duly constituted, represented for these critics a collaborator class, collaborators with a government which was intent on the dissolution or at least the continued exploitation of Indian human and resource capital. These years highlight the problem of establishing a voice for Indian destiny, where Indian intellectuals, politicians and critics vie for the right to claim ownership of legitimate discourse on behalf of true tribal interest.

NOTES

1. Vine Deloria, Jr., and Clifford Lytle, *The Nations Within* (New York: Pantheon Books, 1984), p. 215.
2. "Excerpts from Remarks by Robert L. Bennett, commissioner of Indian Affairs, Before the Indian Rights Association on April 26, 1966,"*Indian Voices,* April/May 1966, pp. 10-11.
3. Alvin M. Josephy, Jr., *Red Power* (New York: McGraw-Hill, 1971), p. 68.
4. *Akwasasne Notes,* June 1969, n.p., quoted from *U.S. News and World Report,* 23 June, 1969.

5. Jack D. Forbes, *Native Americans and Nixon* (Los Angeles: Native American Studies Center-UCLA, 1981), p. 39.

6. Deloria, *The Nations Within*, p. 216.

7. Ibid.

8. Forbes, *Native Americans and Nixon*, p. 119.

9. Josephy, *Red Power,* p. 59.

10. Forbes, *Native Americans and Nixon*, p. 65.

11. Josephy, *Red Power,* p. 55.

12. Ibid., pp. 17-19.

13. *Wall Street Journal,* 30 April, 1969, p. 46.

14. Jack D. Forbes, "Alcatraz: What Its Seizure Means," in *Indian Truth* 47, no. 3, September 1970:14-15.

15. Josephy, *Red Power,* p. 80.

16. *Akwasasne Notes,* September 1970, n. p., article on Wallace "Mad Bear" Anderson from *Esquire,* August 1970.

17. Helen Schierbeck, "Indian Education: A Challenge for the Church," in *Indian Truth* 47, no. 3 (September 1970): 2-6.

18. *Wassaja,* January/February 1983, p. 31.

19. Ibid., p. 32.

20. "Education the Indian Way," *Indian Truth,* no. 217, (April 1977): 5.

21. "Self-determination," *Wassaja,* January 1973, p. 3.

22. "Fake Self-determination,"*Wassaja,* June 1973, p. 2.

23. Vine Deloria, Jr., "Half-truths Charged to Morton,"*Wassaja,* June,1973, p. 7.

24. "Teton Sioux Manifesto," reply of the Teton Sioux to the White House Letter on Negotiations (at Wounded Knee),*Wassaja,* July 1973, p. 10.

9

The Wrong Voices

Felix Cohen, in his classic statement on the meaning of Native American self-government, called Indian tribes the "miner's canary" of American democracy. "When it flutters and droops we know that the poison gases of intolerance threaten all other minorities in our land. . . . We have a vital concern with Indian self-government because the Indian is to America what the Jew was to the Russian Czar and Hitler's Germany."[1] Coming from a managerial liberal like Cohen, an architect of the IRA and arch-New Dealer, his Jeffersonian sentiments about the virtue of inexpert rule sound almost disingenuous. Indeed, liberal thinking about the Indian has always seen his welfare as a polestar by which Euro-America may run its moral/political course. As valuable as this sentiment has been for building generous structures of urban and reservation anti-poverty, pro-education programs, it has been less than perfect as a template against which a vision of unique Indian sovereign self-determination would be drawn.

Along with radical protest at such places as Wounded Knee, the BIA headquarters and along the fishing grounds of the Pacific Northwest, successful lobbying efforts by tribes encouraged the passage of the Self-determination Act in 1975, more closely, if guardedly, outlining BIA delegation of educational authority. In the Northwest Judge George Boldt gave treaty Indians the right to 50 percent of the salmon and steelhead trout in state waters. These other areas of movement indicate some correlation between resistance and legal process. Indian press interests divided on these issues: *Indian Truth* referred to such protest as media events, while *Wassaja* was hailing the activities and supporting their effect on a somnambulant public.[2]

The Declaration of Indian Purpose, submitted at the American

Indian Chicago Conference in 1961, often has been referred to as the first pan-Indian statement of a desire for greater self-government. It is an early statement by the representatives from sixty-seven tribes gathered on the relationship between self-government and self-determination. This relationship has unified "friends of the Indian" and radical Indian alike.[3] Where disunity has occurred along the conservative to radical spectrum, it has occurred over the degree to which the goal of self-government must be allied to the goal of greater Indian political sovereignty.

A number of influential advisory groups continued or emerged during this period, with great agreement on some issues but little on others. Clyde Warrior of the National Indian Youth Council, in a speech before the National Advisory Commission on Rural Poverty, reiterated the theme of self-government and nonexpert grass-roots self rule, but also lashed out at tribal chairmen he called "yes men" of the federal bureaucrats.[4]

The American Indian Task Force, which had served as editorial board for Edgar Cahn's *Our Brother's Keeper* report, also reiterated the theme of self-government and self-determination, but not without a pro-treaty rights proviso.[5] Other groups such as the National Tribal Chairmen's Association (NTCA) and National Council of American Indians (NCAI) supported Indian gains in Washington but were less univocal over time regarding the pursuit of treaty sovereignty. During the 1970s much dissension continued regarding who represented the will of Indian people. At the National Conference on Self-determination, sponsored by the NCIO in 1971, during discussion regarding the creation of a cabinet level Department of Native American Affairs, some Indians argued that all urban and off-reservation Indians be excluded from this group. Despite the protestations of those who resented the exclusion of these groups, the National Tribal Chairmen's Association was born, excluding what its first president Bill Youpee called the "wrong Indian voices." Thus continued deepening fissure between the reservation and off-reservation Indian.[6]

These "wrong voices" were to include many urban activists who had developed their thinking in the Indian ghettos of St. Paul, Los Angeles and Chicago, many the sons and daughters of tribal people who had been relocated after the war and found an alien and hostile America in urban life. This group, among whom were the founders of the American Indian Movement (AIM) and former participants of the fish-ins, were increasingly alienated from conservative tribal spokespersons and federal administrators. Nixon's Interior Secretary Rogers saw these groups as a distinct threat. He wrote, "on the fringe of developments in self-determination policy, and growing up in the wake of the black militant movement is a revolutionary Indian element. Dramatic violence is their pattern. The occupation of Alcatraz, NIKE sites, the federal office building in Washington, the Village of Wounded Knee and others fall into it . . . .They do not represent a group with whom the government can contract or serve."[7]

The persistent division over the treaty rights issue continued to widen during the 1970s. Jack Forbes claimed that many of the divisions split along economic class lines and age lines. He argued that the Native movement had divided roughly along four lines. "On the left are the 'traditionalist-nationalists' whose loyalty is to their tribe, the Indian race and then to the U.S. (or Canada). . .also on the 'left' are the secular nationalists, the urban militants who are, however, less religious. A third group are the 'tribal pragmatists.' These fill the ranks of tribal councils. . .the tribal chairmanship." These are Indians whose concern for sovereignty is dampened by their loyalty to the U.S. and its administrative arm of the BIA. They are not assimilationists, but resist state encroachment on their reservations because "their power and income derive from tribal self-government. Therefore they seek to maximize the power of their governing bodies." In addition, he added that the "Americans of Indian descent, [are] people who would have been absorbed into the white community long ago, had it not been for prejudice . . . income or . . . jobs obtained because of Indian ancestry."[8]

Members of NTCA, who Forbes claimed often belonged to the latter group, came often into direct confrontation with the Indian nationalists over such actions as the BIA takeover and the Wounded Knee occupation. Indeed, part of the Wounded Knee reaction stemmed from grassroots hatred of Oglala tribal police and tribal Chairman Dick Wilson.

Indian politics took shape around these varying ideological positions. Traditional nationalists were often tribal spiritual leaders who exerted significant power. Radical secular nationalists were at the forefront of a very public struggle which was both sensational and significant for its impact. The Indian political center held power in the major councils such as NCAI and NTCA and was officially recognized in Washington. The "Americans of Indian descent," as Forbes referred to them, often played reservation power politics from a base of corporate influence and big money. Self-determination came often to mean very different things to each of these groups.

Until his death in 1972, traditionalist Dan Katchongoa was leader of the Sun clan in the Hopi village of Hotevilla. He was among the many influential spiritual leaders across Native America who opposed the formation of tribal councils after the IRA of 1934. For Katchongoa and other traditionalists, Indian selfhood would be forever compromised by a European representative, that is to say, nonconsensual, form of government. Traditionalist notions of self-government often could not be separated from their belief in sacred and secular traditions. He said, "Now this tribal council was formed, illegally, even according to whiteman's laws. We traditional leaders have disapproved and protested from the start."[9] It is evident that the nature of self-government offered by white Americans through this aspect of the Indian New Deal had active and influential opponents. Their opposition lay in part with the belief that self-government is inseparable from tribal personhood. It was not a structure of representation, but a rooted tradition. This belief has placed slippery ground under the feet of government self-determination advocates throughout the postwar era. The power of the traditionalists was increased by their community standing, knowledge of language, medicine and general power of age veneration, if not by BIA bureaucrats who worked more successfully with younger, BIA-educated reservation Indians.[10]

The middle-road Indian leadership was perhaps better represented in the ranks of tribal council membership and the NCAI. For middle-road Indian leadership, tribal self-government was more legitimate, despite its separation from traditional structure. At the 34th Annual Convention of the NCAI, the "Sovereignty Committee" met. They concluded that sovereignty was of such a nature that each tribe could "take it upon itself to determine the nature and extent of sovereignty it would exercise."[11]

This fragile notion of sovereignty held that tradition, history, treaties and law notwithstanding, tribal destiny is subject to the whim of a passing vote by an IRA tribal council. The NCAI obviously had much more faith in these councils to decide the future of the sovereign than any of the traditionalists.

In July 1975 Richard La Course wrote that the position of NCAI lay somewhere between the right wing assimilationists and left-wing nationalists in the tribes. NCAI, he argued, espoused a "third ideology, a nation-within-a-nation ideology. . .which propounds either economic dependence or interdependence within the dominant national government."[12] Yet, NCAI maintained no clear position on how sovereignty would be developed and maintained in this quasi-dependent relationship. La Course had great faith that quasi-sovereign status was safe both from hostile forces on the tribal council and from the federal government. Yet tribal council leadership, many of whom were also members of NCAI, left ambiguous the future of sovereignty and often appeared hostile to its further definition. Elmer Savilla, executive director of NTCA, issued a public announcement in 1983, warning about the imminent formation of a "Coalition for Tribal Sovereignty." He may have had reasons to dissuade tribesmembers from joining, but the ones he offered are curious. He warned about the development of enemies that keep Indians "divided in our opinion on the many issues."[13]

Savilla appeared here to warn about the danger of a developing discourse on sovereignty which might vary from the official position of NTCA. This appears not extremely healthy for the development of what NCAI argued would become a more representative, therefore meaningful, definition of quasi-dependent sovereignty. Many middle-ground Indian politicians in NCAI appeared indeed during this time to hold two contradictory positions. They appeared to desire on the one hand a moderate definition of sovereign self-determination, somewhere "between paternalism and self-determination."[14] Yet they also argued in 1977 for a position which favored "justice through sovereignty," and some members offered criticism of government harassment of the militant activist American Indian Movement.[15] Yet the weight of middle-ground Indian politics looked with distaste upon the effort to open dialogue with Indian groups and individuals who were not close to the standard tribal government structures. The middle ground kept both the spiritual and secular sovereigntist "fringe" at arm's length throughout years of self-determination in the 1970s.

Indian self-determination had been compromised by an increasingly uncomfortable reality. A class of Indians had developed who did not identify their interests as separate from the corporate and social interest of the white world which surrounded them. Jack Forbes writes:

> As tribal governments become more bureaucratic, with more Indian employees receiving incomes sharply at variance with the general population, a new contradiction emerges to dominate Native life. The local rulers, the local police, the local wealthy will all be Indian, but they will be enforcing the decisions reached by the dominant society or acting out in their own lives the values which they have learned as pupils of that alien society.[16]

Increasingly this class of Indian politicians found their way into positions of great power and influence throughout this period in which having an Indian administrator meant that an agency was conforming to the goal of increased self-determination.[17] The archetype Indian power broker is perhaps "American of Indian descent" W. W. Keeler of the Cherokee. Keeler's role, recounted earlier, included his appointment to chief by Harry Truman. We remember his considerable control, as both chief and executive officer of Phillips Petroleum in Bartlesville, Oklahoma. From 1949 into the 1970s, Keeler built an economic empire, financed with Cherokee tribal funds, little of which benefited the economic straits of his tribesmembers. By 1970 Cherokee income was still $2,000 per year, and though comprising only 12 percent of the population, they made up 35 percent of the welfare rolls. The "Keeler Complex," a group of lavishly appointed buildings near Tallequah, Oklahoma, provided in 1970 stark contrast to the poverty of the tribespeople whose coffers financed its development.[18] In 1969 George Groundhog, chairman of the Original Cherokee Community Organization, sued Keeler, Interior Secretary Hickel and other Cherokee executive committee members, charging racism and discrimination under the Indian Civil Rights Act. The suit charged also that Keeler's appointment by Truman had been unconstitutional.[19] This case perhaps highlights most clearly the rift between some Indian power brokers and their alienated constituency during these years.

Another important example of the distance between conservative Indian leadership and intratribal constituency developed in the relationship between Richard Wilson, Oglalla tribal chair, and the American Indian Movement just prior to the occupation at Wounded Knee on the Pine Ridge, South Dakota reservation. AIM members and others were violently opposed to what they saw as collaboration between Wilson and a hostile occupation government. Indian sovereigntism and tribal government clashed further during the occupation.[20] Wilson referred to the militants as outlaws, and the occupiers saw the tribal police who remained loyal to Wilson as "goons."[21]

The Indian nationalists who protested at Wounded Knee, on Alcatraz and at the BIA headquarters rejected Indian-U.S. relations based on anything but tribal sovereignty. They felt the trust relationship had, in the absence of the firm base of sovereignty, meant the BIA holding Indian resources in trust for whites, not Indians. The Indian nationalist Red Power movement did not shape policy with the most powerful voice during these years, although it was clearly the most focused on the issue of sovereignty. Leaders of the American Indian Movement and other groups, such as United Native Americans, and even to an extent the well established National Indian Youth Council, emphasized the difference between the denial of Native American rights and those of all other minority groups. Russell Means, one of the founders of AIM, referred to this when he said, "The social movements in this country that are non-Indian are after civil rights. We are after sovereign rights...we're a liberation organization."[22] Means' focus on sovereignty, rather than civil rights, was echoed by other influential groups and served to focus attention on treaty obligations rather than concentrating on using self-determination as a means to gain access to certain European values and characteristics which might serve to erode tribal consciousness and homogenize Indian destiny with the goals of the dominant society. These groups would concentrate on issues which highlighted Native sovereign, treaty protected rights.

There were similarities between urban based groups such as AIM and others which were more rural in character. The Akwasasne Ganienkeh Longhouse Mohawk group in New York, for example, spoke out regarding many of the same concerns as the AIM representatives. Both were concerned with promoting health, education and housing issues, yet they insisted on the point of sovereign rights. The Indian Unity Convention held on the Mohawk reserve in 1969, including members from sixty-two Indian nations, discussed travel restrictions between Canada and the United States and religious freedom issues bound up with sacred land use.[23]

United Native Americans, a San Francisco-based group, also centered its concern on a definition of self-determination which included both Indian control of Indian programs and increased recognition of the sovereign status of Native America, including treaty rights, in the areas of resource use and access to public domain lands.[24] Among numerous other small groups, the Navajo Liberation Front argued in the Indian underground press for control over resources on Navajo lands.[25] The disparity between well-to-do Indians negotiating lucrative corporate resource contracts and impoverished and powerless grass-roots Indians continued to fuel the arguments of nationalists who saw any compromise of sovereignty over resources and land use as neo-colonial technique, not fairly negotiated resource interest.

Many of their critics, from tribal chairmen to Reagan administration Interior Secretary James Watt, attacked sovereigntists on the "left" as socialists and subversives. While many in the sovereigntist group may indeed see good in communal values and shared property, most quarrel at the notion that tribal sovereignty derives from Marxist or other "leveler" traditions. Roxanne Dunbar-Ortiz characterizes AIM as "anti-capitalist and anti-imperialist, [yet] the ideology of socialism is officially eschewed because it is seen as a 'Western' philosophy like colonialism or capitalism."[26] She writes:

> During the 1970s American Indian people have concluded they will perish as peoples in the United States and this is the basis for the popular call to struggle today: Nationhood and Self-determination or Genocide. . . . Nationalism is the sole alternative to genocide for Indians and the primary basis for the survival of the Indian people.[27]

Leaders of the Indian nationalist movement have been clearest in their recognition that self-determination, without the commitment to a land base and treaty bound trust protection, is simply another form of termination.[28] The Indian nationalist and Red Power movement in general, sensed clearly, articulated and struggled for the recognition of this fact. However, the era of self-determination should be remembered more as a period of sophisticated competency development, not sovereign recognition. Indeed, any political legitimacy in the struggle of Indian people which was represented, for example, by Wounded Knee, was undermined by official government actions. AIM leaders were harassed into dispersion or jailed. FBI documents later obtained from the office of Attorney General Saxbe showed efforts to discredit and destroy the effectiveness of activist and militant groups including blacks, Indians, and communist spokespersons. Memoranda produced under the Freedom of Information Act directed FBI officials to "expose, disrupt, misdirect, discredit, and otherwise neutralize the groups, activities, and individual names of nationalist hate-type organizations and groupings, their leadership, spokesmen, membership and supporters ... prevent the rise of a 'messiah' who can unify and electrify the nationalist movement."[29]

AIM was not the first group to insist on rightful sovereignty and resist land theft and oppression. Clearly the early spiritual traditionalists preceded them in their opposition to New Deal Indian reorganization. Vine Deloria noted the early contributions of Indian servicemen returning from World War II who emerged as urban Indian leaders. Even as early as the beginning of this century the all-Indian "Society of American Indians," while fundamentally a middle-class Indian support organization, articulated a vision of Native Americans as a permanent "non-vanishing" people in America.[30]

Many tribal leaders have viewed the problems in self-determination policy as an administrative oversight, not a fundamental structural component of a flawed, anti-sovereigntist design. Often, as we have seen, BIA stonewalling of self-determination has been blamed for these problems.[31] It was natural to accuse the BIA for protecting its administrative turf. Yet the resistance of powerful resource companies to Indian control seems a more logical and direct route toward understanding why, during hearings held on treaty trust violation, the American Indian Press Association could record the following testimony:

> Whenever Indian resources are desired by non-Indians, especially commercial interests or state governments, those resources are appropriated for those non-Indian users. Whenever Indians must depend on the Department of the Interior for information, Indians go uninformed. ... Whenever Indian rights come into contact with the interests of the Bureau of Reclamation, the Army Engineers, the Forest Service or the Bureau of Land Management, Indian rights are lost.[32]

Nixon's era of self-determination had sown deep seeds of distrust, despite the rhetoric. There is significant evidence of corporate meddling in the sovereignty based, participatory democracy which would have made self-determination more meaningful. For example, during the struggle for control of north-slope Alaskan oil, oil conglomerates Mobil, Amoco, British Petroleum, Humble-Exxon, Phillips 66, Union 76, and Amerada-Hess sought to prevent Eskimos from organizing their own borough. This would have made it much more difficult to negotiate leases without the impediment of the will of the original inhabitants.[33]

It is indeed treaties which uphold and extend original native sovereignty. Self-determination is best expressed in the language of these rights, not the variations of elite tribal governments and BIA middlemen. If treaties for the sovereign tribes, like the U.S. Constitution for the sovereign United States, are the security of rights for Indian people, accordingly a tribal council vote is not the appropriate place to determine changes in a people's destiny.[34]

The efforts of Indian nationalists during the 1960s and 1970s have highlighted the great difference between the concept of Native American sovereignty and what has become the policy of self-determination. Deloria and Lytle have argued that self-determination is an incomplete notion.[35] Indian activism has, for all its missteps, developed the sharpest critique of unhealthy self-government. As a group they have emphasized the fundamentally radical character of Indian community ideals and of tribal sovereignty. Both are activities which remain incomplete, neither is a fixed structure. Tribal ideals are subjects for tribal discourse and the education of the young. A major challenge and a key to their radical nature lies in the degree of divergence of Indian traditional political, religious, and ethical thinking from that of the dominant culture. Likewise, tribal sovereignty whether expressed in efforts to reform tribal government to enable greater participation, or to press further with land claims and treaty rights, is a process, a struggle, not a structure.[36]

Fundamental differences exist between indigenous peoples whose traditions on the land extend back for thousands of years. Tribal teaching and tradition count this continent as the birthplace of the souls of their people. Along with this comprehension comes culture structures which are radically different in terms of land use, sharing, and ownership, as well as in human interactions.[37]

American Indian selfhood is rooted in the Indian's place on the North American continent. American Indian self-determination is meaningless without the emphasis on sovereignty and treaty based rights which protect Native American heritage. This emphasis does not, however, best characterize the development of self-determination policy during the post-New Deal era. Lacking this emphasis, and acknowledging the hostility with which treaty struggles were received by the administration most closely identified with realizing this policy, it must be concluded that self-determination policy was at best conceived, born, and grew through its infancy as a number of forms of social education, in schooling, economic, and self-help programs—a training ground for a reduction in federal treaty-bound trust responsibility, if not for total eventual termination.

Legitimate self-determination includes not only self-government but the development of educative structures which help refertilize the culture and values from which *self* arises—in this case, tribal community culture. When this effort, the educational effort, loses the truly educational project of self-regeneration, it becomes just economic development; self-help becomes a transitional anti-"termination psychosis" program; and self-determination becomes an empty word, an ironic exercise in the management of Manifest Destiny.

Tribal educational philosophy, if it is tribal at all, is not the subject of traditional Western representational democratic forms. It must be ideological *and* conventional, reflecting traditional will. If an Indian person abandons his past and tribal ideals, he has abandoned his right to speak as a representative of his people. Contemporary Indian life is most meaningful when expressed by those who participate in spiritual and ideological tribal tradition rather than those who are tribal only by virtue of their genetic Indianness. What gives tribal life meaning is its history and culture, as much as by blood quantum or other racial markers. A speaker for Indian interests must be an Indian citizen in the deepest sense of the word—a lover of the community and its ideals.

Adding strength to this argument is the recorded inability of many middle-ground Indian politicians to early recognize and articulate the legitimacy and importance of radical sovereignty activism. Yet given the developing record of resource and labor exploitation, with few concomitant gains in the Indian poverty profile during this period, it appears as a grim design with the limited purpose of involving some Indians in exploitation which would have been impossible to justify and accomplish without such cooperation. If this is true, and if Felix Cohen is correct that American Indian welfare is the miner's canary, the polestar by which the dominant society charts its moral course, tolerance is in grave peril, and human rights about which politicians are inclined to rend their garments, are in more serious danger in our own country than one can imagine, given the height of the rhetoric. For when such sophisticated social-cultural education divides a people against itself, imprisonment can exist without jails, and genocide is possible without extermination.

For self-determination to maintain meaning it must include regeneration and tribal education regarding the unique sovereign nature of tribal life. Those who speak for the people as policymakers must be more than Indians by blood quantum; they must understand and represent the traditional tribal ideals of the people and the ancestral struggle which won the degree of treaty-bound sovereignty which exists.

NOTES

1. Alvin Josephy, Jr., *Red Power* (New York: McGraw-Hill, 1971), p. 28.
2. "Indian Lobbying Successes in the 1970s,"*Indian Truth,* no. 230 (February 1980): n.p..
3. Josephy, *Red Power,* p. 37.
4. Ibid., p. 73.
5. Ibid., p. 133.
6. Jack D. Forbes, *Native Americans and Nixon* (Los Angeles: Native American Studies Center-UCLA, 1981), p. 39.
7. "Secretary Rogers: His Position on Indian Affairs,"*Wassaja,* June 1973, p. 6.
8. Forbes, *Native Americans and Nixon,* p. 109-10.
9. *Indian Truth,* no. 240 (July/August 1980): 5.
10. Vine Deloria, Jr., and Clifford Lytle, *The Nations Within* (New York: Pantheon Books, 1984), p. 215.
11. National Congress of American Indians (NCAI), *Sentinel Bulletin,* November 1977, p. 50.
12. Richard La Course, "Emerging International Native Relations," in *Sentinel Bulletin,* July 1975, p. 19.
13. *Wassaja,* July/August 1983, p. 3.
14. "NCAI Position: Realignment Is Regionalization," *Sentinel Bulletin,* July/August 1973, p. 4.
15. *Indian Truth,* "Report on the National Congress of American Indians Convention," no. 208 (January 1977): 1-2.
16. Forbes, *Native Americans and Nixon,* p. 123.
17. Ibid., p. 42.
18. *Akwasasne Notes,* October 1970, p. 26, from article by Peter Collier, "The Theft of a Nation: Apologies to the Cherokee," *Ramparts,* September 1970.
19. *Indian Truth* 46, no. 1 (1969): 1-3.
20. *Wassaja* , May 1973, p. 6.
21. Forbes, *Native Americans and Nixon,* p. 117.
22. *Akwasasne Notes,* Early Winter 1974, p. 5.
23. "On Travel Freedom Between U.S. and Canada," *Akwasasne Notes,* September 1969, n.p.
24. *Akwasasne Notes,* April 1970, n.p., from the *Warpath* publication of United Native Americans, in San Francisco, Calif.
25. *Akwasasne Notes,* September 1970, n.p.

26. Roxanne Dunbar-Ortiz, "Land and Nationhood: The American Indian Struggle for Self-determination and Survival," *Socialist Review* 63-64 (May-August 1982): 118.

27. Ibid., p. 109.

28. Bruce Johansen and Roberto Maestas, *Wasichu: The Continuing Indian Wars* (New York: Monthly Review Press, 1979), pp. 212-13.

29. Rex Weyler, *Blood of the Land: The Government and Corporate War Against the American Indian Movement* (New York: Everest House,1982), p. 59.

30. Deloria and Lytle, *The Nations Within,* p. 241. See also Weyler, *Blood of the Land,* p. 93; and Hazel Hertzberg, *The Search for American Indian Identity: Modern Pan-Indian Movements* (Syracuse, N.Y.: Syracuse University Press, 1971), pp. 71-79.

31. *Wassaja,* January 1973, p. 13.

32. Forbes, *Native Americans and Nixon*, p. 59.

33. Ibid., p. 62.

34. Rupert Costo, "Indian Treaties: The Basis for Solution of Current Issues," *Wassaja*, July 1973, p. 1.

35. Deloria and Lytle, *Nations Within*, pp. 244-45.

36. William Brandon, "American Indians: The Real American Revolution," *Progressive,* February 1970, pp. 26-30.

37. Russell Lawrence Barsh, "The Nature and Spirit of North American Political Systems," *American Indian Quarterly* 10, no. 3 (Summer 1986): 181.

10

Self-determination
and the Trust Relationship

In order to clearly understand self-determination in American Indian
social and educational policy, we must begin to comprehend that the
complex relationships which have characterized the self-determination
impulse imply independence—independence from government paternalism. Yet government patronage has been fundamental to the career
of the United States Indian Service since the 1860s. The point of
juncture between U.S. government policy and tribal life has been usually
described as a trust relationship. Trust implies a responsibility that the
U.S. government carries to the trust beneficiary—the Indian people.
This responsibility was taken up through the process of treaty ratification
and through subsequent legislation which codified the unique responsibility of the government to the Indian people in perpetuity.

There are, however, varying legal and political interpretations as
to the nature and extent of this trust. The fact that interpretations vary
and that they often are politically conditioned, lays a heavy burden on
our ability to operationally define trust in its special use here. The
strength of the trust is dependent upon the corpus of current political
whim. As such, we must urge caution about any attempt to pin down its
meaning, except as it is seen to be used in practice. What we can certainly
say, however, is that any notion of a trust relationship has defined and
limited the possibilities of the policy practice of self-determination.

The federal government does hold a substantial amount of property
in trust for the sole use/benefit of Indian people. This agreement was
made through treaty negotiation, whereby Indian people ceded larger
tracts of ancestral land in exchange for reserved areas which would be
protected for their use by the federal government. The extent of the trust
varies, from the specific time period of perhaps twenty or fifty years to

agreements in perpetuity. In place of specifics, trust often come to be defined by history through precedent and convention. Regardless of these trust covenants, in practice trust has become a relationship in constant jeopardy of dissolution.

The progress of the trust relationship has been historically determined by the status of American Indian treaty title to land and compensation for lands used or taken. This compensation has taken a variety of forms, principal of which has been the provision of goods and services to tribal people. Self-determination signaled an effort to increase the responsibility of Indian people for the provision of goods and services formerly provided by the trustee, the U.S. government, acting through the plenary power of Congress over commerce with Indian tribes.

In reality, the U.S. government (the trustee) has unilaterally invoked its substantial "plenary" power over the commerce with Indian tribes to blunt and distort its trust responsibility. Evidence for the extent of this trust is to be found in the myriad of treaties and agreements made with Indian peoples, from colonial times through the latter half of the nineteenth century. This extremely large and complex body of law can be found speaking to issues which also go beyond trusteeship over land. Education and social development also are often found as part of the responsibility of the government. However, while the nature and extent of trust has been an issue, behind this lies the considerable power of the government to interpret the trust without consulting the beneficiary and, in some cases, to abrogate its responsibility over the protests of those whom the government is treaty-bound to serve.

Until the year 1871, the treaty was employed as the method of establishing the European-Indian and, later, the U.S.-Indian relationship.[1] Although the method of dealing with tribes by this practice was abandoned with the adoption of the Indian Appropriation Act of 1871, treaties created prior to the act were not abrogated by its passage.[2] In fact, subsequent to this act, Congress continued to treat tribes in a similar fashion as had the Senate before under the authority of Article II, Section I of the Constitution. "Agreements" were made and ratified by both Houses which *de facto* operated as the treaties had before. The only substantial change lay in the fact that now the House of Representatives would cooperate with the Senate in ratification of the new agreements. Along with treaties and agreements, much of the relationship of the federal government to the tribes came by way of special statutes dealing with specific tribes or Indian people generally, and through the adoption of tribal constitutions and charters after the Indian Reorganization Act of 1934.[3]

Between the time of the General Allotment Act of 1887 and the Indian Reorganization Act of 1934, the government developed a tendency to impose regulations and laws upon Indians as a general entity rather than as individual tribes.[4] The fact that these over-generalized statutes and other legal instruments ignored the individual treaty rights of specific tribes prompted a study to be undertaken by the Institute for Government Research. The results of its 1929 study, *The Problem of Indian Administration*, helped fuel a decade of governmental, social and educational reform which led to the evelopment of the Indian Reorganization Act and corporatization of tribal entities.[5] Regardless of the nature of legal instruments, laws, agreements and resolutions made subsequent to 1871, they carry a concomitant legal weight equivalent to that of the treaties and vice versa. Whether treaties and laws related to Indians receive the same status as other legal instruments dealing with the general public is another question. In fact, and indeed, the special unique place of the American Indian in the United States renders problematic his legal status as well.

There is a central paradox which exists with regard to the status of the Indian and which throws Indian policy upon the winds of political fate. On the one hand, Indian people are American citizens with full rights guaranteed, along with concomitant full responsibilities. On the other hand, th quasi-sovereign nature of the tribes and the recognition of this fact during the treaty years is ample evidence for special treatment as a polity. Also, apart from any congressional or court recognition of tribal sovereignty, the Constitution gives Congress plenary power over the commerce with Indian people. This plenary power, along with the developing notion of the Indians as wards of the government, confuses and dilutes the seemingly polar positions of Indians as sovereign and Indians as full U.S. citizens. It allows Congress to decide Indian policy unilaterally. A third problem centers around the extent of the government's trust responsibility. Some argue that the trust only extends to the protection of Indian material resources. Others argue that the trust extends to the development of Indian human capital, even to the extent of saying that sovereignty itself is to be protected.

However, this trust responsibility has itself been a problem for policymakrs throughout history. The trust relationship has been called patronizing and means have been sought to give more control to Indians. However, when Indians have been shown to be capable of maintaining control, they have been rewarded with loss of federal assistance or termination, which has proven anathema to limited tribal sovereignty, and in some cases has resulted in great loss of tribal property through sale and hypothecation.

With all of this, however, most government Indian programs have been geared to preparing Indians to do without special protection to achieve the competency to operate in twentieth-century America. Indian policy has languished along a spectrum of interpretation, from full sovereignty—through dependence and wardship—to competence, to citizenship. Since the legal status of the Indian people is at stake, we are cautioned to heed the warning of logical pitfalls that yawn along this spectrum. The discussion of tribal status has often centered on the argument over degree of tribal sovereignty. Indian legal history turns less on the pull between sovereignty and citizenship than on the issue of competence leading to responsibility. Indian policy and the U.S. government relationship, from the Civilization Acts to self-determination, is a process of providing tribes with the competencies—social, economic and educational—which will lead from tribal status to full citizenship, with all that implies—the responsibility to pay state business and income tax, the abrogation of treaty rights, to full termination of reservation status. The full weight of this claim is supported by the political powers opposed to the legal nature of tribal status throughout history. Regardless of the logic brought to bear on the legal status of treaty rights, the plenary power of Congress can be and has been involved unilaterally to abrogate those treaties.

Federal Indian legal theory takes much of its form and substance beginning with a set of landmark cases adjudicated in the 1830s. The cases began then in conflict as they often do today, although they operated at that time to set a precedent of dependent sovereign interpretation.[6] The development of the dependent sovereign concept begins with the decision of the Supreme Court in the case of *Cherokee Nation v. Georgia*. Georgia had attempted to impose its state laws on the Cherokee people. The Cherokee filed suit with the Supreme Court under Article III of the Constitution, which provides the court with original jurisdiction in cases involving foreign nations and states. At issue was whether the Cherokee constitute a foreign nation in the sense of the Constitution. Chief Justice John Marshall held that the Cherokees and other tribes were not foreign nations but "domestic dependent nations."[7] The domestic-dependent nation concept is important, for it encompasses two key points: (1) that the tribes maintain nation-state, self-governing status, and (2) that they have a special, albeit dependent, relation to the U.S. government. For his opinion, Marshall relied partially on the work of Emerich Vattel, the leading scholar of international law during this period. Vattel held that "weaker nations that submit themselves to alliances with more powerful nations are still Sovereign and, quoting Aristotle, 'the more powerful [nation] is given more honor, and to the weaker, more assistance'."[8]

Later, in *Worcester v. Georgia*, Marshall held that all the power the federal government held over the tribes was limited to that which was representative of tribal consent such as it is expressed in treaties.

In the Cherokee nation case, Marshall argued for the sovereignty of the Cherokee nation, while claiming that this sovereignty is partial and limited because of the dependence of the Cherokee on the U.S. government.[9] They are "acknowledged to have an unquestionable and, heretofore, unquestioned right to the lands they occupy, until that right shall be extinguished by a voluntary cession to our government."[10] He goes on to argue the limits of this power as due to the "dependent" status of Indian nations. In the case of *Worcester,* he went further in his determination of sovereign status. Samuel Worcester, a New England missionary, was imprisoned in the state of Georgia for trespassing on Cherokee land in Georgia. At issue was the right of the Cherokee to accept the presence of Worcester without the consent of Georgia. Marshall declared that the laws of Georgia in this regard were "repugnant to the Constitution."[11] He based his argument on the claim that tribal status was based only on a "condition" of dependence, not on a decision. Thus, dependence was in no way construed to indicate abdication of inherent political rights. Although dependence of condition was an increasing reality in the 1830s, the "language" of dependence often accepted by the tribes in treaties during an earlier period was, Marshall implied, "a pretense, which tribes had tolerated out of ignorance of its legal implications. They were not well acquainted with the words [that] signify dependence—nor did they suppose it to be material whether they were called subjects or the children of their father in Europe."[12]

For Marshall, then, tribes were politically sovereign, limited by their dependence only to the extent of their admission of dependence at the time of treaty, not the *condition* of their dependence. In most cases, tribes had "never been conquered, but together with Europeans, had yielded and compromised in matters of mutual economic interest."[13] They had not forfeited their tribal political authority. Tribal rights and possessions are clearly held by tribes.

In the case of *Worcester,* dependency was redefined as stated in *Cherokee Nation v. Georgia.* U.S.-Indian relations were clearly related to tribal consent and not to any *condition* of dependence.[14] These cases laid the groundwork for a relatively broad interpretation of tribal sovereignty and yet, ironically, solidified the plenary power of Congress, reinforcing its original jurisdiction over commerce with Indian tribes. However, only the doctrine of the plenary power of Congress survived into the years during which the frontier began rapidly to expand— beginning shortly before the Civil War into the late nineteenth century.

Marshall, the ardent federalist, had succeeded in establishing federal power over the state of Georgia with regard to the interpretation of tribal hegemony and immunity from state law. This strong federalist stand and the concomitant broad interpretation of congressional plenary power are, however, Marshall's legacy in the history of Indian power from just before the Civil War to the present. Grant's Peace Policy, the Allotment Period after the Dawes Act, the Indian Reorganization Act and the Indian New Deal, postwar termination and self-determination all were major policy shifts. Each has a separate character springing from a changing constellation of political and reforming forces. Each, however, acted to reaffirm in some way the power of the Congress without impunity and with little legal recourse on the part of tribes, to unilaterally impose policy change in Indian affairs.

This emphasis on congressional unilateral plenary power is exacerbated by the concept dependent sovereign which evolved from the earlier Cherokee decision, yet in a still much weaker form. The *condition* of, rather than the *consent* to, dependence relationship became the leading concept. Sovereignty took a subordinate role in the political relationship, due to the growing emphasis on congressional plenary power over its dependent wards, the Indian.

The years during which the European-American expanded westward up to and beyond the Mississippi were not characterized by great federal toleration for tribal sovereignty. Tribal sovereignty and political self-determination also meant toleration of tribal custom and habit, along with tribal political will. This was clearly inconsistent with the aims of the European-American and his "manifest destiny." For only a brief time after the *Worcester* decision were tribes treated as special political entities through the use of special Indian legislation such as that exempting them from federal taxation. However, as early as 1802 and again in 1819, Congress began stipulating that this special relationship be contingent upon a federal goal of assimilation—the aim to meld the American Indian, socially, economically and morally into the mainstream of the European-American life on the continent.[15] Indian policymakers began to see tribal dependency, and in some ways the limited sovereignty which remained, as a curable condition.

The Civilization Acts of 1802 and 1819 were the first acts specifically to codify the responsibility of the federal government to provide for "Indian social and welfare programs—to help Indians make the transition from the life of the migratory hunter to that of the self-sufficient farmer."[16] Prior to the Civilization Act of 1819, federal laws had dealt with or were intended to implement specific provisions of a treaty.[17] The 1819 act, however, dealt both with treaty and nontreaty tribes and thus established a basis for a federal-Indian relationship apart from, but including, the federal responsibility to treaty tribes.

The federal government's responsibility for Indian welfare, in addition to specific treaty provisions, began perhaps in the Civilization Acts. It is of paramount importance that these efforts reflected mainly a concern for welfare to the extent that welfare put the Indian on a path toward self-sufficiency and civilization. This notion of providing welfare and education until competence was evident in several early treaty provisions as well. As Vine Deloria wrote:

> While the removal of the Chippewas, Potawatomies, and Ottawas from the Chicago area was based on the explicit promise that the United States would provide educational services forever, most treaties promised schooling and other federal services for only a limited time. The Menominee (1831) and Pawnee (1833) treaties, for example, provided federal schools for 10 years; other treaties extended the period to 20 years. Officials in Washington believed that these relatively short periods would be adequate to prepare Indians to till the land, become self-sufficient, and be ready for assimilation into the general population.[18]

The beginnings of Indian welfare as a part of the trust responsibility lay squarely in the effort to civilize and assimilate, these being preconditions for a satisfactory Indian social and economic policy. This effort to assimilate was buried not far beneath the surface of the Indian policy of self-determination, a policy promoted as an extension of tribal sovereignty on matters political, economic, social and educational.

Both tribal political sovereignty as well as federal rather than state jurisdiction are the legacy of the precedent setting Supreme Court decisions regarding the Cherokee. Indian material and human capital is held in trust by the federal government. This trust is, however, to be in force only as long as Indians remain in a dependent state—as wards of the government. The plenary power of Congress is such that Congress may decide when the condition of dependence is weak enough for the trust to end. The question has always been *when* the trust should end—sooner or later—and by what means.

The federal-Indian trust relationship is a complex set of interdependent relationships and mutual responsibilities. However, the unilateral nature of the trust definition became the center of an effort during the 1970s to set a policy on the trust and its extent. These relations and responsibilities were not clearly delineated with regard either to trustee, the federal government, or to the trust beneficiary—the Indian people. Generally, however, despite the lack of clarity as to the scope of this trust, there are three components which make up the corpus of the "trust res" or that which is held in trust—land, tribal self-government and social welfare.[19] These are the components of the trust res, however, which have been at issue. There has not been clear agreement on the extent to which these three are held as trust property, nor even whether all should be included as part of that which is held in trust.

Land is the part of the trust about which there is most agreement.

"The U.S. holds technical legal title while equitable title or the right to use the land is held by the beneficiary—the Indian."[20] Indeed, in 1967-68 fully 90 percent of the bills which came through the Subcommittee on Indian Affairs dealt with Indian land or land claims money.[21] Regardless of the extent or nature of this trust, however, major Indian legislation has always been written around the notion that Indian material or human capital shall be protected, held in trust, until such time as Indian people gain the competence to manage these assets themselves, ending the trust relationship.

Worcester v. Georgia had established the notion of treaty federalism with regard to Indian tribes. Tribes are not to be dealt with "within the scope of the federal-state compact, but relate to the U.S. through separate compacts authorized and enforced under the Treaty Clause: treaty federalism as opposed to constitutional federalism "such as that with states."[22] This interpretation limits the Congress to regulation of "commerce" with Indians, in the same way as commerce is regulated with foreign governments. The political relationship on this interpretation must follow a course of mutual agreement.[23] After 1871, unilateral plenary power began to have a broader interpretation, and the government often adopted so-called legislative "agreements" unilaterally. The U.S. government treated Indian peoples as limited sovereigns for forty years after *Worcester*. Then, however, the government began to more greatly limit its recognition of the tribes to their status as wards rather than limited sovereigns. Indeed, the concept of treaty sovereignty, set by pacts of mutual agreement, became a moot point; in practice, a fiction. For with the total subjugation of the tribes, Indian ward status and capital held in trust through treaty became more and more subject to a broad interpretation of congressional plenary power.

The extent and nature of the federal trust responsibility lacked clarity for years. Assumed in practice, in theory there was no codification of the nature of this trust. Congress terminated the reservation status of much tribal land during the 1950s. This effort brought great concern to Indians and others abou the purpose of U.S. Indian policy and the extent to which the government had an obligation to Indian policy and the extent to which the government had an obligation to Indian people. Although policy had taken a variety of twists and turns, there was no single body of documentation—only a scattering of treaties, agreements, laws, and court holdings which formed the testament of U.S. federal responsibility for its aboriginal people.

In addition, concern over this lack of codification was part of the reason for those who argued for the establishment of an American Indian Policy Review Commission (AIPRC) group made up of congresspersons and Indian representatives. The work of codifying policy through this commission is not as interesting as are the doctrinal disputes which arise over the findings of the commission. The proceedings surrounding these disputes are a classic example of the nature of the doctrine of plenary powers, the extent and meaning of the tribal trust and finally, the direction of Indian policy in general.

The findings of the commission also brought out the paradox of Indian social welfare in policy. That is, is social welfare provided as an insurance that Indian people as well as land is t be protected as part of the trust responsibility? Or is provision of health and educational services an effort to hasten the process when the government may divest itself of its Indian "problem"? Some answers to these questions are suggested in the patterns of dispute presented here in the hearings of the AIPRC.

The AIPRC was established in May 1974 by a joint resolution of Congress. It was established as the result of an admission of failure by the Congress and the Executive to adequately meet their legal and moral responsibility to Indian welfare.[24] It came also as a partial response to nascent Indian radicalism expressed in the BIA office takeover in Washington and the siege of Wounded Knee. Of the fifteen members of the commission, five were senators, five legislators and five Indian leaders.[25] The presiding chairman, Senator James Abourezk, suggested that the commission's purpose was to make a thorough review of federal-Indian policy, for reforms had appeared and disappeared without centrally affecting the deepest concerns of Indian people nor their most pressing problems.[26]

The commission, perhaps, reaffirmed the federal-Indian relationship, yet at no point in the hearings was the ambiguity in that relationship more apparent than in the discussions of the nature of trust.[27] Section III of the AIPRC Final Report sums up the findings of the commission on the status of the federal-Indian trust relationship. It is entitled "Trust Responsibilities in States of Confusion."[28] Section III is an overview of the diverse opinions and forces which have worked to glue the federal-Indian relationship. For example, the National Tribal Chairman's Association (NTCA) claims a "threefold" responsibility of the federal government: (1) There is a special relationship between Indian people and the federal government which is cited in the U.S. Constitution. The Constitution recognizes Indian people as special sovereigns, and from this the NTCA reasons the government has a responsibility to protect this sovereignty; (2) The federal government has a major responsibility to help tribes develop their own resources without outside interference; (3) Flowing from this effort to help tribes develop their *own* resources, the federal government has the "trust responsibility for providing the means by which the tribes can provide community services to the members of the reservation-communities."[29]

The report goes on to cite a dissent to the NTCA opinion on trust, one which was produced in the Office of the Interior Department solicitor. The Department of the Interior position agrees that Indian land and resources are entrusted to the government through the Interior Department for its care. However, beyond land and resources, trust essentially ends. The interior position says that while "the government historically has provided for the social needs of Indian tribes and their members—because of the exclusive power under the Constitution to regulate commerce with Indian tribes—these programs do no [sic] create any trust relationship in the strict legal sense of the word."[30] The central problem surrounding the legal basis of trust is that no clear legal basis exists upon which everyone can agree. Indeed, as the commission reports, "Judgments regarding the origins of the trust relationships are frequently contradictory, and conclusions defining its nature are often inconsistent. Nonetheless, one can find support in authority and evidence for each of the viewpoints."[31]

With all the conflicting legal foundations of trust, the commission fell back on the international legal arguments for sovereignty of Indian tribes. Simply finding, however, that "established relationships between Indian tribes and the U.S. are 'deeply rooted in international law'" is to rely again upon the moral weight of the sovereignty.[32]

Throughout history, whether during the allotment period, with the wholesale of tribal property, or during termination, with the ending of the tribal reservation status, Congress has used its considerable plenary power to cut into the heart of tribal sovereignty. Indeed, the only thing protecting tribal sovereignty from this unilateral power are political exigencies, a moral-based belief in Indian tribal solidarity, arguments from political philosophy on sovereigns, and finally, the direction of the political whim. In addition, the extent to which the government is said to hold land, resources, or whatever in trust for the beneficiary—the Indian people—is clearly related to the condition of dependence of Indians upon the government.

The notion of dependence as we have seen begins with Marshall, where sovereignty is qualified and, in some sense, formed first by the condition of dependence, then by the admission of it. As the sovereignty issue changes with increasing practical actual dependence during the early reservation years, trust is clearly related to this condition, to wardship. Thus land and resources are held alien from their Indian owners, in trust, until such time as the owners are deemed competent to husband or sell the land themselves. Thus the move to civilize, to acculturate, to educate the Indian has historically been an attempt to divest Congress of its trust responsibility, not an effort to create a stronger sovereign Indian nation.

Trust until competence has been the real meaning of the trust relationship. Indeed, those who have not seen the moral force of international law have had little use for its application to Indian people. While the Department of the Interior and the NTCA differ here on the extent of trust, The Interior Department claiming its hold over land, the NTCA adding the responsibility over human capital, Congressman Lloyd Meeds (vice-chair of the commission) took a swipe at the legitimacy of Indian sovereignty which lies at the heart of either limited or extended trust interpretation.

Two years after the beginning of the work of the AIPRC, and two months before the presentation of its final report, the commission met for a mark-up session on the report. At the beginning of this meeting, the executive director, Ernest Stevens, read a list of goals he wished to be part of the general statement of the philosophy of the commission. He said:

> These goals are a reaffirmation of commitment on tribal sover-
> eignty and the strengthening of tribal government [and that] the
> prologue calls for a recognition of the permanency and the right of
> the Indian people to be separate and apart and different from other
> people . . . [and a] reaffirmation of the trust relationship between
> the federal government and the tribes.[33]

Vice-chairman Meeds reported that he disagreed with the notion of tribal sovereignty. He said, "What is tribal sovereignty? It's like pregnance [sic], can you be a little sovereign, or must you be all sovereign? There are a whole host of questions within the question of tribal sovereignty which I think this commission needs to examine in detail."[34] With this, Meeds began to go on record in obstruction to a broad notion of sovereignty, in opposition to most of his colleagues on the commission. An interesting exchange took place between Congressman Meeds and Gill Hall, an assistant to the commission. Hall testified that the essence of the trust responsibility lay in "international law and in treaties, statutory law and in Federal judicial decisions."[35] Yet the beginnings of the trust predate the formation of the United States and lay in agreements made between the tribes and the thirteen colonies during the colonial period. The commission quoted the Northwest Ordinance when it wrote that Indian "lands and property shall never be taken from them without their consent."[36] Meeds questioned whether the ordinance, while binding on the original thirteen colonies, was also binding now on the fifty states. Mr. Hall responded in the affirmative and Meeds said, "As a moral or legal obligation?" Hall replied, "I think as both moral and legal, with the caveat, of course, of Congressional plenary power."[37] Meeds went on to ask rhetorically whether the federal government had the right to condemn Indian land, since it is clear that Congress had exercised its plenary authority to condemn many times without Indian support and often over their protests. Meeds pressed his claim that Congress should have the same right to condemn Indian land for bridge or water projects, as an example, as they do over state land. He asserted that Indian sovereignty was similar, in this case, to that of states. To this Hall replied that the difference was that the Congress had no trust relationship with the states such as it has with Indians.[38]

Since the central issue here is over Indian consent to a condemnation, the question must be asked. Is consent, Indian-informed consent, a part of that which the government must consider in adjudicating its trust responsibility? Consent in this case would indicate that the owner had enough proprietary interest in a property to warrant his consent for use. Consent is much stronger than fair hearing input which is required in state land condemnation proceedings as indicated in the Constitution. Consent is central to an argument for strong sovereignty, an interpretation Meeds was not willing to entertain, given his beliefs about the extent of plenary power. In addition, if a part of the government's trust responsibility includes the protection of the Indian's right to self-direction on land and resource use issues, this was a new direction in interpretation. Fully 1.5 million acres of Indian land had been lost to condemnation proceedings between 1934 and 1977, or approximately 35,000 acres per year, or around 95 acres a day, 4 acres every hour for 43 years. At this rate, it is clear that a strong notion of sovereignty and self-determination through the authority of informed consent is an issue of great import. Even if social and educational programs do fall outside the realm of trust, the loss of land and resource, at a rate of four acres an hour, every hour, put a great deal at stake.[39]

Regardless of the stakes involved, and regardless of the proprietorship of Indian people over reservation land and trust resources, the power of the U.S. government to act unilaterally in resource expropriation and the extent of their trust responsibility has been very great indeed. It was clear during meetings of the AIPRC that a number of the commissioners favored coming out with a policy statement accentuating the sovereignty of Indian tribes as a way of highlighting the right of Indian people to self-determination as separate political entities. Ernest Stevens, staff director of the AIPRC and an Oneida Indian, stated during the hearings that, "Indians for a number of different kinds of reasons should be made a permanent part of the political fabric of the U.S., and as a separate political entity and that they should have the right to be separate and apart forever."[40] Throughout the AIPRC proceedings and findings, many members of the commission reiterated this emphasis on sovereignty for Indian people. However, Congressman Meeds found this interpretation abhorrent to his understanding of the issues involved and appointed a legal consultant to present documentation which he hoped would refute the question of Indian sovereignty.

Congressman Meeds brought in Fred Martone, a Phoenix lawyer, to present his dissent to the commission's emphasis on Indian sovereignty as well as other tangential issues such as reservation taxation. With his public dissent, Meeds put in a clearer light the reality of Congressional plenary power and the inherent political nature of its extent. He and Martone went further, however, in trying to form a legal and constitutional ground for a severely curtailed notion of tribal sovereignty.

While Stevens was arguing for strengthened Indian political status, Meeds claimed that arguments such as these were specious. In addition, Meeds claimed the arguments for strengthened Indian sovereignty contravened his personal views on the issue, which, he claimed, were representative of the "majority of Americans" if "not clearly the majority of Indians."[41] He went on to say: "I think it is a view which has to be expressed out of a personal view that we, our staff and our task force, have laid before us a concept of sovereignty for Indian tribes, which is alien to some of the values in this nation."[42] Meeds believed that "the fundamental error of this report is that it perceives the American Indian tribe as a body politic in the nature of a sovereign as that word is used to describe the United States and the States.... The doctrine of inherent tribal sovereignty, adopted by the majority report, ignores the historical reality that American Indian tribes lost their sovereignty through discovery, conquest, cession, treaties, statutes and history."[43] Meeds was clearly concerned with the commission's emphasis on the political power of tribal entities. He was especially concerned about the extension of Indian jurisdiction over non-Indians.

This attempt to put a corral around the tribal courts and their power could clearly be seen as a move by Meeds to curry the favor of his white constituency prior to what was shaping up to be a tough reelection fight for him in his home district. Indeed, many of his arguments were centered on the issue of the rights of the majority citizenry and the power of their collective will over the moral and judicial logic-chopping which he saw as characteristic of the commission's work.

Much of what the commission attempted was an effort to provide legal, constitutional, and moral arguments for a broader interpretation of the government's responsibility to the Indian. They wanted to provide a base for a "loose construction" of Indian law, extending the "strict constructionist" theory of trust responsibility where that responsibility lies only in the area of land and resources, as in the previous Interior Department interpretation. They wanted to provide a rationale for government *responsibility* for the maintenance of social and educational programs. The maintenance of largesse and a fund of goodwill were not viewed as insurance enough to plan for a future. Moreover, and most importantly, the commission wanted to define sovereignty as an Indian right which is part of the government's responsibility to protect. Sovereignty, here, is not a right of self-government and political self-determination; it is cultural and social hegemony, a part of the Native American "trust res" and part of that which the government, the commission was arguing, has an *obligation* to protect. Should these notions work into policy, however, as Meeds said, "the backlash of the dominant culture would be swift and sure."[44]

Truly, these aims of the commission flew directly in the face of a history in which trust has been only limited. The extent to which trust has been social is that it has been designed to result in the drive to civilize, Americanize—in short, to provide Indians with the competence to share in the responsibilities, as well as the rights. Trust has not been in perpetuity but only until such competence is attained. Indian sovereignty has not been a strong part of the picture.

Historically, Indian reform and reaction has been an ebb and flow, not, however, of the will of the American people to expropriate Indian land. The issue has been—How well are Indian people being prepared for American life? Reform has always been connected to claims by reformers that Indian preparedness is poor and that they have a better plan for accomplishing this. Reactionary forces have been less interested in providing a rationale for resource exploitation, removal plans, or accelerated termination. Beneath the surface, however, the same fundamental forces are at work. Trust until competence, competence, then termination of reservation status. The only difference is in the definition and rationale for a demonstration of competence.

Indeed, this dissent by Meeds is presented here for the way it underscores the power of Congress and the weakness of Indian tribes as governmental entities, and their dependence on the prevailing political will. Chairman Abourezk, along with other members of the commission, was taken aback by the Meeds/Martone dissent. He was, however, supportive of the notion of including a differing viewpoint. He even agreed to the hiring of Martone at a fee of $25,000 during the twilight hours of the commission's existence in an effort to support the idea of what he called "this mini-democracy we are running here."[45]

In addition, Abourezk, for as strongly as he supported arguments for self-determination and trust-protected sovereignty, was clear about the fact that Indian policy will take its course with little guidance from the Courts or this commission. Rather, the adherence to treaties is not a legal issue but a political issue. He said, "If you have a treaty in effect, its *interpretation* [italics mine] becomes a legal matter. Maybe you want to wipe out the treaty or not, that is a *political* matter."[46]

By juxtaposing the lack of integration between legal and moral right and political reality, Abourezk underscored, albeit without the vengeance of Meeds, the chimerical nature of Indian sovereignty, the trust relationship and self-determination. Ernest Stevens's plea for the moral force of the government's trust responsibility was stillborn in its very reference to an Indian nation in alliance with the U.S. against a common enemy. He spoke here of the fact that the U.S. government should realize that the United States was victorious in the War of 1812 only with the help of the Indian people. "Hancock [John] empowered an [Indian] agent to go among the Western tribes [for aid] and they discussed it among themselves, Washington, Jefferson, and so on, and said 'Without these Western tribes we are going to get defeated.'. . Now if it was in 1812 and Congress assumes this position, the Shawnees, the Tuscaroras, the Oneidas, and the various other tribes that remained neutral or pro-U.S., we could have gone to the British and defeated you, and that is a fact."[47] After the applause, following this rejoinder to Meeds, Stevens continued to say that there is a moral argument to protect the rights of Indians, and that, he reminded Martone, "we did not come here only to review the law."[48]

Much earlier, during the hearings relating to the establishment of the commission, Philip Sam Deloria of the American Indian Law Center reminded those contemplating such a Policy Review commission that the question of Indian rights is related to the international dimension of indigenous people's rights. Clearly, for Deloria, much of the discussion would take into account the strongly moral tenor of international legal discourse. Indian rights are to be viewed as a species of a larger right of indigenous peoples worldwide.[49] He warned of the pitfalls in Indian policy, such as the seeming paradox of trust and self-determination. (It is interesting to note the insistence of Stevens and others in the commission on the notion that the conflict could be resolved if sovereignty and self-determination became subsumed under the aegis of the trust.) Deloria went on to cite other conflicts which beset the creation of Indian policy, such as the problem of creating a "first class educational system and the preservation of Indian culture, because to some extent the first class educational system means education in non-Indian culture."[50] He also mentions the conflict between "economic development and traditional Indian, religious and other attitudes toward language."[51] These statements were clearly prophetic of the problems which would confront the commission. They also clearly sum up much of what is paradoxical and problematic in contemporary Indian life. However powerful are the arguments for moral rectitude in policymaking, the political realities loom. Congressional plenary power wields an extraordinary heavy weapon in policy change. Moral sentiment may be fashioned to fit the occasion. In the words of Senator Abourezk, as he discussed Indian treaty law; "Every one of those legal principles can be wiped out with a single law. It can be wiped out with a single political act."[52]

Perhaps we can return to Marshall and witness the words of Andrew Jackson after Marshall had ruled that the forced removal of the Cherokee from the Carolinas and Georgia to Oklahoma was unconstitutional. We recall Jackson's words to this effect, "Mr. Marshall has made his decision, now let him enforce it."

Though the Marshall decisions, and especially *Worcester* and arguments from international law, have been brought to bear on the side of Indian sovereign self-determination, the position of the U.S. government clearly has not been to support strong self-determination by Indian people, except as the road to termination and loss of land. Analysis of the trust relationship shows that trust is not held in perpetuity when it is not in the interest of the government to define it so. Treaty law notwithstanding, trust until competence has been the practice throughout. Only the definition of competence has been at issue. Indian reform arguments most often take the form of squabbles over whether Indians are being assimilated too quickly or too slowly into American life. (Sometimes the question of Indian policy consent is raised. Consent, however, means advice—not consent.)

Beyond the extent of plenary power, the argument between Meeds and the AIPRC highlights a deeper issue here. If we assume that Meeds is right and trust extends only over land, Indian social, educational and welfare policy will continue in a direction to provide competency, leading to a termination of wardship status. If the AIPRC were to carry the day, the increase of social programming would only serve the needs of a traditional aim in policy, that is, to provide competencies which, when they are attained, will provide the basis for any argument for termination. In the end, termination is the final result. The only difference lies in whether or not the government is willing to fund a competency program to help justify that end.

The trust relationship is strongly political rather than strictly legal or moral. Although it began through treaties between sovereigns, it has degenerated. It has become essentially what the U.S. government, the Department of the Interior and the Bureau of Indian Affairs want it to be. Even when the extent of trust is a fluctuating issue, its aims are remarkably uniform—trust over Indian lands, resources and human capital until such time as Indians are deemed competent to cease reservation status. Trust through treaty in perpetuity is a myth.

Indian education policy shifts and social welfare plans are examples of cosmetic change. The underlying theme is and has been education for competence and assimilation. We may appeal to treaty rights by looking at court precedent and the agreements made in treaties, but our appeal is in many ways a moral one, not merely legal. For looming behind the trust relationship lies the awesome legal power of Congress to abrogate those treaties. We may appeal to educational and social rights of Indian people through a broad interpretation of trust, yet we only need to look at history to see the legacy of social and educational programs designed to assimilate and provide competency for a quicker end to the trust relationship. Given this historical and legal precedent, we must keep a critical perspective on the notion of self-determination as a policy development purporting to enhance Indian social, political and cultural hegemony.

NOTES

1. Felix Cohen, *Handbook of Federal Indian Law* (Washington, D.C.: U.S. Government Printing Office, 1945), p. 33. First printed in 1941, Cohen's work was the first attempt to cover the vast and highly complex field of treaties, law, and legal opinion which informs the operation of federal-Indian relations.
2. Ibid.
3. Nathan Margold, "Introduction" to Cohen, *Handbook of Federal Indian Law* (Washington, D.C.: U.S. Government Printing Office, 1945), p. x. Margold was solicitor to the Interior Department when he wrote this introduction.
4. Ibid., p. viii. Briefly, the "General Allotment Act" provided that an Indian, upon passing a test of blood and skill competency, would be given a plot or allotment of land in fee simple, land which formerly was a part of his tribal holding. The Indian Reorganization Act is also a complex piece of legislation, whose chief purpose among its package of provisions was the incorporation of tribal governments and the establishment of tribal constitutions and charters.
5. Ibid., p. ix.
6. See U.S. Commission on Civil Rights, Report, *Indian Tribes: A Continuing Quest for Survival* (Washington, D.C.: U.S. Government Printing Office, 1981).
7. Ibid., p. 24. See also *Cherokee Nation v. Georgia*, 30 U.S. (5 Pet.), 1 (1831).
8. See Emmerich Vattel's *Law of Nations*, first published in 1860.
9. Russel Lawrence Barsh and James Youngblood Henderson, *The Road: Indian Tribes and Political Liberty* (Berkeley: University of California Press, 1980), p. 140.
10. Ibid., p. 53.
11. Ibid., p. 56.
12. Ibid., p. 57.

13. Ibid.

14. Ibid.

15. U.S. Department of Health, Education and Welfare, Office of Education, *A Brief History of the Federal Responsibility to the American Indian* (Washington, D.C.: Printing Office, 1979), p. 19. This report is based on the report *Legislative Analysis of the Federal Role in Indian Education* by Vine Deloria, Jr.

16. Ibid., p. 19.

17. Ibid., p. 20.

18. Ibid., p. 15

19. U.S. Commission on Civil Rights, *Indian Tribes,* p. 25.

20. Edgar Cahn, ed., *Our Brother's Keeper: The Indian in White America,* 2nd ed. (New York: New Community Press, World Publishing Co., 1970), p. 170.

21. Ibid.

22. Barsh and Henderson, *The Road,* p. 59.

23. Ibid.

24. Michael Peter Doss, "The American Indian Policy Review Commission: A Case Study Analysis of an Attempted Large System Change by a Temporary Organization" (Ph.D. dissertation, Harvard University, 1977), p. 48.

25. The AIPRC was comprised of Senator James Abourezk, South Dakota (Chairman); Congressman Lloyd Meeds, Washington (Vice-Chairman); Senator Lee Metcalf, Montana; Senator Mark Hatfield, Oregon; Congressman Sidney Yates, Illinois; Congressman Sam Steiger, Arizona; John Borbridge, Tlingit-Haida; Louis R. Bruce, Mohawk-Sioux; Ada Deer, Menominee; Adolph Dial, Lumbee; Jake Whitecrow, Quapaw-Seneca-Cayuga; Ernest Stevens, Oneida (Executive Director); Kirke Kickingbird, Kiowa (General Counsel); and Max I. Richtman (Professional Staff Member).

26. Doss, p. 46.

27. U.S. Congress, House, *Committee on Interior and Insular Affairs,* 93rd Cong., 2d sess., on H. Res. 881 and S. Res. 133 to provide for the establishment of the AIPRC, 13 May 1974, p. 61. Early in the process several voices were raised concerning the balance of Indian-white representation on the commission. All appeared to be in agreement about the need for Indian representation. There was division, however, over the amount of Indian representation and the method of selection of members. For example, Mike Haney from the American Indian Movement claimed that ten rather than five Indians be represented and that Indian people should participate in the voting for members. He also argued that there be more reservation than urban representatives, and more representatives from west of the Mississippi. These recommendations were not adopted.

28. American Indian Policy Review Commission, *Final Report on Trust Responsibilities and the Federal-Indian Relationship: Including Treaty Review* (Washington, D.C.: U.S. Government Printing Office, 1976).

29. Ibid., p. 47.

30. Ibid., p. 48.

31. Ibid., pp. 52-53.

32. Ibid.

33. *Meetings of the AIPRC,* vol. 4, 19-32 November 1976 (Washington, D.C.: U.S. Government Printing Office, 1977), p. 9.

34. Ibid., p. 11.

35. Ibid., p. 33.

36. Ibid.

37. Ibid., p. 34.

38. Ibid.

39. Ibid., p. 35.

40. Ibid., p. 13.

41. *Meetings of the AIPRC*, vol. 5, 4 February 1977 (Washington, D.C.: U.S. Government Printing Office, 1978).

42. Ibid.

43. Rupert Costo and Jeanette Henry, eds., *Indian Treaties: Two Centuries of Dishonor* (San Francisco: Indian Historian Press, 1977), p. 75-76.

44. Ibid., p. 110.

45. Ibid., p. 150.

46. *Meetings of the AIPRC* 4 February 1977, p. 151.

47. Ibid., p. 156-57.

48. U.S. Congress, House, *Subcommittee on Indian Affairs of the Committee on Interior and Insular Affairs*, 93rd Cong., 2d sess., 13 May 1974 (Washington, D.C.: U.S. Government Printing Office, 1974), p. 52.

49. Ibid.

50. Ibid.

51. Ibid.

52. *Meetings of the AIPRC,* 4 February 1977, p. 153.

11

Conclusion: Managing Manifest Destiny

The rhetorical uses of self-determination are a natural development in a nation whose dominant consciousness was formed in the crucible of what Frederick Jackson Turner would popularize as "manifest destiny" and the associated attempt to liquidate Indian sovereignty. Indian socialization during the self-determination policy period has been, in important ways, an attempt to provide social and institutional competencies, the lack of which were the real impediments to termination and assimilation. After World War II, Indians were to be liberated, free from constraints on their ability to liquidate their property. When this effort proved to be politically unwieldy and socially unjustifiable, the effort was made to provide competency programs of industrial, community and educational development which would remove this impediment to eventual termination.

Many who pointed to the gains made by tribes during the 1960s and 1970s lamented the losses of the Reagan years as a point of comparison. Indeed, Indian social education programs expand and contract the degree to which the government directs its focus to the military or to programming for human capital development. Clearly, one may point to political gains made by tribes; for example, successful efforts to lobby for the attachment of Indian participation in the benefits of most of the compensatory education legislation of the sixties and seventies.

The contract-school movement did not greatly restrain the overall educational emphasis on a rather rigid definition of socialization. Cultural and linguistic assimilation proceeded apace in the schools—regardless of type—in the community, and in the economic sector, each sector mimicking the requirements of resource and human capital development common in the dominant society. Where swift termination had failed to provide an acceptable competency education in the school of hard knocks, liberal social meliorists in industry, the foundations and academia were united in an effort to develop an action social science which would work to provide successful competency education. Perhaps the key to this sophisticated institutional acculturation design was the belief that the most successful program would be one which involved most closely the cooperation of the local people.

There has existed a close relationship between national policy toward developing nations and the effort to apply a "bootstrap" metaphor to the conduct of American Indian social reform. As such, social policy for the Indian must be seen in its close relationship to programs designed to envelop poor nations in the economic orbit of the U.S. There is no mistaking the role of the Ford Foundation in its activities both abroad and within America during this period. Indeed, Mill's "power elite" well describes the cadre of professional reformers who shaped a legitimate grass-roots cry for participatory democracy into this juggernaut of policies with intentions which would be despised by Indian people who speak a different language of self-determination. If self-determination and economic development were an attempt to democratize Indian policy, it is remarkable how such small groups as the Ford Foundation, and the AAIA were able to enjoy such wide latitude to influence the social, economic, and educational policies of this period. From the powerful influence of the Fund for the Republic through the Udall task force and subsequent industrialization and social programming, Ford left its stamp on Indian America. Indian America was one part of a larger plan to rationalize the chaos of the underdeveloped world. Human capital development was a key here. Yet, what were the results of much of this effort? Economic development in both Indian and Latin America has been a code phrase for economic exploitation and the support of local oligarchies, from the petty to the brutal, which have ruthlessly suppressed true popular self-determination in the service of the expanding influence of American capital in the underdeveloped West.

Self-determination has been hailed for its democratizing influence and for its emphasis on development of local economies and local control. On the industrial level, however, local economies were only marginally altered, and development efforts proceeded only with a profusion of promises that the locals would be quiet, docile and manageable. When the local people demanded a role in local economic policy, that was the signal that business as usual was finished, and industry moved on.

On the level of community development and education, control was nurtured as a training in institutional development, not for the virtue of control as an end in itself. Community control was originally designed as training—a demonstration and education for transition—from dependency to potential termination. Neither community nor local economic industrial development were central efforts to secure greater community or tribal power for its own sake; rather, it was a means to an end, to forms of eventual termination. Termination could now be based on a generation of programs which had prepared Indians for western "European" institutional life.

Still, two questions have arisen which apparently work in contradiction to parts of this argument. First, the codification of self-determination, through The Self-determination and Education Assistance Act, has provided only a poor training in institutional management, while it has solidified the control of the BIA. Also, local economic development was often unsystematic and problematic, only marginally involving Indian people in institutional development. How can struggling education and economic contract operations be explained as an effort to prove competency?

History has shown that the proof of competency need not be overstrict. During the allotment period, a tribesmember needed to prove little else than blood quantum and rudimentary literacy to be eligible for an allotment of land. Even during termination, in the early 1950s, tribal ability to handle the withdrawal of federal services was largely ignored—the competency of GI war valor and liberation propaganda often were enough termination justification. True competency would have meant the ability of all tribesmembers to survive and prosper without government and, perhaps, include the capacity of tribesmembers to retain their patrimony—not to sell out. The history of termination and allotment has been, however, the sellout. The issue has only been whether the sellout was fair, whether large Indian properties fell into the right hands or not.

Indeed, the feeble efforts at providing a justifiable termination since 1955 have been more than sufficient effort to justify competency if we take into account that any justification, no matter how feeble, is better than what supported termination before. Indeed, as this is being written, the traditional federal-Indian trust relation, and tribal jurisdiction is in constant danger of being handed over to the states, a form of termination where the federal responsibility to provide education and social services is abrogated, due potentially to the failure or inability of either the states or tribes to pay for services.

Another, perhaps more fundamental question lies with the notion of self-determination itself. One may ask, indeed, if Indian people were given legitimate control over their destiny—sovereignty—is not this tantamount to termination anyway? How can one criticize a self-determination policy which aims at termination when self-determination usually implies sovereignty, which implies separation—indeed, the end of patronage?

Yet we must understand that termination of federal-Indian trust often has meant conferring to tribesmembers the individual parcels of land—ultimately to be sold or kept in the best Anglo-Saxon tradition. The "freedom" to sell land is part of the American heritage, the American Dream, and the sort of privilege which may have been felt too long denied the Indian. Yet, is this sovereignty? When a polity attains sovereignty on the international level, do individuals attain the right to obtain fee patents to the land for sale?

Programs, policies, even the fabric of American law and custom are designed to liquidate, not retain, tribal sovereignty. John Marshall notwithstanding, Jackson and the legacy of manifest destiny put the lie to limited Indian sovereignty except as a transition to termination. Why is this notion so deeply rooted? Reginald Horsman has argued that Anglo-Saxon institutional development takes its inexorability from a deep-seated belief in race destiny—that European, Western and especially "Aryan" movement westward only became a moral and biological imperative as a justification of the exploitation and, finally, the genocide of indigenous peoples of Africa, Asia and North America in the advancing West.[1] In addition to the faith in race destiny, the nineteenth-century notion of progress left little room for impediments to westward expansion and institutional entrenchment. Consistent with this is the progress of the dominant school of social science and its "adjustment" efforts toward Indian America.

Certainly, this "Wheel of Progress" did not slow as resource imperatives and cold war contention heated up after the World War II. Indian sovereignty would not become political sovereignty in any powerful sense of the word, not while it was possible to fracture tribal will and land in the service of continued control of reservation natural and human resources. For self-determination and development to represent a true future for American Indians, it must be a future which includes both tribal "nation-like" sovereignty and Indian cultural renascence.

This analysis of the reality of self-determination attempts to document another chapter in a developing irony, not only of Indian self-determination, but of American democracy in the twentieth century. This has been an attempt to chart the growth of a policy which has fired the imaginations of those who envision a freer and stronger future for Indian community and tribal sovereignty. The irony is that the present vision of self-determination has kept this dream alive.

Liberal progressive social-science policy has not occurred outside the ironies of democratic oligarchy and resource exploitation passing as economic development. Horsman has noted that Indian education and philanthropy was the child of the marriage between humanist Protestant morality and the requirements of westward expansion. Education historian David Adams has shown that it is too simple to see Indian social education as an exercise in forced assimilation. Rather, he notes how social philanthropy and education were "hopelessly intertwined" in a dialectic of humanitarianism and land greed.[2]

This book has been an effort to explore the dialectical and paradoxical dimensions of Native American self-empowerment. Most critics and scholars of twentieth-century Native American social policy have described the postwar contemporary period as a time of increasingly successful tribal and community activism. Truly, it is correct to observe the ongoing and frequently victorious struggles of tribes to gain or retain rightful access to social capital, land and resources. For all the scholarly emphasis on tribal defeat and fragmentation during, for example, the postwar period of termination, there is the story of tribal cooperation and victory. Laurence Hauptman's study of Oneida resistance to termination is an example of the kind of tribal history which demonstrates clearly that policy did not evolve only in a vacuum of liberal think tanks, and philanthropic organizations.[3] Yet, as important as is the story of varieties of resistance, is the story of the forces against which much resistance was directed. Like other Western hemispheric political phenomena, self-determination is a stunted growth, an inevitable mutation from the marriage of social contradiction.

Like many other social-philosophical concepts with human empowerment or extended social-political participation at their heart, self-determination developed a Janus face when it entered the language of American Indian policy. As such, its paradoxical nature must be understood in reference to the contradictions which spawned it. An important characteristic of this form of policy is language development, which uses the shibboleths of democratic participatory language to justify a subaltern agenda, requiring increasingly an unquestioned government service to the power of private property in the interest of human and resource capital development. It is language born in the attempt to reconcile Native American sovereignty with the plenary power of Congress and the subservience of the American polity to the power and rhetoric of a government policy process, and in the contradiction between jurisprudential treaty rights and the siren call of resource mobilization and availability. It was born in the tension between a developing Native American sovereign pluralism and the juggernaut of an American nationalism which grows more and more intolerant of differences out of step with the main agenda of a persistently violent garrison state. It was born, finally, in the power of rhetoric to reconcile the contradiction between democratic dogma and an internal economic colonialism in keeping with the economic colonization of Latin/Indian southern America which was proceeding apace during this period.

Those who point to gains must know that these gains, like those of all liberal programs in the postwar state, have benefitted a privileged class minority, escapees of a permanently festering underclass, mired in structural poverty. Pointing to the relatively small difference in social conditions between the Reagan years and the Great Society is a symptom of the general overconfidence in the power of dissent and a language of self-empowerment to defeat forces of bureaucratization and the social injustice of capital exploitation. It misjudges the power and requirements of capital to impose structural dis-opportunity through educative structures. The reason for the success of the language of self-determination was due not to the sensitivity of policy oligarchies to dissent. It succeeded because it was congruent with a language of social science. It was constructed as a rhetorical reconciliation of the prerogatives of capital development with the ideological requirements of pluralist, democratic dogma.

In *The Structure of Evil* social philosopher Ernest Becker cautioned that social science must reclaim its allegiance to the ethical dimension of policy. The social observer, whether it be a concerned citizen, historian or sociologist, must, for Becker, be aware of the "unique task of social critique."[4] The observation of Native American policy has tended to vacillate between the poles of chronicle, insensitive to the ethical dimensions of policy and shrill polemic, oversensitive and often informative of little more than the passion of indignation. There is not a great deal of critical study in-between.

I believe there is a need to magnify the assumptions locked within the fine chronicles which do exist. When looking at educational and social policy, there must be an intensified focus on the plethora of conceptual baggage which has been carried on the train of twentieth-century liberal social planning. The conceptual terrain is strewn with unexamined positive signifiers—anti-poverty, maximum feasible participation, community control, economic development, self-help, self-determination. The sheen of this terminology threatens to obscure our analysis of its underlying assumptions.

To many policy observers who have lived through the Reagan years, the desire to critically analyze the halcyon days of the OEO, community control or Red Power may be difficult to muster. But these often are the same observers who witnessed over the last ten years the miscarriage of self-determination in community after community, who watched community-control contracts magically convert to block grants, and who saw the threat that these grants would revert to state administration, and then wrongly blamed the conservatives for this and other contractions of autonomy. I believe that it is important to remember that the groundwork for this and other contractions of legitimate self-determination was laid in Camelot.

The contradiction of manifest destiny and Indian sovereignty, along with the history of psychosocial manipulation of developing peoples and nations, is too apparent and too present in the record to be ignored. To be realistic is not to be pessimistic. However, those who would hope for a realization of Indian self-determination in this nation must come to grips with the true place that has been accorded the Indian in this country and with the ideology of self-determination. This examination of that place as it evolved after World War II is simply a confirmation of the power of the ideology of self-determination to shape the economic and social destiny of a people and, indeed, the resistance of the notion that they are "America's Unfinished Business."

It is crucial to understand that both the ideal of self-determination and its rhetorical use were developed from the political, philosophic grounds of liberalism and its ground as part of a dialogue of human freedom and forms of planned social order. On the one hand, this concept and its use in the postwar era resides squarely within the classical liberal political tradition. The emphasis on self-help and self-reliance is consistent with the Enlightenment faith in the individual, social atomism and political localism. Its emphasis on a demand for treaty observance and treaty federalism fits closely with the tradition of independent polities making their own destiny. Its themes echo with the care for political, economic and social freedom dear to the liberal tradition. Self-determination also is tied closely to a belief in human perfectibility, human rationality made manifest through formal and participatory political education. As such, education is a constant requirement for the fruition of social order, an education aimed at the development of intellect and reason, for the development of political virtue. However, there is another, and I believe more important side to the heritage of this notion which helps us understand the concept and its shortcomings more clearly. This is the side of liberalism which grew in the modern period to obscure some of the traditional notions of individual and civil freedom just mentioned.

Joseph Jorgensen has discussed how Indian social reform has been forged in a contradictory context of rugged individualism on the one hand, and a sensitivity to adjustment and compassion on the other. He discusses the tension between the freedom of individuals to succeed on their own terms and the recognition of the humane obligation to provide assistance to minority groups until such time as their members can "strike out on their own."[5] Whether or not he intended this play on words, this quote uncovers that tension in American liberalism which is ambivalent, and in some sense hostile, to group rights as opposed to individual rights (in this case treaty rights) and laws favoring special groups.

In *The Irony of Liberal Reason,* Thomas Spragens provides a persuasive philosophical context in which to understand these tensions. For Spragens, the same liberal tradition that is heir to and protector of Western European humanism has developed within itself tendencies that threaten humane values. He writes:

> these self-destructive tendencies in turn stem from failures within the larger philosophical tradition that undergirds liberalism—especially from failures related to this tradition's conception of human reason. Surviving concepts of Reason are "technocratic" and leave humanistic liberal ideals and practices largely without sustenance and indeed often threaten them more directly.[6]

Indian people have fought for the ideals of treaty federalism and local autonomy throughout this century of policy reform. Yet the Indian leadership's ongoing frustration is the result of the natural tendency of a totalizing federal structure to subsume the legitimate interests of Indian people under the umbrella of national social and educational planning. This planning impulse is a part of the shape of modern government and its reliance on a political philosophy of controlled pluralism, within the guidelines drawn by interlocking cadres of elite policy and administrative social scientists. Ever since *The Problem of Indian Administration* was "solved" by the report of the 1929 Hoover commission, Indian social and education policy have been under the intensifying control of a select group of policy scientists and magistrates, the "true doctors of morality."[7]

During the decades during which modern Indian policy reform has waxed and waned, roughly since the New Deal, Indian policy and the Indian polity has been shaped conforming to the "technocratic legislator" who, armed with the language of the new social science, is "legitimated by his cognitive transcendence and his purity of heart, . . . his task is to fabricate a good political order out of the human matter whose laws are known to him."[8] Spragens reaches back into the Enlightenment tradition and identifies the interest of the French *philosophes* and others in the perfect rationalization of human activity. This rationalization would supersede, through positive science, the haphazard development of social order through traditional politics. As Helvetius described it, the "starting point of the Ideal Legislator, is his knowledge of 'the wires' that move the 'human puppet.' "[9]

The close relationship between legislators, administrators, and functionalist social scientists during the twentieth century is illustrative of the faith of Enlightenment philosophers like Helvetius. Individual policymakers and opinion leaders like Collier, La Farge, Udall and Nash often move smoothly from the academy to social and philanthropic service, to government administration and legislation, and we observe with more frequency the intimate self-referential relations between scientist and legislator. In an important way we see the technocracy which Spragens refers to as a new kind of governance:

> The technocratic tradition gives a peculiarly modern and pro-
> foundly radical twist to the idea of governance. Indeed, the
> technocrat's conception of governance transcends the bounds of the
> traditional notion of governance altogether. Governance, as he
> envisions it, is not a form of leadership. It is not a form of
> representation. It is, instead, a form of creation. The governor
> "ghost" subject relates to the governed "machine" object not as one
> man relates to another but as a potter relates to his clay. . . .
> Governance is envisioned not as a process of reciprocal—if
> asymmetrical—interaction but as a process of unilateral
> control. The technocrat is a maker of society. He assumes
> the role of demiurge, imposing order and form on the chaos
> of human nature. The technocratic ruler, in short, is a *deus
> faber*.[10]

Spragens describes the Enlightenment fascination with the connection between legislation and education. The two were conceived to be one and the same thing by Helvetius and his disciples: "character formation." What the legislator sought to achieve through his system of laws, the educator should achieve through his system of instruction. The ends and the means were the same in both cases. The goal of legislation was not simply obedience; nor was the aim of education mere illumination. The end was what Locke had mandated in his *Thoughts Concerning Education:* "it is virtue, direct virtue, which is the hard and valuable part to be aimed at." And the means were also essentially the same in both cases: make subjects "behave" properly by controlling their environment. In Helvetius's words, "the science of education may be reduced perhaps to the placing a man in that situation which will force him to attain the talents and virtues required in him."[11]

W. Roger Buffalohead has spoken of the paradox of the liberal social reformer by describing John Collier's perplexing intellectual nature in the following way. "John Collier cannot be, at one and the same time, the patron saint of Indian self-determination and the man who disguised assimilation as self-government to make it easier for the federal government and white exploiters to manipulate Indians into signing away their last resources."[12] Collier's case may be generalized to his heirs, social planners who believed their ministrations were in the best interests of tribal people. Yet, imbedded in the logic of liberal social science is a form of rationality which has succeeded in accommodating both termination and self-determination in the same impulse. Michael

Polanyi offers the following generalization which works to explain this ambiguity. He argues that scientism itself, due to the nature of its claim on objectivity, has its salvational aspirations packaged in "neutral and technical language."[13] In many respects this has been the practical rather than the ideal language of self-determination. The social scientist earns a moral intention which is not earned in the democratic market-place of ideas, but by virtue of the science's reputation for objectivity and value-freedom. "The moral content and the scientific pretensions of the ideology exist in symbiosis, since each part performs important services for the other: the moral content gives meaning and motivation to the scientific enterprise and the scientific language gives protection to the moral ends contained within it."[14] The social scientist/legislator is not merely authorized to govern, he is "himself the author of the social order. He is not the 'bearer' of the person of his subjects, . . . so much as he is the creator of these persons."[15]

On this model, the rationality of functionalist social science acts as logical arbiter of the subservience of individuals to the group, and the group to the dominant society. The modern liberal social planner is not just *likely* to subsume minority interests to the rationality of national planning prerogatives, the planner is logically *obliged* to do so. Collier's progeny, including Nash, La Farge, Udall, Roessel and a constellation of other liberal benefactors are not the conspiratorial bearers of a hidden termination agenda, they are following a logic of political development which grows from the natural assumptions of a world view. It is a view which is simply not equipped to make the political distinction between eventual termination and permanent sovereignty. It is a world view in which manifestations of tribalism are at best transitional, and at worst, reactionary revivalism.

The primary tool of the legislator for the technocratic vision of politics is the observation of mankind, and to "infer from these observations the laws of human behavior. . . . His primary tools are legislation and education, both of which involve controlling the environment."[16] If self-determination fails to achieve the ideals of tribal leaders and citizens, part of the reason for this failure is because the blueprint for this policy conforms precisely to its history as a species of liberal technocratic social science and public administration. Federal Indian-policy administration during the years following Eisenhower was characterized by a resurgence of policies which encouraged a symbiosis of education and economic development. This impulse borrows its strength in part from John Collier's New Deal legacy. Indeed, Collier's liberalism clearly reflects the technocratic impulse. The period under discussion here borrows much of the New Deal-era faith in the good offices of government social scientists and experts to solve problems too complicated for mere politics.

The failure to fully realize tribal sovereignty through self-determination is less paradoxical when we realize that these failures are a natural outgrowth of a philosophy, not a failure of policy. The overall self-determination policy equivocation on sovereignty and termination is the result of a political philosophy which subsumes minority tribal interests beneath national capital and human resource prerogatives. It is natural to expect a technocratic liberalism to subsume participatory democratic desires beneath the considered social prerogatives of social scientific expertise.

The practical use of self-determination developed primarily as a form of social therapy rather than political sovereignty. This helps explain its immunity from its more radical political consequences. Political self-determination requires a form of radical rationality which is largely unavailable at the present time—a notion that social good rests with the debates and action of a critically informed polity. This was the message of Red Power, but it is a message philosophically inconsistent with a vision of rational social order efficiently designed by a civic/academic elite with access to the correct theme of social order, within which all sub-polities must orchestrate their activities. Under these conditions it is much easier to see how self-determination can readily devolve, as its critics have charged, into a blueprint for internal colonialism.

The practice of self-determination, as distinct from its ideals, was conceived in the wedding of functionalist social science and government administration, in varying degrees, from the New Deal to the New Federalism of the Reagan era. The policy developments which characterize it are significantly different than the ideals its supporters often say it represents. The ideal is a policy which should represent a clear intent to support treaty-bound federalism and tribal sovereignty. In reality, the policy is operating with an ambiguous notion of sovereignty. Sovereignty is strengthened only the degree to which federal funds work to support tribal development efforts and social infrastructure. The ideal is a policy which confers true control and the right to experiment with policy without the threat of federal interference. In reality, as Hank Adams has noted, self-administration replaces self-determination.

True self-determination would be an end in itself, a realized vision of broadly participatory self-government. In reality, it has been fundamentally manipulative in intent, a form of social conditioning, fashioned largely by administrative elites. In the ideal it would be self-regenerative, where the main function of education is the perpetuation of tribal civic and critical literacy. The reality has been social education for smooth transition and adjustment. Self-determination ideals would reflect, more than they do, the intellectual impact of a wide range of Indian citizens. There is no question that tribal and community desires for radical educational and social reform had a large impact on the dialogue. Yet in a nation where marginalized citizens have seen their struggles shaped to conform to national civic prerogatives, Indian people have not been immune to the "rationalized" exploitation of sacred land, human energy and capital resources, amid the bromides of equal opportunity, guided acculturation, maximum feasible participation, self-help, and indeed, self-determination. The toxin of social therapy poisons the language of self-help, and self-rule. It is a sobering reminder of the elite techno-managerialism which uncomfortably cohabits self-determination along with radical sovereigntist Red Power.

It is crucial to understand that the social education project of the self-determination impulse should be distinguished from ideals of human freedom which are also imbedded within it. Charles Wilkinson has a particularly powerful analysis of sovereignty and the way it may be employed for tribal people to realize the ideals of self-determination. He argues that the uses of sovereignty rest at the heart of the tribal polity itself. "The tribal unity may change when a catastrophic event occurs. . .and a tribe may redefine itself ethnologically. But tribalism continues until the members themselves extinguish it."[17] For Wilkinson, then, the shape of a tribe's will around the issue of sovereignty is the only guarantee of its continuation. If he is right, then this power is defined by the level of critical civic literacy in the tribal community's possession. It is the development of this high literacy which will be mobilized against the fluctuating will of the national sovereign. "The higher sovereign," Wilkinson writes,

> faced with few practical constraints, holds nearly full sway in its ability to sap or energize Indian sovereignty. The power exists to enact everything from the debilitating allotment and termination programs to the beneficent child welfare and tax status laws that offer so much promise to Indian people. With ultimate primacy in Indian law and policy lodged firmly in Congress, Indian leaders know full well that whether tribal sovereignty will decline or progress will depend in important part on the tribes' own skill in presenting their views in the legislative forum.[18]

The developing language of self-determination has been nothing if not equivocal regarding the issue of treaty federalism, tribal nationalism and sovereignty. This equivocation grows directly from a world view which is itself torn between elite control and populist impulse, between national prerogative and local interest, between social stability and tolerance of diversity.

The results of self-determination will depend, as they have already depended, on the nature of the educational impulse. But for its ideals to be realized, it must be allied with continued inter/intra tribal dialogue and education and the development of the ability to aggressively defend sovereignty. Traditional education and community higher education must be the goal of community control, along with, but not subservient to, economic development.

This analysis tries to ask some difficult questions about the nature of modern liberal social/education programming. It draws strength from the critical work of others who have raised the issues of rhetoric and reality in government-Indian relations during the 1960's and 1970s.[19] As such, it is only the beginning of what I hope will be a continuing project toward an ongoing analysis of the impact of social science language and education on the lives of people. It is particularly important to understand the effect of this language on those who who have turned to education as the source of hope in the struggle to live in an America which has turned to more sophisticated methods, toward the social, scientific, and indeed, to the educational management of manifest destiny.

NOTES

1. Reginald Horsman, *Race and Manifest Destiny: The Origins of American Racial Anglo-Saxonism* (Cambridge: Harvard University Press, 1981).

2. David Wallace Adams, "Fundamental Consideration: The Deep Meaning of Native American Schooling, 1880-1900" *Harvard Educational Review* 58, no. 1 (1988): 1-28.

3. Laurence M. Hauptman, "Learning the Lessons of History: The Oneidas of Wisconsin Reject Termination, 1943-1956," *Journal of Ethnic Studies* (Winter 1987): 31-52.

4. Ernest Becker, *The Structure of Evil* (New York: George Braziller, 1968).

5. Joseph G. Jorgensen, "Federal Policies, American Indian Politics and the 'New Federalism'," *American Indian Culture and Research Journal* 10, no. 2 (1986): 4.

6. Thomas A. Spragens, Jr., *The Irony of Liberal Reason* (Chicago: University of Chicago Press, 1981).

7. Ibid., p. 110.

8. Ibid., p. 109.

9. Ibid., p. 110.

10. Ibid., p. 115.

11. Ibid., p. 112.

12. Kenneth R. Philp, *Indian Self-rule: First-hand Accounts of Indian-White Relations from Roosevelt to Reagan* (Salt Lake City: Howe Brothers, 1986), p. 266.

13. Spragens, p. 118.

14. Ibid.

15. Ibid., p. 115.

16. Ibid.

17. Charles F. Wilkinson, *American Indians, Time, and the Law: Native Societies in a Modern Constitutional Democracy* (New Haven, Conn.: Yale University Press, 1987), p. 77.

18. Ibid., p. 86.

19. Important critical studies which suggest the paradoxical nature of the language of economic and educational self-determination include Steve Talbot, *Roots of Oppression* (New York: International Publishers, 1981); Roxanne Dunbar Ortiz, *Indians of the Americas: Human Rights and Self-determination* (New York: Praeger, 1984); Jack Forbes, *Native Americans and Nixon* (Los Angeles: Native American Studies Center-UCLA, 1983). In "Activism and Red Power," Hank Adams has been clear about the position of the main academic interpretation of self-determination impulse, and his opposition to it. "I have read," he writes, "in a number of publications that termination ended in 1958. Termination was going strong in the 1960s under Philleo Nash, James Officer, Stewart Udall and President John F. Kennedy" in (Philp, *Indian Self-Rule*, p. 240).

Bibliography

MANUSCRIPT COLLECTIONS

William A. Brophy Papers. Harry S. Truman Memorial Library, Archives. Independence, Mo.

Dale E. Doty Papers. Harry S. Truman Memorial Library, Archives. Independence, Mo.

Glenn Emmons Papers (Microfilm). University of Toledo Library. Toledo, Ohio.

Harry S. Truman Papers. Philleo Nash Files. Harry S. Truman Memorial Library, Archives. Independence, Mo.

Joel Wolfsohn Papers. Harry S. Truman Memorial Library, Archives. Independence, Mo.

BOOKS

Ambler, Marjane. *Breaking the Iron Bonds: Indian Control of Energy Development.* Lawrence: University Press of Kansas, 1990.

Anderson, Kenneth E.; C. Gordon Colister; and Carl E. Todd, *The Educational Achievement of Indian Children: One Examination of the Question: How Well Are Indian Children Educated?* U.S. Department of the Interior, Bureau of Indian Affairs, Education Division Publication. Washington, D.C.: U.S. Government Printing Office, 1953.

Barsh, Russel Lawrence, and James Youngblood Henderson. *The Road: Indian Tribes and Political Liberty.* Berkeley: University of California Press, 1980.

Beatty, Willard W. *Education for Cultural Change: Selected Articles from "Indian Education."* Washington, D.C.: U.S. Government Printing Office, 1953.

Becker, Ernest. *The Structure of Evil.* New York.: George Braziller, 1968.

Brecher, Charles. *The Impact of Federal Anti-Poverty Policies.* New York: Praeger, 1973.

Burt, Larry W. *Tribalism in Crisis: Federal Indian Policy 1953-1961.* Albuquerque: University of New Mexico Press, 1982.

Cahn, Edgar, ed. *Our Brother's Keeper: The Indian in White America,* 2nd ed. New York: New Community Press/World Publishing Co., 1970.

Chase, Stuart. *Operation Bootstrap in Puerto Rico: Report of Progress, 1951.* Washington, D.C.: National Planning Association, 1951.

Cohen, Felix. *Handbook of Federal Indian Law.* Washington, D.C.: U.S. Government Printing Office, 1945.

Commission on the Rights, Liberties, and Responsibilities of the American Indian. *The Indian: America's Unfinished Business.* Norman, Okla.: University of Oklahoma Press, 1966.

Coombs, L. Madison. Bureau of Indian Affairs. *Doorway Toward the Light: The Story of the Special Navajo Education Program.* Washington, D.C.: U.S. Government Printing Office, 1962.

Costo, Rupert, and Jeanette Henry, eds. *Indian Treaties: Two Centuries of Dishonor.* San Francisco: The Indian Historian Press, 1977.

Dale, George A. In U.S. Department of the Interior, Bureau of Indian Affairs, *Education for a Better Living.* Washington, D.C.: U.S. Government Printing Office, 1955.

Deloria, Vine, Jr., and Clifford Lytle. *The Nations Within: The Past and Future of American Indian Sovereignty.* New York: Pantheon Books, 1984.

Drinnon, Richard. *Facing West: The Metaphysics of Indian Hating and Empire Building.* Minneapolis: University of Minnesota Press, 1980.

_____. *Keeper of Concentration Camps: Dillon S. Myer and American Racism.* Berkeley: University of California Press, 1987.

Dunbar-Ortiz, Roxanne. *Economic Development in American Indian Reservations.* Albuquerque: University of New Mexico, 1979.

_____. *Indians of the Americas: Human Rights and Self-determination.* New York: Praeger, 1984.

Fixico, Donald. *Termination and Recocation: Federal Indian Policy, 1945-1960.* Albuquerque: University of New Mexico Press, 1986.

Forbes, Jack D. *Native Americans and Nixon: Presidential Politics and Minority Self-determination, 1969-1972.* Los Angeles: Native American Studies Center-UCLA, 1981.

Gilbreath, Keith. *Red Capitalism: An Analysis of the Navajo Economy.* Norman, Okla.: University of Oklahoma Press, 1973.

Gross, Emma R. *Contemporary Federal Policy Toward American Indians.* Westport, Conn.: Greenwood Press, 1989.

Hagen, Everett E. *On the Theory of Social Change: How Economic Growth Begins.* Homewood, Ill.: Dorsey Press, 1962.

_____. *Planning Economic Development.* Homewood, Ill.: Richard Irwin, 1963.

Havighurst, Robert, and Estelle Fuchs. *To Live on This Earth: American Indian Education.* New York: Doubleday, 1972.

Hertzberg, Hazel. *The Search for American Indian Identity: Modern Pan-Indian Movements.* Syracuse, N.Y.: Syracuse University Press, 1971.

Horsman, Reginald. *Race and Manifest Destiny: The Origins of American Racial Anglo Saxonism.* Cambridge: Harvard University Press, 1981.

Hough, Henry. W. *Development of Indian Resources.* Denver: World Press, 1967.

Hoxie, Frederick E. *A Final Promise: The Campaign to Assimilate the Indians, 1880-1920.* Lincoln: University of Nebraska Press, 1984.

Iverson, Peter. *The Navajo Nation* Westport, Conn.: Greenwood Press, 1981.

Jackson, Curtis, and Marcia Galli. *History of the Bureau of Indian Affairs and Its Activities among Indians.* San Francisco: R and E Research Associates, 1977.

Johansen, Bruce, and Roberto Maestas. *Wasichu: The Continuing Indian Wars.* New York: Monthly Review Press, 1979.

Johnson, Broderick H. *Navajo Education at Rough Rock.* Rough Rock, Ariz.: Rough Rock Demonstration School, DINE, Inc., 1968.

Josephy, Alvin, Jr. *The American Indian and the Bureau of Indian Affairs.* Toronto: Indian-Eskimo Association of Canada, 1967.

_____. *Red Power: The American Indian's Fight for Freedom.* New York: McGraw-Hill, 1971.

Kaplan, H. Roy, ed. *American Minorities and Economic Opportunity.* Itasca, Ill.: F. E. Peacock, 1977.

Karier, Clarence. *Man, Society and Education* Glenview, Ill.: Scott-Foresman, 1967.

Kickingbird, Kirke, and Karen Ducheneaux. *One Hundred Million Acres.* New York: Macmillan 1973.

Kvasnicka, Robert M., and Herman Viola, eds. *The Commissioners of Indian Affairs 1824-1977.* Lincoln: University of Nebraska Press, 1979.

Landman, Ruth H., and Katherine Spencer Halpern, eds. *Applied An-*

thropologist and Public Servant: The Life and Work of Philleo Nash. Washington, D.C., American Anthropological Association, 1989.

Landsman, Gail H. *Sovereignty and Symbol: Indian-White Conflict at Ganienkeh* Albuquerque: University of New Mexico Press, 1988.

Lasswell, Harold D. and Abraham Kaplan. *Power and Society: A Framework for Political Inquiry*. New Haven: Yale University Press, 1950.

Levine, Stuart, and Nancy Oestreich Lurie, eds. *The American Indian Today*. Deland, Fla: Everett/Edwards, 1968.

Levitan, Sar. *The Great Societies' Poor Law: A New Approach to Poverty*. Baltimore: Johns Hopkins Press, 1969.

Levitan, Sar, and Barbara Hetrick. *Big Brother's Indian Programs— With Reservations*. New York: McGraw-Hill, 1971.

Matson, Floyd W. *The Broken Image: Man, Science and Society*. New York: George Braziller, 1964.

McNickle, D'Arcy. *Indian Man: A Life of Oliver La Farge*. Bloomington: Indiana University Press, 1971.

Mintz, Sidney W. *History, Evolution, and the Concept of Culture: Selected Papers of Alexander Lesser*. Cambridge, U.K.: Cambridge University Press, 1985.

Moynihan, Daniel P. *Maximum Feasible Misunderstanding: Community Action in the War on Poverty*. New York: Free Press, 1969.

National Research Conference on American Indian Education. *Proceedings*. Kalamazoo, Mich.: Society for the Study of Social Problems, 1967.

Noble, David. *The Paradox of Progressive Thought*. Minneapolis: University of Minnesota Press, 1958.

Olson, James S. and Raymond Wilson. *Native Americans in the Twentieth Century*. Provo: Brigham Young University Press, 1984.

Peroff, Nicholas C. *Menominee Drums: Tribal Termination and Restoration, 1954-1974*. Norman, Okla.: University of Oklahoma Press, 1982.

Peterson, Shailer. U.S. Indian Service Education Division. *How Well Are Indian Children Educated?* Washington, D.C.: U.S. Government Printing Office, 1948.

Philp, Kenneth R. *Indian Self-rule: First-hand Accounts of Indian-White Relations from Roosevelt to Reagan*. Salt Lake City: Howe Brothers, 1986.

Prucha, Francis Paul. *The Great Father: The United States Government and the American Indians* Part II . Lincoln: University of Nebraska Press, 1984.

Roessel, Robert A., Jr. *Navajo Education, 1948-1978: Its Progress and Its Problems.* Rough Rock, Ariz.: Rough Rock Demonstration School, Navajo Curriculum Center, 1979.

_____. *Navajo Education in Action: The Rough Rock Demonstration School.* Chinle, Ariz.: Navajo Curriculum Center, Rough Rock Demonstration School, 1977.

Schaw, Louis C. *The Bonds of Work.* San Francisco: Jossey-Bass, 1968.

Sorkin, Alan. *American Indians and Federal Aid.* Washington, D.C.: Brookings Institution, 1971.

Spragens, Thomas A., Jr. *The Irony of Liberal Reason* Chicago: University of Chicago Press, 1981.

Spring, Joel. *The Sorting Machine: National Educational Policy Since 1945.* New York: David McKay, 1976.

Staley, Eugene. *The American Citizens Stake in the Progress of Less Developed Areas of the World.* Menlo Park, Calif.: Stanford Research Institute, 1957.

Stanford Research Institute. *Manual of Industrial Development: With Special Application to Latin America.* Menlo Park: Stanford Research Institute, 1954.

_____. *The San Carlos Apache Indian Reservation: A Resources Development Study.* Menlo Park, Calif.: Stanford Research Institute, n.d., ca. 1954.

Straussman, Jeffrey D. *The Limits of Technocratic Politics.* New Brunswick, N.J.: Transaction Books, 1978.

Striner, Herbert E. *Federal Programs for the Development of Human Resources.* Washington, D.C.: U.S. Government Printing Office, 1968.

Szasz, Margaret. *Education and the American Indian: The Road to Self-determination 1928-1973.* Albuquerque: University of New Mexico Press, 1977.

Talbot, Steve. *Roots of Oppression.* New York: International Publishers, 1981.

Thompson, Hildegard. *The Navajos' Long Walk for Education.* Tsaile, Ariz.: Navajo Community College Press, 1975.

Umozurike, Umozurike Oji. *Self-determination in International Law.* Hamden, Conn.: Archon Books, 1972.

Weyler, Rex. *Blood of the Land: The Government and Corporate War Against the American Indian Movement.* New York: Everest House, 1982.

Wilkinson, Charles F. *American Indians, Time, and the Law: Native Societies in a Modern Constitutional Democracy.* New Haven: Yale University Press, 1987.

Workshop on American Indian Affairs, Department of Anthropology. *Federal Indian Legislation and Policies.* Chicago: University of Chicago Press, 1956.

DISSERTATIONS AND THESES

Doss, Michael Peter. "The American Indian Policy Review Commission: A Case Study Analysis of an Attempted Large System Change by a Temporary Organization." Ph.D. dissertation, Harvard University, 1977.

Fixico, Donald Lee. "Termination and Relocation: Federal Indian Policy in the 1950s." Ph.D. dissertation, University of Oklahoma, 1980.

Flannery, Thomas P. "The Indian Self-determination Act: An Analysis of Federal Policy." Ph.D. dissertation, Northwestern University, 1980.

Jackson, Curtis Emmanuel. "Identification of Unique Features in Education at American Indian Schools." Ph.D. dissertation, University of Utah, 1974.

Reeves, Charles Thomas. "The Fund for the Republic, 1951-1957: An Unusual Chapter in the History of American Philanthropy." Ph.D. dissertation, University of California, Santa Barbara, 1967.

Senese, Guy B. "The Little White School House: The Impact of Progressive Reform on the Social and Educational Policy of the U.S. Indian Service and Bureau of Indian Affairs 1895-1940." M.S. thesis, University of Illinois, 1981. (ERIC Document Reproduction Service, ED 214-712-1982.)

U.S. GOVERNMENT DOCUMENTS

American Indian Policy Review Commission. *Final Report on Trust Responsibilities and the Federal-Indian Relationship: Including Treaty Review.* Washington, D.C.: U.S. Government Printing Office, 1976.

———. *Meetings of the AIPRC,* vol. 4. Washington, D.C.: U.S. Government Printing Office, 1977.

———. *Meetings of the AIPRC,* vol. 5. Washington, D.C.: U.S. Government Printing Office, 1978.

Comptroller General of the United States. *Controls Are Needed Over Indian Self-determination Contracts, Grants and Training and Technical Assistance Activities to Insure Required Services Are Provided to Indians.* Washington, D.C.: U.S. General Accounting Office, 15 February 1978.

_____. *Report to Congress: Improving Federally Assisted Business Development on Indian Reservations.* Washington, D.C.: U.S. Government Printing Office, 1975.

U.S. Code of Federal Regulations (25 CFR).

U.S. Code of Federal Regulations (31 CFR).

U.S. Commission on Civil Rights. *Indian Tribes: A Continuing Quest for Survival.* Washington, D.C.: U.S. Government Printing Office, 1981.

U.S. Congress. "Indian Self-determination and Education Assistance Act." Public Law 93-638. 88 Stat. 2203.

U.S. Congress. Joint Economic Committee. *Federal Programs for the Development of Human Resources.* 90th Cong., 2d sess., 1968.

U.S. Congress. Joint Economic Committee, Subcommittee on Economy in Government. *Toward Economic Development for Native American Communities,* Vol. 1. 91st Cong., 1st sess., 1969.

U.S. Congress. House. *The Education of American Indians: The Organization Question,* 91st Cong., 1st sess., 1970.

_____. *Present Relations of the Federal Government to the American Indian.* 85th Cong., 2d sess., 1959.

_____. Committee on Interior and Insular Affairs. 93rd Cong., 2d sess., 1974.

_____. Subcommittee on Indian Affairs of the Committee on Interior and Insular Affairs. 86th Cong., 2d sess., 1960.

U.S. Congress. Senate. Committee on Indian Affairs. 79th Cong., 2d sess., 1946.

_____. Select Committee on Indian Affairs. 95th Cong., 1st sess., 1977.

_____. Subcommittee of the Committee on Indian Affairs. 78th Cong., 2d sess., 1944.

_____. Subcommittee on Indian Affairs. *Federal Indian Policy.* 85th Cong., 1st sess., 1957.

_____. Subcommittee on Indian Affairs. 93rd Cong., 1st sess., 1973.

_____. Subcommittee on Indian Affairs. 93rd Cong., 2d sess., 1973.

_____. Subcommittee on Indian Education. *The Education of American Indians, A Compilation of Statutes.* 91st Cong., 1st sess., 1969.

U.S. Department of Health, Education and Welfare, Office of Education. *A Brief History of the Federal Responsibility to the American Indian.* Washington, D.C.: U.S. Government Printing Office, 1979.

U.S. Department of the Interior. *Annual Report of the Commissioner of Indian Affairs.* Washington, D.C.: U.S. Government Printing Office, 1943.

_____. *Annual Report of the Commissioner of Indian Affairs.* Washington, D.C.: U.S. Government Printing Office, 1944.

———. *Annual Report of the Commissioner of Indian Affairs.* Washington, D.C.: U.S. Government Printing Office, 1954.

———. *Annual Report of the Secretary of the Interior, 1945-1948.* Washington, D.C.: U.S. Government Printing Office, 1948.

———. *Annual Report of the Secretary of the Interior.* Washington, D.C.: U.S. Government Printing Office, 1950.

———. *A Report of the Secretary of the Interior: Developing America's Resource Base.* Washington, D.C.: U.S. Government Printing Office, 1957.

———. Bureau of Indian Affairs. *Indian Education,* no. 79, 1 December 1942. Washington, D.C.: U.S. Government Printing Office, 1942.

———. *Indian Education,* no. 394 1 November 1963. Washington, D.C.: U.S. Government Printing Office, 1963.

———. *Indian Education: A Fortnightly Field Letter of the Education Division of the U.S. Office of Indian Affairs.* Washington, D.C.: U.S. Government Printing Office, 1943.

———. *Manual for the Indian School Service, 1941.* Washington, D.C.: U.S. Government Printing Office, 1941.

———. Indian Service-Education Branch. *Indian Education,* no. 159, 164. Washington, D.C.: U.S. Government Printing Office, 1947.

———. *Minimum Essential Goals for the Indian Schools, Levels 4 and 5.* Washington, D.C.: U.S. Government Printing Office, 1949.

———. Office of Indian Affairs. *Indian Education,* no. 130, 15 February 1946. Washington, D.C.: U.S. Government Printing Office, 1946.

———."A History of Indian Policy," S. Lyman Tyler, *Report to the Secretary of the Interior by the Task Force on Indian Affairs* (Washington, D.C.: U.S. Government Printing Office, 1973).

U.S. Department of State. *Point Four Cooperative Program for Aid in the Development of Economically Underdeveloped Areas.* Washington, D.C.: U.S. Government Printing Office, 1949.

PERIODICAL AND NEWSPAPER ARTICLES

Adams, David Wallace. "Fundamental Considerations: The Deep Meaning of Native American Schooling, 1880-1900." *Harvard Educational Review,* February 1988.

Akwasasne Notes, June 1969.

———, April 1970.

———, September 1970.

———, October 1970.

———, Early Winter 1974.

Barsh, Russel Lawrence. "The Nature and Spirit of North American Political Systems." *American Indian Quarterly* 16, no. 3 (Summer 1986): 181-98.

Brandon, William. "American Indians: The Real American Revolution." *Progressive,* February 1970, pp. 26-30.

Champagne, Duane. "Organizational Change and Conflict: A Case Study of the Bureau of Indian Affairs." *American Indian Culture and Research Journal* 7, no. 3 (1983): 3-28.

Christian Science Monitor, 9 December 1961.

Cooper, Robert, and Jack Gregory. "Can Community Control of Education Work?" *Journal of American Indian Education* 15 (May 1976): 7-12.

Costo, Rupert. "Fake Self-determination. *Wassaja,* June 1973.

_____. "Indian Treaties: The Basis for Solution of Current Issues." *Wassaja,* July 1973, p. 1.

Danziger, Edmund J. "A New Beginning or the Last Hurrah: American Indian Response to Reform Legislation of the 1970s." *American Indian Culture and Research Journal* 7, no.4 (1983): 69-84.

Deloria, Vine, Jr. "Half-Truths Charged to Morton." *Wassaja,* June 1973.

_____. "Secretary Rogers: His Position on Indian Affairs." *Wassaja,* June 1973.

_____. "Self-determination." *Wassaja,* January 1973.

Dozier, Edward P.; George E. Simpson; and Milton J. Yinger, "The Integration of Americans of Indian Descent." *Annals of the American Academy of Political and Social Science* 311 (May 1957): 41-46.

Dunbar-Ortiz, Roxanne. "Land and Nationhood: The American Indian Struggle for Self-determination and Survival." *Socialist Review,* May-August 1982: 105-120.

Emmons, Glenn. "Broken Arrow." *Time Magazine,* 4 March 1957, pp. 48-49.

Forbes, Jack D. "Alcatraz: What Its Seizure Means." *Indian Truth* 47, no. 3, (n.d.): 14-15.

Hauptman, Laurence M. "Learning the Lessons of History: The Oneidas of Wisconsin Reject Termination, 1943-1956." *Journal of Ethnic Studies,* Winter 1987.

Havighurst, Robert. "Education Among the American Indians: Individual and Cultural Aspects." *Annals of the American Academy of Political and Social Science* 311 (May 1957): 105-116.

_____. "Indian Education: Accomplishments of the Last Decade." *Phi Delta Kappan* 62 (January 1981): 329-332.

"Indian Country is a Frontier Again." *Nations' Business,* September 1969, pp. 74-77.

"Indian Lobbying Successes in the 1980s." *Indian Truth* 230 (February 1980): n.p.

Indian Truth, July-August 1980, editorial (n.p.)

_____. Vol. 46, No. 1, 1969 editorial (n.p.)

Indian Voices, April-May, 1966, pp. 10-11.

"Industry Invades the Reservation,"*Business Week,* 4 April 1970, pp. 72-74.

Jorgensen, Joseph G. "Federal Policies, American Indian Politics and the 'New Federalism.'" *American Indian Culture and Research Journal* 10, no. 2 (1986): 1-13.

_____. "Sovereignty and the Structure of Dependency at Northern Ute." *American Indian Culture and Research Journal* 10, no. 2 (1986): 75-94.

La Course, Richard. "Emerging International Native Relations." NCAI *Sentinel Bulletin* (July 1975): p. 19.

La Farge, Oliver. "Termination of Federal Supervision: Disintegration and the American Indians." *Annals of the American Academy of Political and Social Science* 311 (May 1957): 41-46.

_____. "To Set the Indian Free." *New Republic,* 3 October 1949, pp. 11-13.

Lesser, Alexander. "Education and the Future of Tribalism: The Case of the American Indian." *Social Service Review* 35 (June 1961): 135-43.

McCarty, T. L. "School as Community: The Rough Rock Demonstration." *Harvard Educational Review* 59, no. 4 (November 1989): 484-503.

Nash, Philleo. "The Place of Religious Revivalism in the Formation of the Intercultural Community on Klamath Reservation." *Social Anthropology of North American Tribes,* ed. Fred Eggan. Chicago: University of Chicago Press, 1937, pp. 377-444.

National Congress of American Indians (NCAI). *Sentinel Bulletin,* November 1977.

_____. "NCAI Position: Realignment Is Regionalization." *Sentinel Bulletin,* July-August 1973, p. 4.

Navajo Times, 17 March 1966.

New York Times, 13 July 1961.

_____, 13 March 1966.

_____, 23 July 1967.

"Report on the National Congress of American Indians Convention." *Indian Truth* 208 (January 1977): 1-2.

Schierbeck, Helen. "Education the Indian Way." *Indian Truth* 217 (April 1977): 5.

_____. "Indian Education: A Challenge for the Church." *Indian Truth* 47, no. 3 (September 1970): 2-6.

Sorkin, Alan. "American Indians Industrialize to Combat Poverty." *Monthly Labor Review,* March 1969, pp. 19-25.

Stull, Donald D., Jerry A. Scholtz, and Ken Cadue, Sr. "Rights Without Resources: The Rise and Fall of the Kansas Kickapoo."*American Indian Culture and Research Journal* 10, no.2 (1986): 41-59.

Thompson, Hildegard. "Education Among American Indians: Institutional Aspects." *Annals of the American Academy of Political and Social Science* 311 (May 1957): 95-105.

Wall Street Journal, 30 April 1969.

_____, "Excerpts from Remarks by Robert L. Bennett, Commissioner of Indian Affairs, before the Indian Rights Association on April 26, 1966."

Wassaja, July 1973. "Teton Sioux Manifesto Reply of the Teton Sioux to the White House Letter on Negotiations."

Watkins, Arthur V. "Termination of Federal Supervision: The Removal of Restrictions Over Indian Property and Person." *Annals of the American Academy of Political and Social Science* 311 (May 1957): 747-55.

Index

ABOUT THE AUTHOR

GUY B. SENESE is currently Assistant Professor of Leadership and Educational Policy Studies at Northern Illinois University. He has taught at the Rough Rock Demonstration School on the Navajo reservation, served as youth advocate/counselor with Tlingit-Haida youth in Juneau, Alaska, and worked as Illinois State Board of Education Specialist in Compensatory Education. Dr. Senese's articles have appeared in *Educational Theory, Harvard Educational Review, Educational Foundations,* and *Journal of Thought.*